Bake It to the Limit

Bake It
TO THE LIMIT

Easy-to-Prepare Desserts with Showstopping

Variations for Special Occasions

Dede Wilson

Photography by Dennis M. Gottlieb

William Morrow and Company, Inc.
New York

Library of Congress Cataloging-in-Publication Data

Wilson, Dede.
    Bake it to the limit: easy-to-prepare desserts with showstopping variations for special occasions / Dede Wilson ; photography by Dennis M. Gottlieb. — 1st ed.
    p. cm.
    Includes bibliographical references.
    ISBN 0-688-15972-9
    1. Baking. 2. Desserts. I. Title.
TX765.W53   1999
641.8'15—dc21
                               99-30744
                                 CIP

Printed in the United States of America

First Edition

1 2 3 4 5 6 7 8 9 10

BOOK DESIGN BY NICK ANDERSON

www.williammorrow.com

for David!

my best friend

Acknowledgments

Every book is a collaborative affair, and this one is no exception. Again, there are a few key people I am most grateful to and am indebted to:

Maureen and Eric Lasher, my agents, who always find a good home for my words. Let's keep the ball rolling.

Justin Schwartz, the only editor for me, literally; I'll follow you anywhere.

The visual team of Dennis Gottlieb, Liz Duffy, and Joyce Sangiardi for the photographs, Richard L. Aquan for the jacket and Nick Anderson for the design of the book.

The marketing and publicity team at William Morrow, especially Carrie Weinberg and Corinne Alhadeff.

Production editor Lorie Young for her attention to detail.

Laura Baddish for the amazing publicity on my last book, which got me where I am today.

My recipe testers, Mary McNamara and Debbie Drinker.

Suzanne Lo Manto for her line drawings.

Brian Maynard at KitchenAid for providing a beautiful stainless-steel gas range for recipe testing.

Waring for supplying a quality blender.

All of my friends who ate cake after cookie after brownie after tart after pudding after pie . . . and always asked for more. I appreciated the constructive criticism.

Harry for being a great dad for our children and for all the computer help.

My kids, Ravenna, Freeman and Forrester, for putting up with my baking obsession. . . . I know my time at the stove takes away from time with you. But you will always have love and brownies from me, whenever you want.

Pam Ascher, a great stabilizer in my life. Your great smile lights me up.

And to David!, who literally put me up when I had nowhere to go, made me a home, welcomed me into his life, and provided an emotional and physical mooring when I was in the middle of this book. Thank you. I look forward to more. You are my light, my anchor, my inspiration and my love.

Contents

Introduction

Can you make desserts that look like these? Yes, you can! Consider me your insider connection to professional "tricks of the trade." I want to share my knowledge and help you to produce the desserts of your dreams. I am a self-taught pastry chef, and with a little enthusiasm in the kitchen, your sweets will be a smashing success. And these recipes never compromise taste for looks.

Most of the recipes in this book have a basic version and a "Bake It to the Limit" rendition that offers you optional tips and suggestions. The basic recipe will always taste great and the Bake It to the Limit version will elevate your dessert into something spectacular.

For instance, in the Cakes chapter, a Bake It to the Limit version describes how to turn a simple pound cake into a celebratory cake crowned with a marzipan rose (page 116). In the Ice Cream, Sorbets and Granitas chapter, one extra step can turn Honey Ice Cream into a dazzling sundae with the addition of Blood Orange Sauce (page 148).

Don't worry—these desserts aren't overly fussy. Quite the contrary. The key word here is *accessibility*. The recipes approach technique and presentation in the easiest manner possible. Sometimes it will be as simple as learning how to cut your brownies in an interesting shape so that they look their best on a platter. Other times it will be a more sophisticated matter such as making tempered chocolate bark to turn your Bûche de Nöel into a three-dimensional wonder.

Remember, the balance between taste and presentation is important. In their simplest guise, these desserts will tantalize your taste buds. Baked to the limit, they will dazzle your guests and your palate.

How to Use This Book

This, like any cookbook, can be used literally, but it can also be used quite effectively as inspiration. Mix and match the desserts to your liking. Play with substituting ingredients. You may not come up with a winner every time, but you will learn about flavor, basic baking techniques, timing, and the importance of temperature and texture.

I believe in a democratic dessert world. Anything goes. My taste may not be yours. I love chocolate; you may be a vanilla fan. That's what makes my mixer whir. It's all about experimentation. No one needs dessert, so sweets have to exist for other reasons. They are fun to make, beautiful to look at, and delightful to smell; they can dance all over our tongues and often satisfy an emotional yearning. Be open to new ideas, then get in the kitchen and just bake.

pies and tarts

Pies and tarts are seasonless. Ripe fresh stone fruits and berries beckon in the spring and summer, while apples, pears and pumpkins define autumn. In the depths of winter, citrus can enliven a dreary day and a deep dark chocolate tart can crown a holiday party. Start now, and work your way through the year.

Working with pie and tart doughs may seem daunting to some bakers, but I am here to hold your hand. Pie doughs should be tender and flaky. They can afford to be delicate because they are supported by the pie plate. Tarts, on the other hand, are usually removed from their pans or rings. Their crust needs to be firmer—I prefer a cookielike tart crust. The techniques for making each of these is a little different. For a full treatise on the subject, check out Rose Levy Beranbaum's *Pie and Pastry Bible* (1998) and Carole Walter's *Great Pies and Tarts* (1998).

For pies, I find that Pyrex pie plates work the best. (I use the 9½-inch deep-dish Pyrex pie plate.) For tarts, experiment with loose-bottomed fluted tart pans and open-bottomed tart rings that can be placed directly on a sheet pan (see Equipment, Ingredients and Techniques, page 161, for more information). Always spray pie plates and tart pans or rings with nonstick cooking spray, which makes it easy to remove the dessert, and set them on a parchment-lined sheet pan when you are ready to put them in the oven. Your oven will stay clean (the sheet pan will catch any overflows), and it will be easier to move any dessert with a liquidy filling from the counter to the oven. The sheet pan also provides even heat that will brown the bottom of your crust better. Remove pie plates and tart pans from the sheet pans before cooling on wire racks. Open-bottomed tart rings should be cooled on their sheet pans.

Making Decorative Pie and Tart Crusts

Whether you have a single-crust tart, a single-crust pie or a double-crust pie, there are certain finishing techniques that can make the crust more decorative.

For Single-Crust Tarts: These usually take the least decoration. Clean edges give the tart a professional look. Fold the excess crust inward to reinforce the sides. Then you can pinch the edges gently to create a ripple effect, or you can roll a rolling pin over the tart pan, firmly pressing on the rim of the pan. The rim will cut into the crust from below and make a clean edge.

For Single-Crust Pies: You have a lot of options here. The reinforced dough along the edges provides a surface that can be embellished.

To form a scalloped edge, place the thumb and index finger of your right hand about 1 inch apart against the inside edge of the crust, facing outward. With your left hand, place the index finger between the other two. As you gently push inward with your left finger, push outward with the other two. This forms one "scallop." Repeat all around the edge, spacing the scallops about 1 inch apart.

To make a simple fork-ridged edge, press a fork into the edge to make a pattern. You can turn the fork this way and that to make different designs.

To make an appliquéd edge, cut out small leaf or heart shapes (for example) out of the extra dough. Brush the crust's edge with water, and press the cutouts onto the crust, overlapping as you go around.

For Double-Crust Pies: You can make scalloped or fork-ridged edges as described above. Appliqués can be placed on the top crust too. A nice design can be made by cutting shapes out of the top crust before placing it on the pie, and then applying the cut shapes between the cutouts (brush the crust with water so they will adhere).

Double crusts can also be brushed with milk and sprinkled with sugar for a crystalline effect. Try coarse sugar for a different look.

apple pie with vanilla

Vanilla adds something special to this otherwise classic two-crust apple pie. I like cinnamon in my apple pie, but no nutmeg or other spices. Also, I find that a blend of apples is best, taking advantage of what each one has to offer. Try a mix of Northern Spy and Golden Delicious. Or Granny Smith and Cortland. Or Baldwin (they have a wonderfully complex, winey flavor), Northern Spy and Golden Delicious. Use the lesser amount of sugar with a sweeter blend of apples, and more sugar with the higher proportion of tart varieties—Granny Smith, for example.

Also, peeling apples by hand is certainly doable, but there are apple peelers on the market that make quick work of the job. Some have a viselike clamp that attaches to the table; others have a broad suction-cup base, which I find works better. Both have a rotating spit that holds the apple; when you turn the crank, it pushes the apple against a sharp peeler. The apple is cored, peeled and cut into ¼-inch slices in one action.

P.S. Have you ever sliced into an apple pie and found a large amount of headroom between the cooked-down apple filling and the top crust? That's because the apples were left in large chunks, creating a lot of air space between them when raw. Thin slices eliminate this problem.

Makes one 9½-inch deep-dish pie, 8 servings

1 recipe Basic Pie Crust (page 158)

For the filling
8 apples (6 cups sliced)
⅔ to 1 cup granulated sugar
1 tablespoon instant tapioca
1 teaspoon freshly squeezed lemon juice
½ teaspoon ground cinnamon
½ to 1 teaspoon vanilla extract
2 tablespoons (1 ounce) unsalted butter, cut into large pieces

continued

2 tablespoons whole milk

2 tablespoons granulated sugar

¼ teaspoon ground cinnamon

Spray a 9½-inch deep-dish pie plate with nonstick cooking spray. Roll out the bottom crust and fit it into the pie plate. Refrigerate the crust while you assemble the remaining ingredients.

To make the filling, peel and core the apples. Cut them into ¼-inch slices. Place the apples in a mixing bowl with the sugar, tapioca, lemon juice, cinnamon and vanilla. (Start with the lesser amount of vanilla to see if you like it. Try the full teaspoon next time.) Toss to mix and let sit for 15 minutes.

Pile the filling into the pie crust. Dot with the butter.

Set the filled crust in the refrigerator while you roll out the top crust. Place the top crust over the apples, and seal and crimp the edges. Make a steam vent by cutting a few slashes in the top crust. Brush the top of the pie with the milk. Combine the sugar and cinnamon, and sprinkle over the pie. Freeze the pie for 15 minutes while you preheat the oven to 400°F.

Place the pie on a parchment-lined sheet pan and put it in the oven. Turn the oven down to 375°F and bake for 45 minutes. Check to see how the pie is browning. Continue to bake for approximately 15 more minutes, or until the crust is golden brown and the filling is bubbling.

Cool the pie on a wire rack for 30 minutes to allow the juices to thicken.

This is best eaten the same day it is baked. Serve with Vanilla Ice Cream (page 94) for an à la mode treat.

blueberry pie

If wild blueberries are available, by all means try them in this recipe. They do taste different, and you may prefer them to cultivated berries. I prefer cultivated because that's what my nana used. Whichever you choose, please taste them first and adjust the sugar level as needed.

Makes one 9½-inch deep-dish pie, 8 servings

1 recipe Basic Pie Crust (page 158)

8 cups fresh blueberries

¾ to 1 cup granulated sugar

¼ cup instant tapioca

2 teaspoons freshly squeezed lemon juice

2 tablespoons (1 ounce) unsalted butter, cut into large pieces

Spray a 9½-inch deep-dish pie plate with nonstick cooking spray. Roll out the bottom crust and fit it into the pie plate. Refrigerate the crust while you assemble the remaining ingredients.

To make the filling, wash and sort the berries, removing any stems or leaves. Place the berries in a mixing bowl with the sugar, tapioca and lemon juice. Toss to mix, and let sit for 15 minutes.

Pile the filling into the pie crust. Dot with the butter.

Set the filled crust in the refrigerator while you roll out the top crust. Place the top crust over the berries, and seal and crimp the edges. Make a steam vent by cutting a few slashes in the top crust. Freeze the pie for 15 minutes while you preheat the oven to 400°F.

Place the pie on a parchment-lined sheet pan and put it in the oven. Turn the oven down to 375°F and bake for 45 minutes. Check to see how the pie is browning. Continue to bake for approximately 15 more minutes, or until the crust is golden brown and the filling is bubbling.

Cool the pie on a wire rack for 30 minutes to allow the juices to thicken.

This is best eaten the same day it is baked. Serve warm, with or without Vanilla Ice Cream (page 94).

spiced peach crisp pie

I love peach crisp, but I also love buttery pie crusts. This recipe offers both in one delectable dessert. Make this pie in August, when the peaches are very fragrant and ripe.

Makes one 9½-inch deep-dish pie, 8 servings

For the spiced pie crust

1¼ cups all-purpose flour

1 teaspoon ground ginger

1 teaspoon ground cinnamon

1 teaspoon ground allspice

¼ teaspoon salt

5 tablespoons (2½ ounces) unsalted butter, chilled

1½ ounces (hefty ¼ cup) shortening, chilled

1 to 2 tablespoons ice-cold water

For the filling

12 ripe peaches (6 cups sliced)

¾ cup lightly packed light brown sugar

3 tablespoons instant tapioca

For the topping

⅓ cup rolled oats (not quick or instant)

⅓ cup all-purpose flour

½ cup lightly packed light brown sugar

¼ teaspoon ground cinnamon

¼ teaspoon ground ginger

¼ teaspoon salt

¾ ounce crystallized ginger, minced (about 2 tablespoons plus 1 teaspoon; optional)

4 tablespoons (2 ounces) unsalted butter, cut into large pieces

To make the crust, measure the flour, ginger, cinnamon, allspice and salt into a mixing bowl, mix well, and place in the freezer for 15 minutes.

Cut the butter and shortening into tablespoon-size pieces and scatter over the dry ingredients. Cut in, using a pastry blender or 2 knives, until the crumbs are the size of large flat raisins.

Sprinkle the ice water over the mixture. Toss, using your fingertips or 2 forks, until the dough begins to come together.

Scrape the dough onto a work surface and knead briefly, just enough to bring the crust together into a ball. Divide it into 2 pieces, roll into balls, and flatten. Wrap both pieces in plastic wrap and refrigerate for at least 2 hours, or overnight. The crust may also be frozen for up to a week and defrosted in the refrigerator overnight.

Spray a 9½-inch deep-dish pie plate with nonstick cooking spray. Roll out the bottom crust and fit it into the pie plate. Set the crust in the refrigerator while you preheat the oven to 375°F.

Meanwhile, prepare the filling. Drop the peaches in boiling water for 30 seconds to loosen the skin. Drain, run under cold water, and slip the skin off. Cut each peach into 8 slices, discarding the pit. Place the peach slices in a bowl and toss together with the brown sugar and tapioca; set aside for 15 minutes.

Line the chilled pie crust with foil and weights,

place on a parchment-lined sheet pan and blind bake for 10 minutes.

Meanwhile, make the topping. Combine the oats, flour, brown sugar, cinnamon, ginger, salt and crystallized ginger, if using, in a bowl. Add the butter and cut it in with a pastry blender or 2 knives until the mixture is rough and crumbly.

Remove the pie crust from the oven, remove the foil and weights, and pile the peach filling into the crust. Cover the filling with an even layer of topping, patting it gently into place.

Return the pie to the oven and bake for 45 to 55 minutes, or until the filling is bubbling and the topping is crisp and golden brown.

Cool the pie on a wire rack for 30 minutes to allow the juices to thicken.

This is best eaten the day it is baked. Serve warm, with or without Vanilla Ice Cream (page 94).

cranberry sour cherry pie

This ruby red filling is perfect for the Thanksgiving or Christmas dessert table. Both of these tart fruits are perked up with just enough sugar to keep you pleasantly puckered. Either freeze pitted sour cherries in July for winter use, or feel free to use the canned variety—they work perfectly. (The Thank You brand of water-packed sour cherries comes in 14½-ounce cans, which yield 1½ cups of cherries; so you'll need 2 cans.)

Makes one 9½-inch deep-dish pie, 8 servings

1 Recipe Basic Pie Crust (page 158)

For the filling
4 cups fresh or defrosted frozen cranberries
3 cups sour cherries, pitted
2 cups granulated sugar
5 tablespoons instant tapioca
2 tablespoons (1 ounce) unsalted butter, cut into large pieces

Spray a 9½-inch deep-dish pie plate with nonstick cooking spray. Roll out the bottom crust and fit it into the pie plate. Refrigerate the crust while you assemble the filling.

Wash and sort the cranberries, removing any stems or leaves. Place them in a mixing bowl with the cherries, sugar and tapioca. Toss to mix, and let sit for 15 minutes.

Pile the filling into the pie crust. Dot with the butter.

Refrigerate the filled crust while you roll out the top crust. Place the top crust over the filling, and seal and crimp the edges. Make a steam vent by cutting a few slashes in the top crust. Freeze the pie for 15 minutes while you preheat the oven to 400°F.

Place the pie on a parchment-lined sheet pan and put it in the oven. Turn the oven down to 375°F and bake for 45 minutes. Check to see how the pie is browning. Continue to bake for approximately 15 more minutes, or until the crust is golden brown and the filling is bubbling.

Cool the pie on a wire rack for 30 minutes to allow the juices to thicken.

This is best served the day it is baked. Serve warm, with or without Vanilla Ice Cream (page 94).

✦ BAKE IT TO THE LIMIT

This variation transforms a homey double-crust pie into a chic open-faced tart. The glorious color of the cranberries and cherries will be on full display, and the optional pastry stars make it perfect for New Year's Eve. For this version, the filling is cooked on top of the stove because the tart spends less time in the oven than the pie does.

½ recipe Sweet Tart Dough (page 159)
½ the ingredients for Cranberry Sour Cherry Pie
filling (above), omitting the butter

Spray a 10-inch loose-bottomed fluted tart pan with nonstick cooking spray. Roll out the dough and fit it into the pan (there will be leftover dough). Place the tart pan in the freezer for 30 minutes. If desired, roll out the extra dough and cut it into half a dozen various-size stars. Place these on a parchment-lined sheet pan and freeze for 30 minutes.

Preheat the oven to 375°F.

Line the tart shell with foil and weights, place on a parchment-lined sheet pan, and blind bake for 12 minutes. Remove the foil and weights, and bake for 5 to 7 minutes more. The crust should just be turning golden around the edges, and the bottom should be dry and beginning to crisp. Place the tart pan directly on a wire rack to cool. Meanwhile, if you are using them, bake the stars for 5 to 10 minutes (depending on size), until they're just turning golden around the edges. Place the sheet pan directly on a wire rack to cool.

Meanwhile, make the filling. Wash and sort the cranberries, removing any stems or leaves. Place them in a saucepan with the cherries, sugar and tapioca, and bring to a boil over medium heat. Turn the heat down and simmer for 10 to 15 minutes, or until the cranberries have popped, the fruit has broken down a bit, and the mixture has begun to give off some juice and thicken. Remove from the heat and scrape immediately into the tart shell. Use an offset spatula to spread the fruit evenly across the bottom of the tart. Place the tart in the oven and bake for 1 to 2 minutes, or until the filling has begun to set in the shell. Set the tart pan directly on a wire rack to cool.

If you are using them, arrange the cooled cookie stars here and there on top of the tart just before serving. Remove the tart from the pan before serving. This is best if eaten the day it is baked. Serve warm or at room temperature.

key lime pie
à la ravenna

Ravenna is my daughter, and her favorite pie is key lime—so of course I wanted to create the best rendition ever to satisfy her craving. This version has a lime-scented graham cracker crust, a dense sweet/tart lime layer and a tangy, creamy lime curd layer. Fresh key limes are not normally available on the market, but you can find bottled key lime juice. I have found that regular freshly squeezed lime juice (from Persian limes) works perfectly well too.

Makes one 9½-inch deep-dish pie, 8 servings

For the crust

1½ cups graham cracker crumbs

½ cup (4 ounces) unsalted butter, melted

2 tablespoons granulated sugar

Freshly grated zest of ½ lime

For the filling

One 14-ounce can sweetened condensed milk

½ cup lime juice

4 large egg yolks

Freshly grated zest of ½ lime

For the topping

1 cup granulated sugar

⅔ cup lime juice

8 large egg yolks

¼ to ½ teaspoon lime oil (optional; see Note)

For the whipped cream

1½ cups heavy cream

5 tablespoons granulated sugar

Preheat the oven to 350°F. Spray a 9½-inch deep-dish pie plate with nonstick cooking spray.

To make the crust, place the graham cracker crumbs, melted butter, sugar and zest in a bowl. Stir to combine. Pour the mixture into the prepared pie plate, and press with your fingers to create an even layer on the bottom and up the sides. Use a flat-bottomed glass to facilitate pressing the crumbs along the bottom and to help with the edges. Keeping the glass flat, move toward the edges; it will press the crumbs along the sides, creating an even layer all around. Blind bake the crust for 5 to 7 minutes, or just until it starts to brown. Place on a wire rack to cool slightly.

Meanwhile, prepare the filling. Whisk together the condensed milk, lime juice, egg yolks and zest. Pour the mixture into the partially baked crust. Bake for 10 minutes. Then return the pie to a wire rack to begin cooling.

While the filling is baking, prepare the topping. Place the sugar, lime juice and egg yolks in the top of a double boiler. Cook over simmering water until the mixture is thick enough to coat the back of a spoon, about 15 minutes. When you draw a spoon across the bottom of the pan, it should leave a small path. Stir in the lime oil, if using, off the heat.

Gently pour the curd topping over the pie, completely covering the filling. Let the pie cool to room temperature on the wire rack. Then refrigerate it for at least 4 hours, or overnight.

Right before serving, prepare the whipped cream. Whip the heavy cream and sugar together until medium-firm peaks form. The cream should be whipped beyond the soft-peak stage, but not too stiff. Spread the whipped cream over the pie, all the way to the edges. Make peaks by repeatedly touching the cream with the back of a spoon, drawing the cream up and out. Serve immediately.

continued

Note: Lime oil, made by Boyajian, can be ordered from Williams-Sonoma or found at some specialty food stores. It is the distillation of oils from lime zest and has an incomparable flavor. If necessary, substitute the finely grated zest of 1 lime for the oil.

chocolate banana pecan pie

Here the perennial favorite, pecan pie, gets dressed up with chocolate, a dose of banana liqueur and creamy slices of banana. Chocolate, bananas and nuts: heaven in a pie plate.

Makes one 9½-inch deep-dish pie, 10 servings

For the crust

1 recipe Chocolate Pie Crust (page 158)

1 large egg white, beaten

For the filling

6 tablespoons (3 ounces) unsalted butter, melted

1 cup lightly packed dark brown sugar

½ teaspoon salt

4 large eggs

1 cup light corn syrup

3 tablespoons banana liqueur (I use Leroux's Crème de Banana)

8 ounces semisweet chocolate, cut into ½-inch chunks (1⅓ cups)

7½ ounces (about 1½ cups) pecan halves, toasted (page 152)

1 ripe medium-size (6- to 7-ounce) banana, peeled and sliced into 1-inch chunks

Spray a 9½-inch deep-dish pie plate with nonstick cooking spray. Roll out the dough and fit it into the pie plate, making a high crimped edge (see page 2). Freeze for 30 minutes.

Fifteen minutes into the freezing time, preheat the oven to 375°F.

Place the pie pan on a parchment-lined sheet pan. Line the pie crust with foil, fill it with weights, and blind bake for 10 minutes. Remove the foil and weights, and brush the crust with the egg white. Bake for 1 to 2 minutes more, to dry out the egg and crust. Cool slightly on a wire rack. Turn the oven down to 350°F.

Meanwhile, prepare the filling. Whisk together the melted butter, brown sugar and salt. Beat in the eggs one at a time, whisking well after each addition. Beat in the corn syrup and liqueur. Fold in the chocolate, pecans and banana chunks. Pour the filling into the partially baked pie crust.

Bake for 45 to 55 minutes. The filling will be puffed with a few tiny cracks, but should still be a little soft and wiggly in the center. It will firm up tremendously upon cooling.

Set the pie plate directly on a wire rack to cool for at least 20 minutes before serving.

This can be made a day ahead, but I think it is best made the morning of the day you plan to serve it.

★ **BAKE IT TO THE LIMIT**

Nothing fancy—just whip some cream that has been lightly sweetened and flavored with banana liqueur.

1 cup heavy cream

3 tablespoons granulated sugar

2 tablespoons banana liqueur or dark rum

Place the cream, sugar and liqueur in a chilled bowl. Beat until soft peaks form. Make right before using, or store for up to 2 hours in the refrigerator. Serve wedges of the pie topped with dollops of the whipped cream.

rhubarb raspberry cream tart

Rhubarb signals spring for me. Here this dessert vegetable is paired with raspberries and spooned over a lemony cream cheese filling, all set in a pecan crust.

Makes one 8½- by 2½-inch deep tart, 10 to 12 servings

For the crust

> 1¼ cups all-purpose flour
>
> 2 ounces (about ½ cup) pecan halves, toasted
>   (see page 152)
>
> Pinch salt
>
> ½ cup (4 ounces) unsalted butter, chilled and
>   cut into large pieces
>
> 2 to 3 tablespoons ice-cold water

For the filling

> 8 ounces cream cheese, at room temperature
>
> ¾ cup granulated sugar
>
> 1 teaspoon freshly squeezed lemon juice
>
> 1 teaspoon vanilla extract
>
> 1 large egg

For the fruit topping

> 10 ounces fresh rhubarb, cut into ½-inch dice (2 cups)
>
> 1 pint fresh or defrosted IQF (individually quick
>   frozen) raspberries (2 cups)
>
> ¾ cup granulated sugar
>
> ¼ cup all-purpose flour

To make the crust, place the flour, nuts and salt in a food processor fitted with the metal blade and process until the nuts are finely ground. Add the pieces of butter and process by pulsing the machine on and off until the mixture resembles coarse meal. With the machine running, dribble the water in through the feed tube, bit by bit, until the dough starts to come together. Scrape the dough out onto a floured surface and knead it together into a smooth ball. Flatten and wrap in plastic wrap. Refrigerate for at least 2 hours.

Lightly flour your work surface and roll the dough out to a 14-inch circle, ¼ inch thick. Spray an 8½-inch, 2¼-inch-deep, loose-bottomed fluted tart pan with nonstick cooking spray. Fit the dough into the pan, folding the edges in on themselves so that the upper edges are double-thick. Freeze for 30 minutes. After 15 minutes, preheat the oven to 375°F.

Place the tart pan on a parchment-lined sheet pan. Line the frozen tart shell with foil and fill with weights. Blind bake for 15 minutes. Remove the foil and weights and bake for 5 more minutes. The shell should be dry to the touch. Set the tart pan directly on a wire rack to cool slightly.

While the crust is baking, prepare the filling. In the bowl of a heavy-duty mixer, beat the cream cheese with the flat paddle attachment until smooth and lightened. Add the sugar gradually, beating on high speed until light and creamy. Add the lemon juice, vanilla and egg, and beat until smooth. Pour the filling into the tart shell and bake for 10 minutes, until just beginning to set.

While the filling is baking, prepare the fruit topping. In a bowl, combine the rhubarb, raspberries, sugar and flour. When the tart comes out of the oven, spoon the fruit filling over the top. Bake for 40 minutes, or until the filling is a little puffed and firm. The tart will continue to firm up during chilling.

Set the tart pan directly on a wire rack to cool to room temperature. Then refrigerate for 6 hours, or overnight, before serving. Remove the tart from the pan before serving.

chocolate peanut butter tart

This is as rich and sweet as a candy bar—a kid's dream dolled up in adult guise. It is based on a recipe I found years ago in *Chocolatier* magazine, a great resource for all chocolate-related information.

Makes one 10-inch tart, 12 servings

½ recipe Sweet Tart Dough (page 159)

For the nut filling

5 ounces (1 cup) walnut halves, toasted (see page 152)
¼ cup (2 ounces) unsalted butter, cut into large pieces
½ cup plus 2 tablespoons lightly packed dark brown
*   sugar*
¼ teaspoon salt
⅓ cup heavy cream
⅓ cup honey

For the peanut butter filling

2 cups smooth hydrogenated peanut butter
1 cup confectioner's sugar
1 teaspoon vanilla extract

For the ganache topping

8 ounces semisweet chocolate, finely chopped
⅔ cup heavy cream

Spray a 10-inch loose-bottomed fluted tart pan with nonstick cooking spray. Roll out the tart dough and fit it into the tart pan. Freeze the tart shell for 30 minutes.

Fifteen minutes into the freezing time, preheat the oven to 375°F.

Place the tart pan on a parchment-lined sheet pan. Line the tart shell with foil and fill with weights.

Blind bake for 10 to 12 minutes, or until the crust is turning a light golden brown. Cool thoroughly on a wire rack. Remove foil and weights.

To make the nut filling, chop half of the walnuts. Melt the butter in a medium-size saucepan over medium heat. Add the brown sugar and salt, stirring to blend. Add the cream and honey. Bring to a boil, turn down the heat and simmer for 1 minute. Stir in all the nuts.

Pour the nut filling into the cooled tart shell and bake for about 20 minutes, or until the filling is bubbling. Set the tart pan directly on a wire rack to cool completely.

Meanwhile, make the peanut butter filling. Cream the peanut butter in the bowl of a heavy-duty mixer, using the flat paddle attachment on medium speed, until smooth, about 1 minute. Sift in the confectioner's sugar and beat on low speed until it is completely incorporated, about another 2 minutes, scraping down the bowl once or twice. Beat in the vanilla.

Using an offset spatula, spread the peanut butter filling over the cooled nut layer. Place the filled tart in the refrigerator.

To make the ganache topping, place the chopped chocolate in a heatproof bowl. In a small saucepan, bring the cream to a boil over medium heat. Pour the hot cream over the chocolate, let sit a few minutes, then whisk to melt the chocolate and combine with the cream. Cool the ganache until you can see whisk streaks, about 30 minutes at room temperature (or stir over ice to shorten the chilling time).

Spread the ganache over the chilled tart, covering the peanut butter layer. Refrigerate for at least 2 hours before serving. Or the tart may be refrigerated for a day before serving. Serve cold. Remove the tart from the pan before serving.

continued

Making a Parchment Cone

Once you've made a parchment cone, it will be easy to do again. It's just explaining it that's difficult. I always use one when working with melted chocolate.

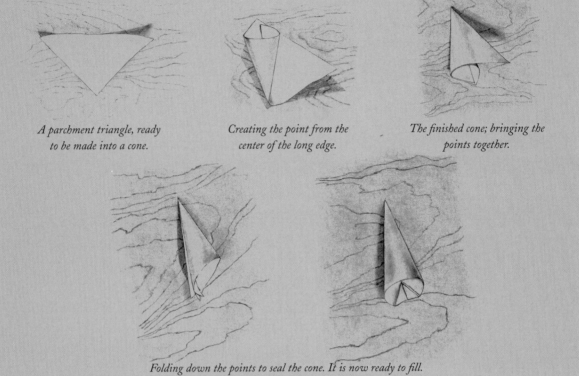

A parchment triangle, ready to be made into a cone.

Creating the point from the center of the long edge.

The finished cone; bringing the points together.

Folding down the points to seal the cone. It is now ready to fill.

Cut a wide triangle from parchment paper, so it has two equal shorter sides and one longer side. The center of the long edge will form the point of the cone. Holding the triangle in front of you, with the long side facing left, place your left thumb and index finger on the center point of the long side. Take the top corner and fold it down and under itself, pulling it toward the right, until it meets the point opposite the long side. Remove your left hand from the center point and now use that thumb and index finger to hold these two points together. Flip the cone over so that they are on the left. Take the remaining extended corner and wrap it around the entire outside of the cone so that it meets the first two points. Jiggle the paper back and forth until the fit is perfect and the point is tight. Fold the section with the three corners inward. The cone is ready to fill.

Fill the cone (never more than halfway), and then fold the open edge over itself several times to make a seal. Snip off the point with sharp scissors. Make a very tiny opening for most chocolate work. To use pastry tips with the cone, cut a larger opening prior to filling it. Discard the bag when finished.

For a final flourish, you can pipe a free-form peanut butter design on top of the ganache.

¼ cup peanut butter filling (above)
1 teaspoon whole milk

Remove and reserve ¼ cup of the peanut butter filling before spreading the remainder over the nut layer. After the tart is assembled, combine the reserved filling with the milk in a small bowl, whisking together well. Place the mixture in a parchment cone and pipe a free-form zigzag design over the ganache. Chill and serve as above.

gianduja truffle tart

This is a chocolatey, decadent, rich dessert. Serve small slices with a cup of coffee. Gianduja is a specialty chocolate, a flavorful blend of hazelnuts and chocolate, which comes in block form like regular baking chocolate (I use Callebaut brand). Look for it in specialty food stores. For this recipe, use a milk chocolate gianduja.

Makes one 11-inch tart, 10 to 12 servings

For the crust

One 9-ounce box Nabisco Famous Chocolate Wafers, roughly crumbled by hand

1¼ ounces (about ¼ cup) hazelnuts, skinned and toasted (see page 152)

6 tablespoons (3 ounces) unsalted butter, melted

For the filling

8 ounces gianduja, finely chopped
1½ cups heavy cream
11 ounces bittersweet chocolate, finely chopped

Preheat the oven to 375°F. Spray an 11-inch loose-bottomed fluted tart pan with nonstick cooking spray.

To make the crust, grind the cookies and nuts in a food processor fitted with the metal blade until fine. Pour in the melted butter and pulse the machine on and off to combine well. Press the crumb crust over the bottom and up the sides of the prepared tart pan. Use a flat-bottomed glass to facilitate pressing the crumbs along the bottom and to help with the edges. Keeping the glass flat, move toward the edges; it will press the crumbs along the sides, creating an even layer all around.

Place the tart pan on a parchment-lined sheet pan. Blind bake the crust for 10 minutes. Set the tart pan directly on a wire rack to cool completely.

To make the filling, melt 6 ounces of the gianduja with ¼ cup of the cream in a double boiler or microwave. Whisk until smooth and pour into the cooled tart shell. Refrigerate for 30 minutes.

Melt the bittersweet chocolate with the remaining 1¼ cups cream in a double boiler or microwave. Whisk until smooth and pour over the chilled gianduja layer.

Melt the remaining 2 ounces gianduja, place in a parchment cone, and make a random design over the bittersweet ganache. Refrigerate until firm, at least 3 hours.

This tart may be refrigerated for up to 2 days; cover it with plastic wrap after it has chilled for the initial 3 hours. Serve cold, in thin slices. Remove the tart from the pan before serving.

continued

Serve this tart with Crème Anglaise, flavored with hazelnut liqueur if you like. A cocoa dusting completes the plate. You need luncheon or dinner-size plates for this.

½ recipe Crème Anglaise (page 146)
8 ounces bittersweet chocolate, finely chopped
Dutch-process cocoa

Have the Crème Anglaise made, cooled, and poured into a squeeze bottle.

Melt the chocolate in a double boiler or microwave, and place in a parchment cone. Make a large star design on each plate, about 7 inches from point to point, with the melted chocolate. Refrigerate the plates until the chocolate sets, about 5 minutes.

Fill in the chocolate star outline with the Crème Anglaise. Then place a slice of the tart slightly off-center. You should be able to see the star's points radiating beyond the slice.

Dust the plate's edges with cocoa (a mesh-top dredger, page 162, works best). Serve immediately.

pumpkin brûlée tart in a gingersnap crust

This thin tart features a pumpkin pie–like filling—only it's creamier. The gingersnap crust and caramelized topping add flavor and crunch.

Makes one 9-inch tart, 10 to 12 servings

For the crust

Half a 12-ounce box of Sunshine brand gingersnap cookies (1½ cups fine crumbs) or any other commercially packaged gingersnap
1 tablespoon granulated sugar
6 tablespoons (3 ounces) unsalted butter, melted

For the filling

7 large egg yolks
⅓ cup granulated sugar
2½ cups heavy cream
½ cup canned pumpkin puree
½ teaspoon ground cinnamon
½ teaspoon ground allspice
½ teaspoon ground ginger
3 tablespoons (1½ ounces) unsalted butter, at room temperature

For the topping

¼ cup lightly packed light brown sugar

Preheat the oven to 350°F. Spray a 9-inch loose-bottomed fluted tart pan with nonstick cooking spray.

To make the crust, process the cookies in a food processor fitted with the metal blade until they are reduced to a fine crumb. Add the sugar and melted butter. Pulse the machine on and off to combine.

Press the crumb mixture into the prepared tart pan, building up the sides to ¼-inch thickness. Use a flat-bottomed glass to facilitate pressing the crumbs along the bottom and to help with the edges. Keeping the glass flat, move toward the edges; it will press the crumbs along the sides, creating an even layer.

Place the tart pan on a parchment-lined pan. Blind bake the crust for 8 to 10 minutes, or until it is fragrant and just turning brown. Cool thoroughly on a wire rack.

To make the filling, whisk the yolks and sugar together in the top of a double boiler. Set over simmering water; do not let the water come to a rolling boil and do not let it touch the bottom of the double boiler insert.

Whisk constantly for about 10 minutes, or until the mixture has lightened in color, increased in volume and acquired the texture of hollandaise; it should be thick enough to coat the back of a spoon.

Add the cream, pumpkin puree and spices, and continue to cook and stir for about 20 minutes, or until the mixture is very, very thick. The whisk should leave definite marks. Be patient with this step. It must be done slowly over low heat or the eggs will curdle. Whisk in the softened butter. Immediately pour the filling into the cooled tart shell and refrigerate until chilled and set, at least 4 hours, or overnight.

Immediately before serving, sift the brown sugar evenly over the tart and caramelize it with a propane torch (see page 89). Serve immediately. Remove the tart from the pan before serving.

fig tart with lemon honey mascarpone

This tart features fresh Black Mission figs, which have a nearly purple black skin covering flesh that is a beautiful combination of rose, pink, cream and green. The rich lemony, honey-sweetened filling and tangy port glaze make this an unusual fresh fruit tart. Prepare this in the summer or fall, when these figs are in season.

Mascarpone is a soft Italian cheese similar to crème fraîche or sour cream combined with cream cheese. You can find it in better cheese stores and spe-cialty food stores. The bottomless tart ring used here is an alternative to a loose-bottomed tart pan. Either type of pan will work perfectly well. The shell should be baked the day of serving.

Makes one 14 by 4½-inch rectangular tart, 8 servings

½ recipe Sweet Tart Dough (page 159)

For the filling

1 cup (8 ounces) mascarpone cheese
Grated zest of ½ lemon
¼ cup freshly squeezed lemon juice
3 tablespoons honey
¼ cup heavy cream

For the fruit

8 fresh Black Mission figs

For the glaze

½ cup apple jelly
2 tablespoons port wine

Spray a 14 by 4½-inch rectangular tart ring with nonstick cooking spray, and place it on a parchment-lined sheet pan. You may also use a similar-sized loose-bottomed pan.

Roll out the tart dough into a large rectangle and fit it into the prepared tart ring, folding some of the excess toward the inside and building up the sides about ½ inch above the edge. Make sure the dough does not fold over the edge of the ring, or you will not be able to lift the ring off. Freeze for 30 minutes.

Fifteen minutes into the freezing time, preheat the oven to 375°F.

Place the tart pan on parchment-lined sheet pan. Line the frozen tart with foil and fill with weights. Blind bake for 10 minutes. Remove the foil and weights and bake for 10 more minutes, or until the

tart shell is just turning light brown. Set the sheet pan directly on a wire rack to cool thoroughly.

To make the filling, place the mascarpone in a medium-size mixing bowl and stir to loosen it up a little bit. Add the zest (you can grate it directly over the mascarpone). Add the lemon juice and honey, and stir gently but thoroughly until smooth. In another bowl, whip the cream until stiff peaks form. Fold about a quarter of the whipped cream into the mascarpone to lighten it; then fold in the rest.

Cut each fig into 8 slices. Run a sharp knife between the crust and the ring and lift the ring up and off. Place the tart shell on a serving platter. Spread the filling over the bottom; this is accomplished most easily by using a small offset spatula. Arrange the figs, cut side up, in rows over the filling.

To make the glaze, melt the jelly in a small heavy-bottomed saucepan over medium-low heat. Stir in the port and continue to heat until there are no lumps, about 5 minutes.

Brush the glaze over the fruit. It will not be thick—it just gives a nice sheen and flavor to the tart.

Refrigerate for at least 1 hour, or until the glaze has jelled. Serve slightly chilled, the day it is assembled.

blackberry cream strawberry tart

This tart is light and fresh-tasting, but what will strike you immediately is the way it looks. The buttery crust is filled with a violet-colored pastry cream and topped with sliced ripe red strawberries. The contrast of the red over the violet is vivid and unusual.

Makes one 10-inch tart, 10 to 12 servings

½ recipe Sweet Tart Dough (page 159)
1 pint fresh blackberries
1 recipe Vanilla Pastry Cream (page 151),
    using the larger quantity of flour
2 pints fresh strawberries

Spray a 10-inch loose-bottomed fluted tart pan with nonstick cooking spray. Roll out the tart dough, and fit it into the tart pan. Freeze for 30 minutes.

Fifteen minutes into the freezing time, preheat the oven to 375°F.

Place the tart pan on a parchment-lined sheet pan. Line the tart shell with foil and fill with weights. Blind bake for 10 to 12 minutes. Then remove the foil and weights, and bake for 10 to 15 minutes more, until golden brown. Place on a wire rack to cool completely.

Puree the blackberries in a food processor fitted with the metal blade. Strain through a fine-mesh strainer to remove the seeds.

Make the pastry cream and let it cool for 10 minutes. Then fold in the berry puree. Cool for 15 minutes. Pour the filling into the cooled tart shell and refrigerate until set, about 4 hours.

Hull the strawberries and cut them in half vertically. Arrange the berries, cut side down, in concentric circles over the pastry cream—or in any pattern you like. Just make sure that some of the gorgeous violet-colored pastry cream is visible in between the fruit.

Serve immediately, or refrigerate for up to 6 hours. Remove the tart from the pan before serving.

chocolate truffle raspberry tart

You want easy? This is mega-easy and packs a chocolate wallop. Make this tart when raspberries are in season—or, for pure chocolate indulgence, make it berry-less.

Makes one 11-inch tart, 12 servings

For the crust

One 9-ounce box Nabisco Famous Chocolate Wafers, roughly crumbled by hand

½ cup (4 ounces) unsalted butter, melted

For the filling

15 ounces semisweet chocolate, finely chopped

1½ cups heavy cream

½ pint fresh raspberries

Preheat the oven to 350°F. Spray an 11-inch loose-bottomed fluted tart pan with nonstick cooking spray.

To make the crust, process the cookies in a food processor fitted with the metal blade until they are reduced to a fine crumb. Add the melted butter and pulse the machine on and off to combine.

Pat the crust into the prepared tart pan, building up the sides to ¼-inch thickness. Use a flat-bottomed glass to facilitate pressing the crumbs along the bottom and to help with the edges. Keeping the glass flat, move toward the edges; it will press the crumbs along the sides, creating an even layer all around.

Place the tart pan on a parchment-lined sheet pan. Blind bake the crust for 12 to 15 minutes, or until it is fragrant and dry. Set the tart pan directly on a wire rack to cool thoroughly.

To make the filling, place the chocolate in a heat-proof bowl. Bring the cream to a boil over medium heat, and pour it over the chocolate. Let sit for a few minutes, then whisk together until smooth.

Remove half a dozen of the best berries and set them aside; scatter the remaining berries across the bottom of the cooled crust. Pour the ganache filling over the berries. Immediately use a small offset spatula to push the ganache into all the spaces and smooth it over the berries. You will see the raspberries underneath the ganache, but they should not prominently poke through.

Refrigerate until set, at least 6 hours, or overnight. Immediately before serving, arrange the reserved berries here and there on top of the tart. Serve chilled, in thin slices. Remove the tart from the pan before serving.

✦ BAKE IT TO THE LIMIT

This tart is easy to make, and should remain so. However, by simply changing the type of pan, you can create a very different look. There are petal-shaped tart rings on the market that can lend a decorative touch. They are usually imported from Europe and come in many sizes. I used one for this recipe that averaged about 10 inches in diameter and had 7 "petals." You may have a little crust and filling left over, depending on the size of your tart ring. Make one or two little individual tarts with the remains to give to a friend.

plum tart

Fresh, juicy purple or dark red plums (not prune plums) work best for this tart, which is chock-full of fruit with just a tiny bit of cream and cognac holding it together.

Makes one 10-inch tart, 8 to 10 servings

½ recipe Sweet Tart Dough (page 159)

For the filling

6 (4-ounce) ripe purple- or dark-red-skinned plums

⅓ cup granulated sugar

1 teaspoon ground cinnamon

1 teaspoon vanilla powder, or ½ teaspoon vanilla extract

1 tablespoon heavy cream

1 tablespoon cognac or brandy

Spray a 10-inch loose-bottomed fluted tart pan with nonstick cooking spray.

Roll out the dough on a floured surface and fit it into the prepared tart pan. Freeze for 30 minutes.

Fifteen minutes into the freezing time, preheat the oven to 375°F.

Place the tart pan on a parchment-lined sheet pan. Line the frozen tart shell with foil and fill with weights. Blind bake for 12 minutes. Remove the foil and weights, and bake for 10 minutes more. The edges should be just tinged with golden brown. Set aside on a wire rack. It does not need to cool thoroughly.

Meanwhile, prepare the filling. Remove the pits and cut each plum into 8 slices. Place the plums in a nonreactive pan and sprinkle with the sugar, cinnamon and vanilla powder (wait to add if using vanilla extract). Toss to coat. Bake for 15 minutes, or until the fruit is very soft and has given off a lot of juice.

Remove the pan from the oven and stir in the extract, if using. Using a slotted spoon, scoop the plums into the baked tart shell, spreading the fruit evenly to cover the bottom of the tart. Drizzle the cream evenly over the fruit, and then do the same with the cognac. (The leftover plum juices make a nice sauce for ice cream or yogurt, or combine them with club soda for a nonalcoholic cocktail.)

Bake the tart for 5 to 7 minutes, until the fruit is set and firmed up. Cool to room temperature. Remove the tart from the pan before serving.

This is best served the day it is baked.

crystallized ginger pear tart

Pears and ginger have a natural affinity for each other. Here fresh pears are fortified with Poire William, a pear liqueur, and accented with both crystallized and ground ginger. All of this is cushioned by a rich custard . . . autumnal heaven in a crust.

Makes one 8½-inch by 2½-inch-deep tart, 10 servings

½ recipe Sweet Tart Dough (page 159)

For the filling

4 large (7- to 8-ounce) Bartlett pears

¼ cup granulated sugar

1 ounce crystallized ginger, minced (about 3 tablespoons)

½ teaspoon ground ginger

For the custard

⅔ cup heavy cream

¼ cup granulated sugar

¼ cup Poire William (pear liqueur, available in most liquor stores), or dark rum or brandy

2 large eggs

Spray an 8½-inch, 2¼-inch-deep loose-bottomed fluted tart pan with nonstick cooking spray.

Roll out the dough on a floured work surface to ¼-inch thickness. Fit it into the prepared tart pan, reinforcing the sides by folding the edges over to form a double thickness of dough. Freeze for 30 minutes.

continued

Fifteen minutes into the freezing time, preheat the oven to 375°F.

Place the tart pan on a parchment-lined sheet pan. Line the frozen tart shell with foil and fill with weights. Blind bake for 12 minutes. Remove the foil and weights and bake for 8 minutes more. The pastry should be dry to the touch. Place on a wire rack to begin cooling.

Meanwhile, core the pears and cut them into ½-inch slices (do not peel them). Place the slices in a nonreactive pan and sprinkle with the sugar, crystallized ginger and ground ginger. Toss to coat.

Bake the pears for 15 to 20 minutes, or until fork-tender.

Meanwhile, prepare the custard. Whisk together the cream, sugar, liqueur and eggs.

Pour the fruit into the cooled tart shell, and pour the custard over it. Bake for 25 minutes, or until the custard is just set (it will jiggle slightly).

Cool on a wire rack for at least 30 minutes for the custard to firm up.

This tart may be served warm or at room temperature, and is best served the day it is made. Remove the tart from the pan before serving.

✳ **BAKE IT TO THE LIMIT**

An easy crackly sugar glaze adds some texture to this tart.

2 tablespoons granulated sugar

Sprinkle the sugar evenly over the cooled baked tart. Caramelize with a propane torch (see page 89). Serve immediately.

apricot almond tart

This sweet tart crust is enhanced with almond paste, which complements the fresh apricots beautifully. Make this tart when apricots are at their peak, usually in July. The recipe uses a bottomless tart ring as an alternative to a loose-bottomed tart pan. Either type of pan will work. The tart in the photograph was made in an 8-inch by 1½-inch loose-bottomed tart pan.

Makes one 8-inch tart, 8 servings

For the crust

1 cup (8 ounces) unsalted butter, at room temperature

4 ounces almond paste

½ cup granulated sugar

¼ teaspoon salt

1 large egg

1 large egg yolk

3 cups all-purpose flour

For the filling

8 large (3-ounce) ripe fresh apricots

1 cup granulated sugar

4 teaspoons cornstarch

1 teaspoon freshly squeezed lemon juice

1 teaspoon almond extract

For the streusel

⅓ cup all-purpose flour

2 tablespoons granulated sugar

*2 tablespoons (1 ounce) unsalted butter,
    cut into large pieces*

To make the crust, beat the butter, almond paste and sugar together in the bowl of a heavy-duty mixer, using the flat paddle attachment on medium-high speed, until creamy and light, about 3 minutes. Beat in the salt, egg and egg yolk. Add the flour and beat on low speed until the dough just begins to come together. Use your hands to gather it together in the bowl; it will be sticky. Scrape the dough out onto a work surface, flatten it into a round disc, and wrap it in plastic wrap. Refrigerate for at least 2 hours, or overnight.

Spray an 8-inch, 2-inch-high tart ring with non-stick cooking spray, and set it on a parchment-lined sheet pan.

Halve the dough; put half back in the refrigerator until needed. Roll out the other half on a floured surface to ¼-inch thickness. Fit the dough into the prepared tart ring, and press it down into the bottom and along the sides. Reinforce the sides by folding the dough inward, creating double-thick walls. The crust should be even with the pan's upper edge. Freeze for 30 minutes.

Fifteen minutes into the freezing time, preheat the oven to 375°F.

Meanwhile, roll out the other half of the dough to ⅛-inch thickness on a floured surface. Cut it into 1-inch-wide strips, using a fluted pastry wheel, if desired, place them on a clean board or sheet pan, and place back in refrigerator.

Line the frozen tart shell with foil and fill with weights, making sure the sides are supported with both. Blind bake for 10 minutes. Remove the foil and weights, and set the sheet pan directly on a wire rack to begin cooling.

To make the filling, remove the pits and cut each apricot into 6 slices. Toss the slices in a bowl with the sugar, cornstarch, lemon juice and almond extract.

To make the streusel, combine the flour, sugar and butter in a small bowl and mix together, using your fingers.

Mound the fruit filling in the tart shell. Sprinkle with the streusel. Remove the pastry strips from the refrigerator and lay 4 or 5 of them across the tart, then 4 or 5 perpendicular to those. You may weave them over and under, if desired, making a lattice crust. Cut the ends of the strips to meet the edges of the tart. Press the edges to adhere.

Bake for 1 hour, or until the filling is bubbling and the crust is turning pale golden brown. Set the sheet pan directly on a wire rack to cool for 20 minutes. Then run a sharp knife tip between the crust and the ring, and lift the ring up and off. Cool the tart completely, and serve at room temperature.

This tart is best served the day it is made. Any leftovers make a superlative breakfast when topped with a large dollop of yogurt.

four-berry crisp

Every now and then I find a product that is of excellent quality and makes my life in the kitchen much easier. Red Valley's frozen Burst O' Berries is one such item. It is a mixture of blueberries, strawberries, blackberries and raspberries that have been individually quick frozen (IQF) without any sugar or other additives. With this convenience item, this dessert is easy to make at any time of year. Red Valley products are available nationwide. Preparation time is a mere 10 minutes, max.

Makes one 9½-inch deep-dish pie, 6 servings

Two 12-ounce packages frozen Red Valley Burst O'
*   Berries*
1 cup lightly packed light brown sugar
¾ cup all-purpose flour
¾ cup rolled oats (not quick or instant)

½ teaspoon ground cinnamon

¼ teaspoon salt

½ cup (4 ounces) unsalted butter, chilled and cut into large pieces

Preheat the oven to 375°F. Spray a 9½-inch deep-dish pie plate with nonstick cooking spray.

Pour the frozen fruit into the prepared pie plate.

In a medium-size mixing bowl, combine the brown sugar, flour, oats, cinnamon and salt. Sprinkle the butter pieces over the dry ingredients and cut in, using a pastry blender or 2 knives, until the topping resembles a chunky granola. Scatter the topping evenly over the fruit.

Place the pie pan on a parchment-lined sheet pan. Bake for 30 to 35 minutes, or until the topping is golden and the fruit is bubbling around the edges. Let sit for 10 minutes before serving. Serve the crisp at room temperature, or rewarm it after cooling. Best eaten the day it is made.

BAKE IT TO THE LIMIT

This one's easy. Serve the warm crisp with Crème Fraîche Sorbet (page 111) for a great contrast of flavors and temperatures.

grilled peach tart

This fruit pizza is really just an open-faced rustic tart. Grilled pizzas are the delicious brainchild of George Germon and Johanne Killeen of Al Forno restaurant in Providence, Rhode Island. They make only savory ones, as far as I know, but I've found that the slightly smoky flavor from the hardwood charcoal livens up peaches wonderfully.

You will need a charcoal grill, hardwood charcoal,

tongs, two sheet pans, a cutting board, a pizza wheel, and two work tables right near the grill. An extra set of hands is quite helpful, too. This is major assembly-line work. Read these directions several times before starting (reversing the left and right if you're a lefty). And please make sure your grill rack is very clean. Believe me, it's worth it.

Makes eight 10-inch pizza tarts, 8 to 10 servings

For the pizza dough

2 cups warm water

Pinch granulated sugar

2 envelopes dry yeast

5½ to 7½ cups all-purpose flour

½ cup coarse-ground yellow cornmeal

5 teaspoons salt

¼ cup light-colored and -flavored olive oil

2 cups clarified butter (page 150)

For the toppings

4 large (7-ounce) firm ripe peaches

2 cups (1 pound) mascarpone cheese

1 cup lightly packed light brown sugar

1 cup dark rum

Three to 6 hours before you plan to grill the tart, prepare the pizza dough. Measure out the warm water, stir in the sugar, and then sprinkle in the yeast and stir. Place in a warm area until it foams and bubbles, about 5 minutes.

Pour the yeast mixture into the bowl of a heavy-duty mixer, and add 5 cups of the flour, the cornmeal and the salt. Mix with the dough hook attachment on low speed until the dough begins to come together. It should be soft, but smooth and elastic. Add more flour as needed. Keep mixing until it becomes springy,

which indicates that some of the gluten has developed. The dough should be dry enough to just come away from the walls of the bowl. Then let the machine run for 1 minute to further develop the gluten.

Turn the dough out onto a lightly floured surface and knead it briefly by hand. Coat a large mixing bowl with the ¼ cup oil, place the dough in the bowl, and turn the dough over a few times to coat it with the oil. Cover the bowl with plastic wrap and place it in a warm area, away from drafts, to rise. (I put mine in my turned-off gas oven with the pilot light on.) Let rise until doubled in bulk, about 1½ hours. While the dough is rising, make the toppings:

Drop the peaches into boiling water for 30 seconds to loosen the skins. Drain, run under cold water, and slip the skins off. Cut each peach into about twenty ⅛-inch-thick slices. Set them aside in a bowl and refrigerate until needed.

Whisk together the mascarpone, brown sugar and rum in a small bowl. Set aside and refrigerate until needed.

Punch the dough down, gather it into a ball, and let it rise again for 40 minutes. The dough is now ready to use, or it may be held, well covered with plastic wrap, in the refrigerator for 3 hours.

Make a fire using hardwood charcoal, with the coals all piled on the left side of the grill. (You need a hot side and a cold side.)

Divide the dough into 8 equal balls and place them on a sheet pan that has been heavily coated with liquid clarified butter. Cover with plastic wrap.

Have a work table set up to the right of the grill with your equipment in place as follows: to the extreme right of the table, the sheet pan with the dough balls; then, moving left toward the grill, a clean sheet pan heavily coated with liquefied clarified butter (about ⅛ inch deep); then the peaches with a set of tongs, and the mascarpone mixture with 2 teaspoons; then a jar with liquefied clarified butter and a pastry brush; then another set of tongs and a hot-mitt.

The table on the other side of the grill should hold a cutting board, a pizza wheel and a serving platter.

When the coals have all turned ashen, you are ready to go.

Take one ball of dough and place it on the empty buttered sheet pan. Use your fingers to press it out into a very thin flat circle. Don't worry about making a perfect circle—just keep pressing and patting the dough out as thin as possible. You should be able to see the pan through it.

Quickly lift the pizza with your fingers and place it on the hot side of the grill, over the coals. Cook until the bottom begins to brown and blister, usually 3 to 5 minutes. Keep peeking by lifting it with the tongs. Meanwhile, give the top a good coating of clarified butter. When the bottom is browned, flip it over and immediately drag it to the cool side of the grill.

Very quickly brush the pizza with clarified butter, then dot the surface with about ⅓ cup of the mascarpone mixture, which may be sticky. The 2 teaspoons will help make this easier. Using the tongs, scatter about 10 peach slices over the pizza. Drag the pizza back over the coals, drizzle with a little clarified butter, and continue to cook until the mascarpone begins to bubble, about 2 minutes.

Immediately drag the pizza over onto the cutting board on the left-hand table and hand it off to a helper who can cut and serve it while you begin again. Each pizza should be cut into 6 to 8 wedges. It is possible to do 2 or 3 pizzas at a time, all at staggered stages, but this takes practice.

These must be served immediately.

Dressing Up the Plate

Of course these desserts can be served as is—a soft-crumbed, moist cake with a rich buttercream is gorgeous as a solitary wedge on a plate. But sometimes a sauce can add that little something extra.

Oftentimes desserts in restaurants have several components and look very impressive. But sometimes a chef goes overboard. The one caution, and it is a big one, is that all the components on the plate must work together, and all of them should be there for a reason. For a general rule of thumb, think about the dessert's qualities on its own. Is it fruity and warm? Then something cool and creamy will accent it nicely. Is it thick and creamy? Then a crunchy tidbit will enhance it.

For instance, if it is a birthday or other such celebration, the addition of chocolate initials piped onto the plate would be appropriate. A frozen ice cream can be improved by the textural and temperature contrast of a crisp cookie. But a mint leaf on top of a scoop of fruit crisp is not necessarily bringing anything to the dish. It is a touch of green, but usually the mint flavor is not considered a necessary component, and if the crisp is made correctly, the crunchy, nubby topping and vibrantly colored fruit will shine without an herb sprig. If anything, a warm fruit crisp can be enhanced by a cool, creamy sorbet or ice cream.

As you may have noticed by now, the "Bake It to the Limit" suggestions in many of the recipes are indeed these fillips that make the difference. However, sometimes you want even more. Here are some suggestions for you to experiment with.

Sauces

Place the sauce of your choice in a squeeze bottle. Apply the sauce to the plates, over or under the dessert, in a free-form design or in a defined design that you have chosen. One sauce can be used, or more than one for a colorful and flavorful effect.

Ring of Hearts

To create a ring of hearts around the plate, place dots of sauce the size of M&M's around the plate's perimeter. Using a toothpick or a very thin sharp knife, draw through the dots, dragging and extending the end (which will be the heart's point) a little bit. Continue around the plate. Individual hearts, of all sizes, can be made this way as well.

Outline Drawing

Place melted semisweet chocolate in a parchment cone and draw the outlines of any designs you like. You can draw realistic shapes, like butterflies, or free-form silhouettes. Chill the plates for a few minutes to harden the chocolate; then fill in the outlines with one or more liquid sauces. The colors of a caramel and a berry sauce, for example, will bleed into one another within the same outline and create an interesting effect. Play!

Dry Ingredients

Confectioner's sugar, cocoa and cinnamon can all be dusted onto plates. Thoroughly dried edible flowers can be pulverized in a coffee grinder or spice mill. They will have subtle colors that look quite unusual on the plate. A fine-mesh strainer can work for this technique, but a dredger (see page 162) is best.

Gold and Silver Powder

These powders are made of actual gold and silver and can be purchased at cake decorating stores. They are expensive and extravagant, and I reserve them for special occasions like birthdays or anniversaries. You can dust plates with them or sprinkle them over desserts. They look especially nice on top of a chocolate glaze (see Broken Heart Coeur à la Crème, page 82).

Chocolate Designs and Initials

Simply put melted semisweet or bittersweet chocolate in a parchment cone and pipe designs or initials on the edge of each plate. This should be done ahead of time because the plates need to be chilled so that the designs firm up. To gild the lily, brush the designs with some gold or silver powder.

cookies

Cognac Apricot Rugelach ✳ Shortbread Fiori di Sicilia ✳ Adrienne's Gianduja Chocolate
Chunk Cookies ✳ Chunky Raisin Chip Cookies ✳ Espresso White Chocolate Chunk Cookies ✳ Chocolate
Espresso Shortbread ✳ Florentines ✳ Sesame Lace Cookies ✳ Ménage à Trois Cookies ✳ Ginger Crackle Cookies ✳
Macadamia Oat Crisps ✳ Hazelnut Macaroons ✳ Cornmeal Walnut Anise Biscotti ✳ Chocolate Almond Biscotti ✳
Coffee Pecan Oat Shortbread ✳ Tuiles

I love cookies. They can be either elegant or homespun. Some are best eaten the day they are made, but many others keep well in a cookie jar for impromptu snacking. The easier recipes here are perfect for mixing up with the help of the children in your life. A little flour on the floor never hurt anyone—get in there and get your hands dirty.

cognac apricot rugelach

These little crescents are filled with tart cognac-soaked apricots and crunchy walnut bits. Most rugelach recipes use either cream cheese or sour cream; this one uses both, with buttery, rich, flaky results. A drizzle of semisweet chocolate is an optional crowning touch.

Makes 32 cookies

For the dough

4 cups all-purpose flour

¼ teaspoon salt

2 cups (1 pound) unsalted butter, at room temperature

8 ounces cream cheese, at room temperature

½ cup granulated sugar

½ cup sour cream

2 teaspoons vanilla extract

For the filling

1 cup (7 ounces) dried apricots

¼ cup cognac or brandy

3 ounces (about ¾ cup) walnut halves, finely chopped

½ cup granulated sugar

½ cup lightly packed light brown sugar

½ cup apricot fruit spread (do not use jam, which has a high sugar content and would be too sweet)

For the topping

¼ cup whole milk

¼ cup granulated sugar

2 teaspoons ground cinnamon

To make the dough, sift the flour and salt together in a bowl; set aside.

In the bowl of a heavy-duty mixer, beat the butter and cream cheese with the flat paddle on high speed until light and creamy, approximately 3 to 5 minutes. Add the sugar gradually and continue beating until fluffy. Gently beat in the sour cream and vanilla by pulsing the machine on and off a few times.

Add the flour mixture to the wet ingredients in 2 or 3 batches, beating briefly after each addition and scraping down the bowl once or twice. Beat just until combined.

Divide the dough in half, wrap each piece in plastic wrap, and shape each into a flat disc. Refrigerate at least 2 hours, or overnight.

To make the filling, place the apricots and cognac in a food processor fitted with the metal blade. Pulse on and off until the apricots are finely chopped. Scrape into a mixing bowl and add the walnuts, sugar, brown sugar and fruit spread. Stir well to combine. Set aside until needed. The filling may be made 2 days ahead and stored in an airtight container in the refrigerator.

To make the topping, pour the milk into a measuring cup; set aside. Combine the sugar and cinnamon in a small bowl; set aside. Have a pastry brush ready.

Roll out each piece of dough on a floured surface into a 14-inch circle, approximately ⅛ inch thick. Spread the filling over the dough thinly and evenly.

Use a sharp knife or a pizza cutter to divide each circle into 16 wedge-shaped pieces. Starting at the outer edge, roll each piece up. Place the rugelach, center point down, 2 inches apart on a parchment-lined sheet pan. Bend them gently into a crescent shape, if desired. Refrigerate for 1 hour, or cover with plastic wrap and chill overnight.

Fifteen minutes before baking, preheat the oven to 350°F. To prevent the bottoms from burning, place each pan of rugelach on top of another, creating doubled pans. Or use insulated sheet pans if you have them.

Brush the rugelach with the milk and top with a sprinkling of the cinnamon-sugar.

Bake for approximately 30 minutes, rotating the pans front to back halfway through. The rugelach should be puffed and very lightly golden brown. The bottoms burn easily, so be careful not to overbake them. Remove the pans from the oven and place them directly on wire racks to cool.

These are best eaten the day they are made, but they may be stored at room temperature in an airtight container for up to 4 days.

✹ BAKE IT TO THE LIMIT

Top the rugelach with chocolate. Apricots, cognac and chocolate—you've got to try this.

4 ounces semisweet chocolate, finely chopped

Melt the chocolate in a double boiler or microwave. Place it in a parchment cone and snip a small opening at the point of the cone. Drizzle melted chocolate over the cooled apricot rugelach while they are still on the sheet pan, for easy cleanup. Refrigerate briefly to set the chocolate.

VARIATIONS

Raspberry Fig Filling

Prepare this filling as a substitute for the apricot filling in the main recipe.

2 cups (12 ounces) whole dried Calmyrna figs, quartered
1 cup raspberry fruit spread (do not use jam, which has a high sugar content and would be too sweet)

Place the figs in a food processor fitted with the metal blade. Pulse on and off until the figs are finely

chopped. Scrape into a mixing bowl and add the fruit spread. Stir well to combine. Set aside until needed. The filling may be made 2 days ahead and stored in an airtight container in the refrigerator.

Cherry Pecan Filling

Prepare this filling as a substitute for the apricot filling in the main recipe.

1 cup dried tart cherries
½ cup water or Amaretto
3 ounces (about ¾ cup) pecan halves, finely chopped
1 cup raspberry or apricot fruit spread (do not use jam, which has a high sugar content and would be too sweet)
½ cup granulated sugar
½ cup lightly packed light brown sugar

Place the cherries and liquid in a microwaveable bowl, cover with plastic wrap, and microwave on full power for 1 to 2 minutes. This will plump the cherries. Drain the cherries, if necessary, and place them in a food processor fitted with the metal blade. Pulse on and off until the cherries are finely chopped. Scrape into a mixing bowl and add the remaining ingredients. Stir well to combine. Set aside until needed. The filling may be made 2 days ahead and stored in an airtight container in the refrigerator.

Baking Cookies

Whether your cookies are scooped straight out of the mixing bowl or chilled and rolled out, you must prepare your sheet pans in a way that will give the best results. Cookie bottoms have a tendency to burn, but there are precautions you can take to prevent this.

Start with heavy-gauge pans. If you own some insulated cookie sheets, which are double sheets with an air cushion in between, by all means try them with these recipes. However, these pans insulate the cookie bottoms so well that they prevent a desired degree of caramelization in some recipes, and therefore many pastry chefs do not like them. I use sheet pans that have a small raised edge all the way around. They are strong, will not warp, and conduct heat well.

If you have repeated problems with burnt cookie bottoms, try doubling up your sheet pans. Simply stack one on top of another. This creates a layer of air, which will prevent burning.

I always line my sheet pans with parchment. It makes a great nonstick surface for cookies. Even chocolate chip cookies, which are usually baked on a nongreased, bare cookie sheet, will bake better on parchment. You may be able to reuse parchment on occasion, if after removing the cookies the paper is still pretty clean.

Some cookies should be cooled on their sheets, and others are immediately removed to a wire rack. Follow the individual recipe instructions. Proper cooling yields optimum texture. Also, if you have more dough than room in your oven, the pans will have to be reused for a second, or perhaps third, batch; always cool the pans between batches.

Proper storage is crucial too. If the recipe says to store the cookies in an airtight container, do it. Likewise for any other particular directions.

shortbread fiori di sicilia

This shortbread is basically the same as the one in Nick Malgieri's essential book *How to Bake*. I had been searching for a perfect shortbread recipe for years, and Nick offers it up. His technique of completely creaming the butter and sugar, and then adding the flour by hand, results in a truly tender, luscious shortbread. I've just added an unusual flavoring. Fiori di Sicilia is a complex Italian flavoring with notes of orange, lemon and vanilla; you can order it from The Baker's Catalogue (see page 173). It adds an elusive, sophisticated flavor to these cookies.

Makes 24 cookies

2 cups (1 pound) unsalted butter, at room temperature
1 cup granulated sugar
1 teaspoon Fiori di Sicilia (optional)
5 cups all-purpose flour

Using 4 sheet pans, line 2 pans with parchment paper and place them on top of the other 2 sheet pans

There are several chocolate chip cookies recipes in this book, and they all start with melted butter, instead of beginning with soft butter and creaming it with the sugar. Using melted butter yields a very chewy cookie—just the way I like my chocolate chip cookies. However, overbaking the cookies will make them crisp, regardless, so take care.

to create doubled pans to prevent burning. Or use insulated sheet pans, if you have them.

In the bowl of a heavy-duty mixer, beat the butter with the flat paddle attachment until creamy. Add the sugar gradually and continue beating on high speed until very light and fluffy. This may take as long as 10 minutes. Do not rush this stage. The mixture should be almost white in color. Beat in the flavoring, if desired.

Gently stir and fold in the flour using a rubber spatula, until just incorporated. This is important to retain the delicate texture of the shortbread.

Roll the dough out to ½-inch thickness on a lightly floured surface, and cut out cookies with the cookie cutter of your choice. These baking directions are for cookies that are 3 inches across; if yours are smaller, reduce the cooking time, and if larger, increase the cooking time. Reroll any extra dough and cut out as many cookies as possible. Place the cookies on the prepared pans and chill for at least 1 hour.

Fifteen minutes before baking time, preheat the oven to 325°F.

Bake for 15 to 20 minutes. The cookie bottoms should just be turning golden, but the tops should remain as white as possible.

Set the pans directly on wire racks to cool for 5 minutes. Then remove the cookies to a rack and allow to cool completely. These cookies are best eaten within 1 week; store them at room temperature in an airtight container.

adrienne's gianduja chocolate chunk cookies

The Adrienne in the title is Adrienne Welch, an amazing cookbook author (*Sweet Seduction*), baker, and chocolatier. She loves hazelnuts and chocolate, and these cookies are a tribute to her. Gianduja is an Italian blend of chocolate and hazelnut. It comes in block form and has the same smoothness as regular chocolate, but with the added nuance of roasted nuts. I use Callebaut brand, which is a milk chocolate–hazelnut blend. (Gianduja does come in dark chocolate also.) Cacao Barry makes a good version as well.

You can substitute semisweet for the bittersweet chocolate. The bittersweet is preferred because it complements the very sweet gianduja better.

Makes 36 cookies

continued

4½ cups all-purpose flour

1 teaspoon salt

1 teaspoon baking soda

1½ cups (12 ounces) unsalted butter, melted

2 cups lightly packed light brown sugar

1 cup granulated sugar

3 large eggs

1 tablespoon vanilla extract

9 ounces gianduja chocolate, cut into ½-inch chunks (1½ cups)

9 ounces bittersweet chocolate, cut into ½-inch chunks (1½ cups)

3 ounces (¾ cup) hazelnuts, toasted, skinned (see page 151), and coarsely chopped

Preheat the oven to 325°F. Line 2 sheet pans with parchment.

In a bowl, stir together the flour, salt and baking soda; set aside.

In another bowl, whisk together the melted butter, brown sugar and sugar. Whisk in the eggs one at a time, blending well after each addition. Stir in the vanilla. Add the dry ingredients and stir just until combined. Add the chocolates and nuts. The dough may be refrigerated in an airtight container at this stage for up to 4 days, or it may be frozen, tightly wrapped in plastic wrap, for a month.

Form the dough into ¼-cup-size balls, using a ¼ cup measuring cup or ice cream scoop. If the dough has been refrigerated, roll it between your palms. If it is at room temperature, it is easier to scoop the dough.

Place the balls on the prepared pans, leaving 2 inches between them. Bake for 15 to 18 minutes, or until the edges are golden, rotating the pans front to back halfway through the baking time. The centers will be lighter in color, soft and a bit puffed up.

Remember that any cookie will become crisp if over-baked, so watch carefully. One minute too long can make a difference.

Set the sheet pans directly on racks to cool. The cookies are best eaten immediately, while still warm, with a glass of ice-cold milk. Or store them for up to 3 days at room temperature in an airtight container, separating the layers with clean parchment or waxed paper.

chunky raisin chip cookies

Reminiscent of the Chunky candy bar, with one big difference—these raisins are soaked in rum.

Makes 36 cookies

4½ cups all-purpose flour

1 teaspoon salt

1 teaspoon baking soda

1½ cups raisins

½ cup dark rum

1½ cups (12 ounces) unsalted butter, melted

2 cups lightly packed light brown sugar

1 cup granulated sugar

3 large eggs

1 tablespoon vanilla extract

9 ounces (1½ cups) semisweet chocolate chips

6 ounces (about 1 cup) coarsely chopped dry-roasted peanuts

Preheat the oven to 325°F. Line 2 sheet pans with parchment.

In a bowl, stir together the flour, salt and baking soda; set aside.

Place the raisins and rum in a small microwaveable bowl. Cover with plastic wrap and heat in the microwave on full power for 1 to 2 minutes, just enough to plump the raisins and infuse them with rum flavor. Set aside to macerate while you proceed with the recipe.

In another bowl, whisk together the melted butter, brown sugar and sugar. Whisk in the eggs one at a time, blending well after each addition. Stir in the vanilla. Add the dry ingredients and stir just until combined. Add the chocolate, nuts and raisins, including any rum.

The dough may be refrigerated in an airtight container at this stage for up to 4 days, or frozen, tightly wrapped in plastic wrap, for a month.

Form the dough into ¼-cup-size balls, using a ¼ cup measuring cup or ice cream scoop. If the dough has been refrigerated, roll it between your palms. If it is at room temperature, it is easier to scoop the dough.

Place the balls on the prepared pans, leaving 2 inches between them. Bake for 15 to 18 minutes or until the edges are golden, rotating the pans front to back halfway through the baking time. The centers will be lighter in color, soft and a bit puffed up. Remember that any cookie will become crisp if overbaked, so watch carefully. One minute too long can make a difference.

Set the sheet pans directly on racks to cool. The cookies are best eaten immediately, or they may be stored for up to 3 days at room temperature in an airtight container; separate the layers with clean parchment or waxed paper.

espresso white chocolate chunk cookies

These are great with that afternoon cup of coffee or with a glass of ice-cold milk. They are a classic chocolate chip cookie, adding white chocolate and flavored with espresso.

Makes 36 cookies

4½ cups all-purpose flour

2 tablespoons freshly and finely ground espresso

1 teaspoon salt

1 teaspoon baking soda

1½ cups (12 ounces) unsalted butter, melted

2 cups lightly packed light brown sugar

1 cup granulated sugar

3 large eggs

1 tablespoon vanilla extract

12 ounces white chocolate, cut into ½-inch chunks (2 cups)

5 ounces (about 1 cup) walnut or pecan halves, toasted (see page 152) and coarsely chopped

Preheat the oven to 325°F. Line 2 sheet pans with parchment.

In a bowl, stir together the flour, espresso, salt and baking soda; set aside.

In another bowl, whisk together the melted butter, brown sugar and sugar. Whisk in the eggs one at a time, blending well after each addition. Stir in the vanilla. Add the dry ingredients and stir just until combined. Add the chocolate and nuts. The dough may be refrigerated in an airtight container at this stage for up to 4 days, or it may be frozen, tightly wrapped in plastic wrap, for a month.

Form the dough into ¼-cup-size balls, using a ¼ cup measuring cup or ice cream scoop. If the dough has been refrigerated, roll it between your palms. If it is at room temperature, it is easier to scoop the dough.

Place the balls on the prepared pans, leaving 2 inches between them. Bake for 15 to 18 minutes, or until the edges are golden, rotating the pans front to back halfway through the baking time. The centers will be lighter in color, soft and a bit puffed up. Remember that any cookie will become crisp if overbaked, so watch carefully. One minute too long can make a difference.

Set the sheet pans directly on racks to cool. The cookies are best eaten immediately, or they can be stored for up to three days at room temperature in an airtight container; separate the layers with clean parchment or waxed paper.

✳ BAKE IT TO THE LIMIT

Espresso Kahlúa Ice Cream Sandwiches Dipped in Bittersweet Chocolate

Ice cream sandwiches appeal to kids, but these are a grown-up incarnation. Filled with Espresso Kahlúa Ice Cream and dipped in dark chocolate, this is one extravagant ice cream sandwich!

Makes 10 sandwiches

1 recipe Espresso Kahlúa Ice Cream (page 99)
20 Espresso White Chocolate Chunk Cookies,
*   completely cooled*
20 ounces bittersweet chocolate, finely chopped

Scoop the ice cream into ten ½-cup balls and flatten them with your hands so that they are the shape of hockey pucks. They should be the same diameter as the cookies. Place the ice cream discs on a sheet pan and freeze until solid, at least 1 hour. This may be done a day ahead.

Sandwich each disc of ice cream between 2 cookies, pressing the cookies so they adhere to the ice cream. Return the sandwiches to the sheet pan and place in the freezer.

Meanwhile, melt the chocolate in a double boiler or microwave. Pour the melted chocolate into a small deep bowl, to create a deep pool of chocolate. Cool to room temperature; the chocolate should still be fluid. Have a parchment-lined sheet pan ready.

Grasp an ice cream sandwich as though you were going to eat it, and dip half of the sandwich into the chocolate. Let the excess chocolate drip off, and then place the sandwich on the prepared sheet pan, flat side down. Repeat with the remaining sandwiches. Freeze until the chocolate is solid, about 10 minutes, or until serving time.

These may be made a day ahead. Let them soften at room temperature for 5 or 10 minutes before serving. The ice cream should be frozen but not rock-hard. The cookies need to defrost a bit too.

chocolate espresso shortbread

A rich, buttery, crumbly shortbread with a deep chocolate taste, accented with espresso.

Makes 30 cookies

2 cups (1 pound) unsalted butter,
   at room temperature
1¼ cups granulated sugar
4¼ cups all-purpose flour
¾ cup Dutch-process cocoa
1 teaspoon instant espresso powder
¼ teaspoon salt

In the bowl of a heavy-duty mixer, beat the butter with the flat paddle attachment on medium speed until creamy. Add the sugar gradually and continue beating until light and fluffy, about 5 minutes.

In another bowl, stir together the flour, cocoa, espresso powder and salt. Add to the creamed mixture and beat on low speed until incorporated.

Scrape the soft dough onto a large piece of plastic wrap and gather together into a ball. Refrigerate for 1 to 2 hours, or until firm enough to roll out. You may chill it overnight; just let it soften a bit at room temperature before proceeding.

Preheat the oven to 325°F. Line 2 sheet pans with parchment.

Roll out the dough on a lightly floured surface to ½-inch thickness. Cut out cookies with a cookie cutter of your choice. These baking instructions are for 3-inch cookies. If you make small cookies, reduce the baking time, larger cookies will require a longer baking time. Reroll any extra dough and cut out as many cookies as possible. Transfer the cookies to the prepared pans, keeping them at least 1 inch apart.

Bake for 20 to 25 minutes, rotating the pans front to back halfway through the baking time. These cookies are so dark that it is impossible to see if they are beginning to color. Use the time suggested and check to see if the edges and bottoms are completely dry. You should be able to lift a cookie up with a spatula to peek at the bottom; the cookie should be baked enough to remain stiff and not break.

Set the pans directly on a wire rack to cool for 5 minutes. Then remove the cookies to the rack and cool completely. The sheet pans must be cooled completely between uses, but you will probably be able to reuse the parchment.

The cookies are best eaten within 1 week; store them at room temperature in an airtight container.

✶ BAKE IT TO THE LIMIT
Chocolate Espresso Shortbread Hearts with Edible Gold and Silver

These chocolate cookies can be cut into small heart shapes for Valentine's Day and embellished with edible gold and silver powder (found at cake decorating stores).

Makes 30 hearts

1 recipe Chocolate Espresso Shortbread dough, chilled
2 shot glasses or other small containers
Edible gold and/or silver powder
Vodka
2 small, soft artist's paintbrushes

Roll out, cut and bake heart-shaped shortbread cookies (any size or assorted sizes) as described in the main recipe. Cool completely.

continued

Sprinkle some gold powder in one glass, some silver in the other—about ½ teaspoon in each. Drizzle a tiny bit of vodka into each glass; start with about ¼ teaspoon and add more if necessary. Stir the powders with the brushes. You want the mixture to have the consistency of paint. Now paint free-form or planned designs on the cookies. The metallic paint looks gorgeous against the dark chocolate background. The paint will dry almost immediately. Store the cookies as described above.

florentines

Caramel, chocolate, orange, cherries and almonds. Chewy and crunchy. The best.

Makes 18 cookies

6 tablespoons (3 ounces) unsalted butter,
*   cut into large pieces*
⅔ cup granulated sugar
⅓ cup heavy cream
3 tablespoons honey
⅓ cup dried tart cherries
⅓ cup water or Amaretto
3 ounces (about 1 cup) sliced almonds,
*   blanched or natural, half of them chopped*
⅓ cup diced candied orange peel
¼ cup all-purpose flour
6 ounces semisweet or bittersweet chocolate,
*   finely chopped*

Preheat the oven to 350°F. Using 4 sheet pans, line 2 pans with parchment paper and place them on top of the other 2 pans to create doubled pans to prevent burning. Or use insulated pans, if you have them.

Melt the butter in a medium-size saucepan. Add the sugar, cream and honey and bring to a simmer. Cook to 230°F. (If you dip a spoon into the mixture and dribble it in a glass of cold water, it will spin a thread.)

Meanwhile, place the cherries and liquid in a microwaveable bowl, cover with plastic wrap, and microwave on full power for 1 to 2 minutes. This will plump the cherries. Drain, if necessary.

Stir the cherries, almonds, candied orange peel and flour into the cream mixture.

Drop 2-tablespoon-size mounds of the batter onto the prepared pans. Dampen your hands with cold water and flatten the cookies with your fingers.

Bake in the middle of the oven for 10 to 15 minutes, rotating the pans front to back halfway through the baking time. The cookies will spread, the edges will darken, and the centers will just begin to bubble. Do not overbake.

Place the pans directly on racks to cool. Some of the cookies may not have a nice round shape. Coax them into a rounder shape by pulling in the stray edges with a large round cookie/biscuit cutter as follows: The cookie cutter must be larger in diameter than the Florentines. Place the cookie cutter over a misshapen Florentine. Use the inside edges of the cookie cutter to draw in the edges of the Florentine. Rotating the cookie cutter in a circular motion also helps form the Florentine into a nice round shape. Completely cool the cookies on the pans.

Meanwhile, melt the chocolate in a double boiler or microwave.

Carefully remove the cooled cookies from the sheet pans with a spatula. Using a small offset spatula, spread chocolate over the bottoms of the cookies. Make a wavy pattern with a decorator's comb, if desired. Place the cookies, chocolate side up, back on the sheet pans. Place in the refrigerator until the chocolate is set, about 10 minutes.

Store in single layers, separated by waxed paper or parchment, in an airtight container in the refrigerator. Best when eaten within 4 days.

sesame lace cookies

These light, sweet, crunchy cookies are a great foil for summery sorbets and ice creams. They are quick to mix up in one pot, leaving you with little cleanup. One caveat: they are as fragile as can be, so take care when stacking them for storage.

Makes 60 cookies

½ cup sesame seeds

½ cup (4 ounces) unsalted butter, cut into large pieces

¾ cup lightly packed light or dark brown sugar

⅓ cup light corn syrup

1 cup rolled oats (not quick or instant)

2 tablespoons all-purpose flour

1 teaspoon vanilla extract

¼ teaspoon salt

Preheat the oven to 350°F. Line 2 sheet pans with parchment and lightly spray them with nonstick cooking spray. (If you have 4 sheet pans, your baking will go more quickly because you can have 2 in the oven and 2 cooling at the same time). Have an additional bare sheet pan ready for toasting the seeds.

Spread the sesame seeds out on the unlined sheet pan and toast until golden and fragrant, approximately 5 minutes. Set aside to cool.

Place the butter in a medium-size saucepan and melt over medium heat. Add the brown sugar and corn syrup, and stir to combine. Bring to a boil, turn down the heat, and simmer for 1 minute. Remove from the heat.

Add the oats, flour, vanilla and salt, and stir with a wooden spoon to combine. Stir in the toasted sesame seeds.

Drop the batter by ½ teaspoons at least 2 inches apart on the prepared sheet pans. It is important to keep the cookies small because they really spread out. Bake the cookies for 6 to 8 minutes, rotating the pans front to back once during baking. The cookies should be evenly golden brown.

Place the sheet pans directly on racks to cool. The cookies will harden up in a few minutes. The sheet pans must be cooled completely between uses, but you will probably be able to reuse the parchment.

When they have cooled, transfer them to airtight containers, keeping them as flat as possible and separating the layers with parchment or waxed paper. They must be stored at room temperature in an airtight container. Humidity will soften and ruin these cookies.

ménage à trois cookies

These trufflelike cookies are packed with white, milk and dark chocolate. I have been sitting on this recipe for almost ten years, waiting to publish it. Make these right now!

Makes 30 cookies

12 ounces semisweet chocolate, finely chopped

4 ounces unsweetened chocolate, finely chopped

¾ cup (6 ounces) unsalted butter, cut into large pieces

4 large eggs

1½ cups granulated sugar

1 tablespoon vanilla extract

½ cup all-purpose flour

½ teaspoon baking powder

1 teaspoon salt

12 ounces semisweet or bittersweet chocolate, cut into ½-inch chunks (2 cups)

9 ounces milk chocolate, cut into ½-inch chunks (1½ cups)

9 ounces white chocolate, cut into ½-inch chunks (1½ cups)

Preheat the oven to 350°F. Line 2 sheet pans with parchment. (If you have 4 sheet pans, your baking will go more quickly because you can have 2 in the oven and 2 cooling at the same time.)

Melt the finely chopped semisweet and unsweet- ened chocolates together with the butter in a double boiler or microwave. Stir occasionally until smooth. Cool slightly to a warm room temperature.

Place the eggs, sugar and vanilla in the bowl of a heavy-duty mixer and beat with the balloon whip attachment on high speed until light and fluffy, 2 to 5 minutes. Fold in the chocolate mixture until no streaks remain (an extra-large rubber spatula works best).

Place the flour, baking powder and salt in a bowl and stir together with a whisk to aerate lightly.

Fold the flour mixture into the batter just until combined. Fold in all of the chocolate chunks.

Use a ¼-cup-size measuring cup or ice cream scoop to drop the batter onto the prepared sheet pans. Leave 3 inches between the cookies.

Bake for 14 minutes. Rotate the pans front to back once during baking. With these cookies it is hard to judge doneness. Depending on your oven, they will be done after 14 to 17 minutes, when the tops and edges have become dull but the insides and middles are still soft. It will go against your instincts to pull them out of the oven now, but they are done. Do not overbake! They will firm up a bit when cool, but they will remain chocolate truffle–like inside. Bake one or two at first and play around with the timing until you get it right before embarking on the rest of the batter.

Place the pans directly on racks to cool. If you try to remove the cookies too soon, they will fall apart. When they are cool, remove them from the pans with a spat- ula that is large enough to support the entire bottom of each cookie. Keeping them as flat as possible, store them in single layers separated by parchment or waxed paper. They must be stored at room temperature in an airtight container. Don't worry about storing them for long, though—these go fast. Eat within 2 days.

★ BAKE IT TO THE LIMIT

This is very easy and makes a big difference. Reserve about a quarter of the chocolate chunks, all flavors. Scoop the batter onto the sheet pans. Then manually press the chocolate chunks into the cookie tops before baking. The chunks will remain quite visible and make the cookies look as if they are bursting with chocolate.

ginger crackle cookies

These gingerbreadlike cookies have a crackly appearance with an extra-crunchy sugar topping. You can substitute regular granulated sugar for the coarse sugar if necessary, but the results will be different.

Makes 12 large or 24 small cookies

1 cup (8 ounces) unsalted butter, at room temperature

1 cup granulated sugar

1 cup molasses

1½ teaspoons ground ginger

1 teaspoon ground cinnamon

½ teaspoon ground nutmeg

½ teaspoon ground cloves

2 large eggs

4 cups all-purpose flour

1 teaspoon baking soda

1 teaspoon salt

1 cup coarse sugar (see Note)

In the bowl of a heavy-duty mixer, beat the butter with the flat paddle attachment on medium speed until creamy. Add the sugar gradually and beat on medium-high speed until light and fluffy, about 3 minutes. Beat in the molasses and spices until blended. Add the eggs one at a time, beating well after each addition and scraping down the bowl once or twice.

In another bowl, stir together the flour, baking soda and salt. Add the dry ingredients in 2 or 3 batches to the wet ingredients, pulsing the beater on and off to incorporate gently. Cover the bowl with plastic wrap and refrigerate for 2 hours.

Fifteen minutes before baking, preheat the oven to 350°F. Line 2 sheet pans with parchment.

Use a ¼-cup-size measuring cup or ice cream scoop to scoop out the dough. (These cookies can also be made in miniature size. Use an ⅛-cup-size scoop and bake for 10 to 15 minutes.) Roll each one between your palms to form a ball. Dip the cookies in the coarse sugar, covering half of the ball. Place, sugar side up, on the sheet pans and flatten with the palm of your hand or the flat bottom of a water glass. Leave 2 inches between cookies. You should be able to accommodate 6 large cookies on each pan.

Bake for 15 to 20 minutes, rotating the pans front to back once during the baking time. The cookies will be slightly darker around the edges, puffed and lighter in the middle.

Place the pans directly on wire racks to cool. Store the cookies at room temperature in an airtight container for up to 4 days.

Note: Coarse sugar, sometimes called sugar crystals, can be found at cake-decorating stores or mail-ordered from Sweet Celebrations (see page 176).

BAKE IT TO THE LIMIT

Pumpkin Ice Cream Sandwiches with Ginger Crackle Cookies

I love Thanksgiving—it's a real family-and-friends holiday. Oftentimes, when the adults are reminiscing, the kids get a bit bored. Here's something for them to look forward to.

Makes 6 sandwiches

1 recipe Ginger Crackle Cookies (12 large cookies)

3 cups Pumpkin Ice Cream (page 98)

Scoop the ice cream into six ½-cup balls and flatten them into discs that resemble a hockey puck. They should be the same diameter as the cookies. Place the ice cream discs on a sheet pan and freeze until solid, at least 1 hour. This may be done a day ahead.

Immediately before serving, sandwich each ice cream disc between 2 cookies, pressing the cookies so they adhere. (You can also make mini-sandwiches. Use 24 small cookies to make 12 tiny ice cream sandwiches. For these, the ice cream should be shaped into ¼-cup-size balls before flattening.)

These may be made a day ahead and stored on the pan in the freezer. Let them soften at room temperature for 5 to 10 minutes before serving. The ice cream should be frozen but not rock-hard. The cookies need to defrost a bit too.

macadamia oat crisps

These crispy, lacy cookies are excellent with ice creams and sorbets. They are very fragile, however, so store them carefully. They appear in a photograph with Lemon Velvet Ice Cream on page 102.

Makes 24 cookies

¼ cup (2 ounces) unsalted butter, cut into large pieces

½ cup lightly packed light brown sugar

¼ cup light corn syrup

1½ cups rolled oats (not quick or instant)

2½ ounces (about ½ cup) unsalted macadamias, lightly toasted (see page 152) and finely chopped

Preheat the oven to 350°F. Line 2 sheet pans with parchment and lightly spray them with nonstick cooking spray. (If you have 4 sheet pans, your baking will go more quickly because you can have 2 in the oven and 2 cooling at the same time.)

Melt the butter in a medium-size saucepan over medium heat. Stir in the brown sugar and corn syrup. Bring to a boil, turn down the heat, and simmer for 1 minute. Remove from the heat and stir in the oats and nuts.

Drop the batter by tablespoon at least 2 inches apart onto the prepared sheet pans. It is important to keep the cookies relatively small because they really spread out. Bake the cookies for approximately 15 minutes, rotating the pans front to back once during baking. The cookies should have flattened out and turned evenly golden brown.

Place the sheet pans on racks and let the cookies cool on the pans. The sheet pans must be cooled completely between uses, but you will probably be able to reuse the parchment. Keeping the cookies as flat as possible, store them in single layers separated by parchment or waxed paper. They must be stored at room temperature in an airtight container. Eat within 4 days.

hazelnut macaroons

These are French-type macaroons, not the Jewish-American coconut type. They are crisp and chewy at the same time, and worth the effort.

Makes 36 cookies

5½ ounces (1 cup plus 2 tablespoons) hazelnuts, toasted and skinned (see page 151)

2 tablespoons granulated sugar

1¾ cups plus 2 tablespoons confectioner's sugar, sifted

3 large egg whites

⅛ teaspoon cream of tartar

Preheat the oven to 450°F. Line 2 sheet pans with parchment.

continued

Place the nuts, granulated sugar and ¾ cup plus 2 tablespoons of the confectioner's sugar in a food processor fitted with the metal blade. Process until the nuts are ground to a fine meal. Set aside.

Using a heavy-duty mixer, beat the egg whites in a clean, grease-free bowl with the balloon whip attachment on low speed until frothy. Add the cream of tartar and continue beating on medium-high speed until soft peaks form. Gradually add the remaining 1 cup confectioner's sugar and continue to whip until stiff, but not dry, peaks form.

Fold the dry mixture into the egg whites. Place in a large pastry bag fitted with a ½-inch plain round tip. Pipe cookies the size of silver dollars about 2 inches apart on the prepared sheet pans. They will look like large Hershey's Kisses. Dip your index finger in cold water and pat down the points to make a more rounded shape.

Place the pans in the oven and immediately turn the oven down to 375°F. Bake for approximately 10 minutes, or until the cookies are dry and you can lift one from the parchment. Place the sheet pans directly on a wire rack to cool completely before removing the cookies from the pan.

✳ BAKE IT TO THE LIMIT

Sandwiching these cookies with a bittersweet chocolate ganache takes them to a higher level of sophistication.

3½ ounces bittersweet chocolate, finely chopped
¼ cup heavy cream

Place the chocolate in a heatproof bowl. Bring the cream to a boil in a small saucepan over medium heat, and pour over the chocolate. Let sit for a few minutes, then whisk to melt the chocolate and combine with the cream. Place the bowl over another bowl filled with ice, and stir until the mixture is thick enough to spread (or refrigerate until the consistency is right), stirring occasionally, about 1 hour.

Using a pastry bag fitted with a coupler and a small star tip, such as a #18, pipe a swirl of ganache on the bottom of half of the cookies. (Alternatively, use a small offset spatula to spread the ganache on.) Top each cookie with another one to make a ganache sandwich.

Refrigerate for 5 minutes to firm up the ganache. Then store at room temperature until ready to serve. These should be eaten the day they are assembled.

cornmeal walnut anise biscotti

These have a sandy quality from the cornmeal and a licorice bite from the anise seed. Wayne Brachman, the inventive pastry chef at New York's Mesa Grill and Bolo, offers a blue cornmeal/pecan version in his book *Cakes and Cowpokes*. The anise seed and walnuts add a new dimension, and I prefer the color of an all-yellow-cornmeal version.

Makes 36 biscotti

2¾ cups all-purpose flour
1 cup fine-ground yellow cornmeal
1½ teaspoons baking powder
1 teaspoon baking soda
1 teaspoon salt
¼ cup anise seed
6 large eggs
1 cup granulated sugar
5 ounces (1 cup) walnuts, toasted (see page 152)
    and finely chopped

Preheat the oven to 325°F. Line 2 sheet pans with parchment.

In a mixing bowl, sift together the flour, cornmeal, baking powder, baking soda and salt; set aside.

Spread the anise seed on a chopping surface. Use the flat bottom of a metal measuring cup to crush the seed, pressing down and out, a little at a time. Or you can place the seed between waxed paper and roll with a rolling pin.

In the mixing bowl of a heavy-duty mixer, beat the eggs and sugar with the balloon whip on high speed until light and fluffy. Add the dry ingredients and incorporate by pulsing the machine on and off. Stir in the anise seed and walnuts.

Form the dough into 3 logs, and place 2 on one prepared sheet pan, 1 on the other. The logs should be the length of the pan and about 2 inches in diameter. The dough will be wet; use a spatula to help shape and smooth the logs.

Bake for 30 minutes or until dry and just turning light brown, rotating the pans front to back once during baking. Remove the pans from the oven and place them directly on wire racks to cool for 10 minutes. Turn the oven down to 275°F.

Place the logs on a cutting surface and slice them on the diagonal into ½-inch-thick pieces. Arrange the slices on the sheet pans, cut sides down. Bake for 20 minutes or until drier and crispy. Remove the cookies from the pans and let them cool completely on wire racks. Store in an airtight container for up to 3 weeks.

chocolate almond biscotti

These biscotti are crunchy and chocolatey, with extra chocolate chips and nuts packed into the dough.

Makes 45 biscotti

4¼ cups all-purpose flour

¼ cup Dutch-process cocoa

1 tablespoon baking powder

1 teaspoon salt

4 ounces semisweet chocolate, finely chopped

1 cup (½ pound) unsalted butter, at room temperature

¾ cup granulated sugar

¾ cup lightly packed light brown sugar

4 large eggs

1 tablespoon Amaretto liqueur

9 ounces (1½ cups) chocolate chips

7½ ounces (about 1½ cups) whole blanched almonds, roughly chopped

Preheat the oven to 325°F. Line 2 sheet pans with parchment.

In a mixing bowl, sift together the flour, cocoa, baking powder and salt; set aside.

Melt the chocolate in a double boiler or microwave; set aside.

Meanwhile, in the bowl of a heavy-duty mixer, beat the butter with the flat paddle attachment on high speed until creamy. Gradually add the sugar and brown sugar, and continue beating until light and fluffy, about 2 minutes. Add the eggs one at a time, scraping down the bowl and beating well after each addition. Beat in the melted chocolate and the Amaretto. Add the dry ingredients in 3 batches by pulsing the machine on and off, scraping down the bowl once or twice. Stir in the chocolate chips and nuts.

Form the dough into 3 logs, and place 2 on one prepared sheet pan, 1 on the other. The logs should be the length of the pan and about 2 inches in diameter. The dough will be wet but firm; use floured hands to help roll the logs into shape.

Bake for 35 to 45 minutes, or until dry and firm, rotating the pans front to back once during baking. Remove the pans from the oven and place them directly on wire racks to cool for 10 minutes. Turn the oven down to 275°F.

Place the logs on a cutting surface and slice them on the diagonal into ½-inch-thick pieces. Arrange the slices on the sheet pans, cut sides down. Bake for 20 minutes or until drier and crispy. Remove the cookies from the pans and let them cool completely on wire racks. Store in an airtight container for up to 3 weeks.

✦ BAKE IT TO THE LIMIT

Chocolate-covered almonds can be found in specialty food stores. They are dusted with cocoa and make delicious tidbits on their own. They are expensive, but folded into this biscotti batter they add an unexpected treat. They replace the chocolate chips and almonds in the basic version.

12 ounces (2¼ cups) cocoa-dusted chocolate-covered almonds, halved

Simply fold these into the batter instead of the chocolate chips and almonds.

coffee pecan oat shortbread

This is a dry, crumbly cookie, perfect to serve with a bowl of fresh sliced peaches or strawberries. I started with the basic shortbread recipe, added instant coffee, and replaced some of the flour with ground oats and finely chopped pecans. Don't be afraid to play with recipes like that; it is how new recipes are born.

Makes 18 cookies

2 cups (1 pound) unsalted butter, at room temperature
1 cup lightly packed light brown sugar
1 tablespoon plus 1 teaspoon instant coffee or espresso powder
3 cups all-purpose flour
1 cup rolled oats (not quick or instant)
5 ounces (1 cup) pecan halves, toasted (see page 152)

Preheat the oven to 325°F. Line 2 sheet pans with parchment.

In the bowl of a heavy-duty mixer, beat the butter with the flat paddle attachment until creamy. Add the brown sugar gradually and beat on high speed until very light and fluffy, about 3 to 5 minutes. The mixture will also lighten in color. Beat in the coffee.

Meanwhile, sift the flour and set aside. Place the oats in a food processor fitted with the metal blade and process until finely ground, with the consistency of wheat germ. Add the oats to the flour. Now place the nuts in the food processor and pulse on and off until finely chopped. Add them to the flour/oat mixture.

Add the dry ingredients to the creamed butter/sugar mixture and stir in by hand just until combined.

Using a ¼-cup measuring cup or ice cream scoop,

scoop the dough onto the prepared sheet pans, placing the cookies 2 inches apart. Bake for 20 to 25 minutes, or until the edges are just turning golden and the tops are dry, rotating the sheet pans front to back once during the baking. Place the pans directly on racks to completely cool. Then remove the cookies and store them in an airtight container for up to 4 days.

★ BAKE IT TO THE LIMIT

These cookies can be finished off nicely with a drizzle of bittersweet chocolate.

4 ounces bittersweet or semisweet chocolate, finely chopped

Melt the chocolate in a double boiler or microwave. Meanwhile, arrange the cookies close together on parchment-lined sheet pans.

Place the melted chocolate in a parchment cone, and cut a tiny opening in the tip. Drizzle the chocolate, sweeping your arm back and forth to make horizontal lines all over the cookies. They don't have to be parallel, just random.

Place the pans in the refrigerator for 5 minutes to harden the chocolate. Store at room temperature up to 2 days.

tuiles

Tuile batter is a classic cookie batter that makes an extremely thin, crispy cookie. It is spread within the confines of a template or stencil. You can make your own stencils using the opaque white plastic meant just for this purpose (found at sewing and craft stores).

Simply use an X-acto knife to cut out shapes of your choice. See Note for information on making templates.

Makes dozens of cookies, depending on size of stencil

¼ cup (2 ounces) unsalted butter, at room temperature
½ cup confectioner's sugar, sifted
2 large egg whites
¼ teaspoon vanilla extract
½ cup cake flour, sifted

Preheat the oven to 400°F. Line 2 sheet pans with parchment and lightly spray them with nonstick cooking spray.

Cream the butter and confectioner's sugar together in the bowl of a heavy-duty mixer, using the flat paddle attachment on medium-low speed, until light and fluffy, about 1 minute. Add the egg whites, one at a time, beating well after each addition. Beat in the vanilla. Add the flour and beat in carefully, pulsing the machine on and off. Do not overmix. Make sure the batter is completely smooth.

Lay a stencil over one of the sheet pans and spread a thin, even layer of batter inside the stencil, using a small offset spatula. Lift off the stencil and repeat, keeping the cookies at least 1 inch apart. If you are making tuile bowls (see below), bake only 2 or 3 at a time. (They firm up very quickly, and you won't be able to drape them in time.) For spoons, you can make several at a time.

Bake for approximately 5 minutes (depending on the size of the stencil), until the edges are brown but the cookie center is still pale. Rotate the pans front to back once during baking. Watch carefully—they can turn dark brown very quickly. Remove from the oven and place the pans directly on a wire rack.

For tuile bowls, immediately remove the cookies with a spatula and drape each one over the bottom of a glass. Use your hand to mold the cookie down and around the glass, forming an upside-down bowl. Let the cookies cool on the glasses. These are best used the day they are baked, but they can be stored in an airtight container for up to 3 days.

The spoon-shaped cookies can be cooled on the pans, then stored in single layers in an airtight container, with parchment or waxed paper between the layers. They are very fragile.

Tuiles may be stored at room temperature for up to 3 days. Any moisture, however, will leave you with soggy, inedible cookies.

Note: For a teaspoon stencil, trace a realistically sized teaspoon onto plastic. Make sure the handle is wide enough that it will not break, at least ½ inch. If you want to make a bowl, trace a circle 5 or 6 inches in diameter.

breakfast sweets and snack-time treats

Oat Scones ✳ Pear Bread ✳ Calvados Applesauce Date Cake ✳ Chocolate Chunk

Peanut–Butter Banana Crunch Cake ✳ Buttermilk Poppy Seed Muffins ✳ Honey Maple Carrot Muffins ✳

Apricot Vanilla Bean Muffins

This chapter includes snack cakes, muffins and a very special scone—simple recipes all,

even in their Bake It to the Limit incarnations. Most of these whip up easily, so if you are

looking for a quick sweet fix, look no further.

oat scones

These simple scones are powerfully addictive. When I owned a bakery—Harvest Moon, in Amherst, Massachusetts—they were our most popular item, outselling our all-butter croissants, fancy tortes, and all of our pastries. They are rich, but what a special weekend treat they make. They are essentially the same scones as in Susan Purdy's *A Piece of Cake*, but the Sucanat gives them their special quality. You may substitute granulated or brown sugar, but the results will be very different. Sucanat, which you can find in natural-foods stores, stands for SUgar CAne NATural and is organic sugar cane that has been dried but minimally processed. Its full, complex flavor enriches the scones in a unique way.

Makes 21 scones

1¼ cups (10 ounces) unsalted butter, melted

⅔ cup whole milk, at room temperature

2 large eggs, at room temperature

3 cups all-purpose flour

2½ cups rolled oats (not quick or instant)

½ cup Sucanat

2 tablespoons baking powder

2 teaspoons cream of tartar

¾ teaspoon salt

1 cup raisins, dried tart cherries or dried cranberries

Preheat the oven to 375°F. Line 2 sheet pans with parchment.

In a mixing bowl, whisk together the melted butter, milk and eggs.

In a large bowl, stir together the flour, oats, Sucanat, baking powder, cream of tartar, salt and dried fruit.

(You may plump the dried fruit in advance—soak it in hot water for about 30 minutes, then drain. Or, microwave for 1 to 2 minutes.)

Pour the wet mixture over the dry and stir just until combined.

Using a ¼-cup measuring cup or ice cream scoop, place scoops of the batter on the prepared pans, forming 2 rows of 4 scones each on each pan. Fit the extra scones in between. Dip the bottom of a glass in flour and use it to flatten the scones.

Bake for 12 to 17 minutes. The scones should be lightly browned around the edges. The tops should be dry but not too highly colored, and the bottoms lightly colored but not too dark. Place the pans on a wire rack to cool for 5 minutes, then remove the scones to the rack.

These are best served warm and must be eaten the day they are made.

Tip: The night before, prepare the dry mix and combine the milk and eggs in a bowl; cover and refrigerate the milk mixture. In the morning, melt the butter and mix the batter together. It goes quite quickly.

pear bread

Pears and ginger are a combination I adore (see Crystallized Ginger Pear Tart, page 21). Here, this sweet bread is filled with both fresh and dried pears, pecans and ginger.

Magi-Cake Strips (see page 163) really help this bread bake evenly.

Makes one 9¼ × 5¼-inch loaf, 12 slices

2 cups all-purpose flour

1½ teaspoons baking soda

¼ teaspoon salt

*5 ounces (about 1 cup) pecan halves, toasted
(see page 152) and chopped*

*6 dried pear halves (4 ounces), chopped into ¼-inch
pieces (about ¾ cup)*

*2 ripe (7- to 8-ounce) Comice or Anjou pears, peeled,
cored and diced*

¾ cup (6 ounces) unsalted butter, at room temperature

1 cup granulated sugar

1½ teaspoons ground ginger

1 teaspoon vanilla extract

2 large eggs

Preheat the oven to 325°F. Spray a 9¼ × 5¼-inch loaf pan with nonstick cooking spray and dust it with flour.

In a mixing bowl, stir together the flour, baking soda and salt. Add the pecans, dried pears and fresh pears; toss to coat. Set aside.

In the bowl of a heavy-duty mixer, beat the butter with the flat paddle attachment on medium speed until creamy. Add the sugar gradually and continue beating until light and fluffy, about 2 minutes. Beat in the ginger and vanilla. Add the eggs one at a time, beating well after each addition and scraping down the bowl once or twice.

Stir the dry mixture into the wet mixture by hand just until combined. Scrape the batter into the prepared pan. Wrap the pan with Magi-Cake Strips (see page 163). Bake for 65 to 75 minutes. To test for doneness, insert a toothpick: it should come out clean.

Cool in the pan on a wire rack for 10 minutes, then turn the bread out of the pan and let it cool thoroughly on the rack before slicing.

This bread is best if allowed to sit for 6 hours, or overnight, before serving. Store at room temperature wrapped in plastic wrap. Best if eaten within 2 days.

calvados applesauce date cake

This is a moist, flavorful snack cake. It's great with tea, for breakfast or to bring in the bucks at a bake sale.

Makes one 10-inch ring, 8 to 10 slices

1 cup chopped pitted Medjool dates (about 12 dates)

¼ cup Calvados (apple brandy)

2¼ cups all-purpose flour

1 teaspoon baking soda

1 teaspoon ground cinnamon

½ teaspoon ground nutmeg

½ teaspoon salt

¼ teaspoon ground cloves

*5 ounces (1 cup) pecan halves, toasted (see page 152)
and chopped*

¾ cup (6 ounces) unsalted butter, at room temperature

⅔ cup granulated sugar

⅔ cup lightly packed light brown sugar

2 large eggs

1 Granny Smith apple, peeled and grated

1 cup unsweetened applesauce, preferably homemade

For the glaze

1 cup (4 ounces) confectioner's sugar, sifted

1 tablespoon plus 1 teaspoon Calvados

1 tablespoon heavy cream

continued

Preheat the oven to 350°F. Spray a 10-inch (6- to 8-cup) ring mold with nonstick cooking spray.

In a small bowl, combine the dates and Calvados; set aside to macerate.

Into a mixing bowl, sift the flour, baking soda, cinnamon, nutmeg, salt and cloves. Toss together with the pecans; set aside.

In the bowl of a heavy-duty mixer, beat the butter with the flat paddle attachment on high speed until creamy. Add the sugar and brown sugar gradually, and beat until very light and fluffy, about 3 minutes. Add the eggs one at a time, beating well after each addition and scraping down the bowl once or twice.

In a small bowl, stir together the grated apple, applesauce, dates and any Calvados that hasn't been absorbed by the dates.

In alternating batches, fold the dry ingredients and the apple mixture into the creamed butter/sugar mix. Stir in just until blended.

Spread the batter evenly in the prepared ring pan. Bake for 40 to 50 minutes, or until an inserted toothpick comes out clean. Cool in the pan on a wire rack for 10 minutes, then unmold the cake onto a rack to cool completely.

Meanwhile, make the glaze. In a small bowl, combine the confectioner's sugar, Calvados and cream, whisking together until smooth. Pour into a parchment cone, and pipe zigzags back and forth over the top of the cake after it has completely cooled.

Store at room temperature for up to 24 hours. Loosely cover with foil, if necessary, until serving time.

Note: To chop dates easily, refrigerate them first and then chop them with a flour-coated knife.

chocolate chunk peanut-butter banana crunch cake

The idea for the banana chip topping came from Elinor Klivans, in her book *Bake and Freeze Desserts*. The combo of chocolate, peanut butter and banana came from my desire to meld these flavors, which go so well together. Use Magi-Cake Strips (see page 163) to help this cake bake evenly.

Makes 9 to 12 bars

For the batter

½ cup (4 ounces) unsalted butter, at room temperature

½ cup smooth hydrogenated peanut butter (like Jif or Skippy)

½ cup granulated sugar

½ cup lightly packed light brown sugar

1 teaspoon vanilla extract

2 large eggs

1 ripe medium-size (6- to 7-ounce) banana, peeled and cut into 1-inch chunks

1 cup all-purpose flour

1 teaspoon baking powder

¼ teaspoon salt

6 ounces semisweet chocolate, cut into ¼-inch chunks (1 cup)

For the topping

1 cup sweetened banana chips, roughly chopped

½ cup lightly packed light brown sugar

¼ cup (2 ounces) unsalted butter, melted

¼ cup all-purpose flour

continued

Preheat the oven to 350°F. Spray an 9 × 9-inch square cake pan with nonstick cooking spray.

To make the batter, place the butter and peanut butter in the bowl of a heavy-duty mixer and beat with the flat paddle attachment on medium speed until smooth. Add the sugar and brown sugar gradually, and beat on high speed until light and fluffy, about 3 minutes. Beat in the vanilla. Then add the eggs one at a time, beating well after each addition and scraping down the bowl once or twice. Add the banana and pulse the machine on and off a few times to incorporate the banana pieces. They should break down a bit and blend in with the batter.

In a separate bowl, stir the flour, baking powder and salt together. Add to the batter, mixing just until incorporated. Fold in the chocolate chunks. Scrape the batter into the prepared pan.

To make the topping, combine the banana chips, brown sugar, melted butter and flour in a small bowl. Mix well. Sprinkle this mixture over the top of the batter. Wrap the pan with Magi-Cake Strips (see page 163).

Bake for 45 to 55 minutes. The cake should look golden, and the sides should be just coming away from the pan; an inserted toothpick will come out clean. Cool the cake in the pan thoroughly on a wire rack before cutting, about 30 minutes.

Store at room temperature, covered with plastic wrap, for up to 3 days.

⭐ **BAKE IT TO THE LIMIT**

This may push it over the top, but we all need that every now and then.

Confectioner's sugar
3 ounces semisweet chocolate, melted

Sprinkle the confectioner's sugar over the cooled cake. Place the melted chocolate in a parchment cone and drizzle it over the top of the cake.

buttermilk poppy seed muffins

Poppy seeds have a subtle taste and crunch; grinding them maximizes their flavor. Here they are added to a soft-crumbed buttermilk muffin.

Makes 12 muffins

¼ cup poppyseeds
1 cup buttermilk
½ cup (4 ounces) unsalted butter, at room temperature
1 cup granulated sugar
½ teaspoon vanilla extract
½ teaspoon orange oil (optional; see Note)
3 large eggs
2 cups all-purpose flour
1½ teaspoons baking powder
½ teaspoon baking soda
½ teaspoon salt

Preheat the oven to 350°F. Heavily spray a 12-cup muffin pan with nonstick cooking spray, spraying the top of the pan as well as the inside of the cups.

Grind the poppy seeds in a clean coffee or spice grinder. In a large measuring cup, combine the ground poppy seeds with the buttermilk; set aside to soak while preparing the rest of the batter.

In the bowl of a heavy-duty mixer, beat the butter with the flat paddle attachment on medium speed until creamy. Add the sugar gradually and continue beating until light and fluffy, about 2 minutes. Beat in the vanilla and orange oil, if using. Add the eggs one at a time, beating well after each addition and scraping down the bowl once or twice.

In another bowl, stir together the flour, baking powder, baking soda and salt. In alternating batches, add the dry mixture and the buttermilk mixture to the batter, stirring in by hand just until blended.

Divide the batter among the prepared muffin cups. Bake for 25 to 30 minutes, or until an inserted toothpick comes out clean and the tops spring back when lightly pressed.

Cool in the pan set on a wire rack for 5 minutes, then unmold the muffins onto a wire rack. These are best served warm. Store at room temperature, covered with foil, but eat the same day.

Note: Orange oil, made by Boyajian, can be ordered from Williams-Sonoma or found at a local specialty food store. It is the distillation of oils from orange zest and has an incomparable flavor. Do not substitute orange extract, which has an artificial flavor; if necessary, substitute the grated zest of 1 orange.

⭐ **BAKE IT TO THE LIMIT**
Serve these muffins with Marmalade Butter for a little something extra.

½ cup (4 ounces) unsalted butter, at room temperature
¼ cup orange marmalade
1 tablespoon orange juice
1 tablespoon Grand Marnier (optional)

Combine the butter, marmalade, orange juice and Grand Marnier, if using, in a small bowl. Stir together until thoroughly mixed. Pack into a ramekin or other similar serving dish, and serve alongside the warm muffins.

honey maple carrot muffins

These are like mini carrot cakes, ready to brighten up your breakfast or midday snack. The muffins are sweetened with honey and maple syrup and are made with half whole wheat flour, so you can feel a bit more virtuous eating them first thing in the A.M. Check to see if your natural-foods store has dark, grade B maple syrup in the bulk food section; it is much more flavorful and less expensive than fancy grade A bottled syrup, although either will work perfectly.

Makes 12 muffins

12 ounces carrots
½ cup canola oil
⅓ cup honey
⅓ cup maple syrup
3 large eggs
¾ cup all-purpose flour
¾ cup whole wheat pastry flour
1½ teaspoons baking powder
1½ teaspoons baking soda
½ teaspoon salt
1½ teaspoons ground cinnamon
¾ teaspoon ground nutmeg
⅓ cup raisins

Preheat the oven to 350°F. Heavily spray a 12-cup muffin pan with nonstick cooking spray, spraying the top of the pan as well as the inside of the cups.

Wash and peel the carrots. Trim both ends and grate in a food processor, using the medium grating attachment; or grate on the largest holes of a hand grater. Set aside.

In a large bowl, combine the oil, honey and maple

syrup, whisking together well. Add the eggs one at a time, whisking well after each addition.

In another bowl, stir together the flour, whole wheat pastry flour, baking powder, baking soda, salt, cinnamon and nutmeg. Add the dry ingredients to the wet, stirring just until the mixture is combined. Stir in the carrots and raisins.

Divide the batter among the prepared muffin cups. Bake for 25 to 30 minutes, or until an inserted toothpick comes out clean and the tops spring back when lightly pressed.

Cool in the pan for 5 minutes, then unmold the muffins onto a wire rack. These are best served warm. Store at room temperature, covered with foil, but eat within 24 hours.

✴ BAKE IT TO THE LIMIT

A lightly sweetened Honey Vanilla Cream Cheese Frosting makes these a complete breakfast for on-the-run mornings. Great for kid's lunch boxes too. You can make these the night before.

10 ounces cream cheese, at room temperature

3 tablespoons honey

¼ teaspoon vanilla extract

In the bowl of a heavy-duty mixer, beat the cream cheese with the flat paddle attachment on medium speed until creamy. Add the honey and vanilla and beat until smooth, about 30 seconds.

Spread the frosting on the completely cooled muffins, using an icing spatula; or pipe the frosting out of a pastry bag fitted with a large star tip to make a swirl on top of each muffin. Store as described above.

apricot vanilla bean muffins

Fragrant with vanilla and chewy with dried apricots, these will wake you up in the morning. Vanilla extract can be substituted for the vanilla bean, but the flavor will not be as full.

Makes 12 muffins

½ cup (4 ounces) unsalted butter, at room temperature

1 cup granulated sugar

1 vanilla bean, split, or 1 teaspoon vanilla extract

2 large eggs

3 cups all-purpose flour

1 tablespoon baking powder

½ teaspoon baking soda

¼ teaspoon salt

1½ cups buttermilk

7 ounces (1 cup) dried apricots, finely chopped

Preheat the oven to 375°F. Heavily spray a 12-cup muffin pan with nonstick cooking spray, spraying the top of the pan as well as the inside of the cups.

In the bowl of a heavy-duty mixer, beat the butter with the flat paddle attachment on medium speed until creamy. Add the sugar gradually and beat until light and fluffy, about 2 minutes. Scrape the vanilla bean seeds into the mixture and beat them in briefly (or add the extract, if using). Beat in the eggs one at a time, beating well after each addition and scraping down the bowl once or twice.

In another bowl, stir together the flour, baking powder, baking soda and salt; set aside.

In alternating batches, add the buttermilk and dry ingredients to the batter, stirring in by hand just until combined. Stir in the apricots.

Divide the batter among the prepared muffin cups.

Bake for 20 to 25 minutes or until the tops are lightly golden. Cool in the pan for 5 minutes, then unmold the muffins onto a rack.

These are best served warm. Store at room temperature, covered with foil, but eat the same day.

⭐ BAKE IT TO THE LIMIT

An extra topping of almond paste and coarse sugar makes these extra-special, great for a birthday brunch. The vanilla powder can be found in specialty stores, or mail-ordered through Williams-Sonoma. It is pure powdered vanilla and boosts the flavor.

2 ounces almond paste
¼ cup coarse sugar (see Note)
1 tablespoon all-purpose flour

1 tablespoon (½ ounce) unsalted butter, at room temperature
½ teaspoon vanilla powder

Crumble the almond paste into a small mixing bowl. Add the sugar, flour, butter and vanilla powder and mix together well. Pat a small amount on top of the uncooked batter in each muffin cup. Bake, cool and serve as directed.

Note: Coarse sugar, sometimes called sugar crystals, can be found at cake-decorating stores or mail-ordered from Sweet Celebrations.

brownies and bars

Easy to whip up and baked in one pan, brownies and bars will always have their place in the baker's repertoire. Some of these store better than others. Individually wrapping the bars in plastic wrap, whether they are refrigerated or stored at room temperature, will keep them at their freshest.

fudgy bittersweet brownies

These are pure unadulterated chocolate. No nuts, no cakey texture—just smooth, fudgy brownies.

Makes 24 brownies

10 ounces bittersweet chocolate, finely chopped

¾ cup (6 ounces) unsalted butter, cut into large pieces

1¾ cups granulated sugar

5 large eggs

2½ cups all-purpose flour

½ teaspoon baking powder

½ teaspoon salt

Preheat the oven to 350°F. Spray a 13 × 9-inch baking pan with nonstick cooking spray.

Melt the chocolate and butter in a double boiler or microwave. Whisk together until smooth and set aside.

Meanwhile, place the sugar and eggs in the bowl of a heavy-duty mixer. Using the balloon whip attachment, whip on high speed until light and fluffy, about 3 minutes.

Add the melted chocolate mixture to the eggs, and beat just until combined.

In another bowl, whisk together the flour, baking powder and salt. Add to the batter, stirring in by hand just until combined.

Scrape the batter into the prepared pan. Bake for 25 to 35 minutes. When the brownies are done, the top will look dull and a bit puffed, and the edges will be barely coming away from the pan's sides. A toothpick inserted in the center will come out with some wet batter attached. The longer you bake them, the drier they'll be, so don't overbake.

Cool completely in the pan on a wire rack before cutting into bars. If you like, trim off the edges before cutting. Store at room temperature covered with plastic wrap. Best eaten within 24 hours.

marzipan apricot brownies

These multitiered bars consist of a shortbread base covered with a layer of apricot preserves, topped with a layer of almond paste, and crowned with a layer of Fudgy Bittersweet Brownie.

Makes 32 brownies

For the almond shortbread

½ cup (4 ounces) unsalted butter, at room temperature

¼ cup granulated sugar

¼ teaspoon almond extract

1¼ cups all-purpose flour

For the middle layers

½ cup apricot preserves

10 ounces almond paste

For the brownie layer

5 ounces bittersweet chocolate

6 tablespoons (3 ounces) unsalted butter, cut into large pieces

¾ cup granulated sugar

2 large eggs

1¼ cups all-purpose flour

¼ teaspoon baking powder

¼ teaspoon salt

continued

Preheat the oven to 325°F. Spray a 13 × 9-inch baking pan with nonstick cooking spray.

To make the almond shortbread, place the butter in the bowl of a heavy-duty mixer and beat at medium-high speed with the flat paddle attachment until creamy. Add the sugar gradually and continue beating on high speed until very light and fluffy. This may take as long as 10 minutes. Do not rush this stage. The mixture should be almost white in color. Blend in the almond extract.

Gently stir in the flour by hand, just until incorporated. A light hand is necessary to retain the delicate texture of the shortbread. Pat the shortbread dough into the prepared pan, using your fingertips to make an even layer completely covering the bottom.

Bake for 10 to 12 minutes, or until dry and just starting to color. Set on a wire rack to begin cooling. Increase the oven temperature to 350°F.

To make the middle layers, heat the apricot preserves in a small pan over low–medium heat. Brush or spoon an even layer of the warmed preserves over the still-warm shortbread.

Roll out the almond paste to the dimensions of the pan and about ¼ inch thick. Place on top of the apricot layer. It's okay if it is in pieces.

Make the brownie layer. Melt the chocolate and butter in a double boiler or microwave. Whisk together until smooth and set aside.

Meanwhile, place the sugar and eggs in the bowl of a heavy-duty mixer. Using the balloon whip attachment, whip on high speed until light and fluffy, about 3 minutes.

Add the melted chocolate mixture to the eggs, and beat just until combined.

In another bowl, whisk together the flour, baking powder and salt. Add to the batter, stirring in by hand just until combined. Pour the batter over the almond paste layer, using an offset spatula to spread it evenly.

Bake for 15 to 20 minutes, or until the brownie layer is dull and a bit puffed and the edges have barely come away from the pan's sides. A toothpick inserted in the center of just the brownie layer will come out with some wet batter attached.

Cool completely in the pan on a wire rack before cutting into bars. These are rich, so you can cut small pieces; if you like, trim off the edges before cutting. Store at room temperature covered with plastic wrap. Best eaten within 24 hours.

chocolate chunk ginger bars

These have a buttery brown sugar base filled with chocolate chunks and crystallized ginger. The combination may surprise you, but it works. The hit of ginger is enhanced with a ginger liqueur called Canton. You can buy little "nips" of Canton, so you won't break the bank mixing up a batch.

Makes 24 bars

¾ cup (6 ounces) unsalted butter, at room temperature

1½ cups lightly packed light brown sugar

½ teaspoon vanilla extract

4 teaspoons Canton ginger liqueur, or 4 teaspoons water

2 large eggs

2 cups all-purpose flour

2 teaspoons baking powder

1 teaspoon ground ginger

½ teaspoon salt

12 ounces semisweet chocolate, cut into ½-inch chunks (2 cups)

2 ounces crystallized ginger, finely chopped (⅓ cup)

Preheat the oven to 350°F. Spray a 13 × 9-inch baking pan with nonstick cooking spray.

In the bowl of a heavy-duty mixer, beat the butter with the flat paddle attachment on medium speed until creamy. Add the brown sugar gradually and continue beating until light and fluffy, about 2 minutes. Beat in the vanilla and Canton liqueur. Then add the eggs one at a time, blending well after each addition and scraping down the bowl once or twice.

In a separate bowl, stir the flour, baking powder, ginger and salt together. Add to the batter, mixing just until incorporated. Fold in the chocolate chunks and crystallized ginger. Scrape the batter into the prepared pan.

Bake for 30 to 40 minutes, or until golden and a bit puffed, with the edges just coming away from the sides of the pan. An inserted toothpick will come out clean.

Cool completely in the pan on a wire rack before cutting into bars. Store at room temperature covered with plastic wrap. Best eaten within 24 hours.

lemon espresso bars

These are for coffee-lovers. They have a pleasantly bitter coffee flavor, just like a good shot of espresso. The lemon oil and peel add a subtle nuance. These are not for your kid's bake sale. Save them for an adult afternoon tea or indulge in one for a major midday pick-me-up.

Doubling up the pan or using Magi-Cake Strips (see page 163) is highly recommended to help this bar bake evenly.

Makes 16 bars

¾ cup (6 ounces) unsalted butter, melted
¾ cup granulated sugar

¾ cup lightly packed light brown sugar
½ teaspoon vanilla extract
½ teaspoon lemon oil (see Note)
3 large eggs
¼ cup instant espresso powder
1 cup all-purpose flour
¾ teaspoon baking powder
¼ teaspoon salt
2½ ounces bittersweet chocolate, finely chopped
1½ ounces diced candied lemon peel

Preheat the oven to 350°F. Spray an 8 × 8-inch square baking pan with nonstick cooking spray. Place it inside another 8 × 8-inch pan (or use Magi-Cake Strips, below).

In a mixing bowl, whisk together the melted butter, sugar, brown sugar, vanilla and lemon oil. Add the eggs one at a time, whisking well after each addition. Stir in the instant espresso.

In another bowl, stir together the flour, baking powder and salt. Add the chocolate and lemon peel, and toss to coat. Stir the dry ingredients into the butter/espresso mixture just until combined. Scrape the batter into the prepared pan. Wrap the pan with Magi-Cake Strips if you did not double the pan.

Bake for 50 to 60 minutes, or until a toothpick inserted in the center comes out clean.

Cool to room temperature in the pan on a wire rack before cutting into squares. Store at room temperature, covered with plastic wrap. Best eaten within 24 hours.

Note: Lemon oil, made by Boyajian, can be ordered from Williams-Sonoma or found at specialty food stores. It is the distillation of oils from lemon zest and has an incomparable flavor. Do not substitute lemon extract. If necessary, substitute the finely grated zest of 1 lemon.

double-layer truffle brownies

My bakery manager, Lori Maki, gave me this recipe. I have never seen another one quite like it. It has a fudgy brownie base filled with walnuts, and a ganache layer that is baked right on top for a richer-than-rich flavor and texture. Very decadent.

Makes 32 brownies

For the bottom layer

½ cup (4 ounces) unsalted butter, cut into large pieces

2½ ounces semisweet chocolate, finely chopped

1½ teaspoons vanilla extract

1 teaspoon instant coffee or espresso powder

Pinch salt

1 cup granulated sugar

2 large eggs

½ cup all-purpose flour

6 ounces (about 1¼ cups) walnut halves, toasted (see page 152) and coarsely chopped

For the top layer

8 ounces semisweet chocolate, finely chopped

½ cup (4 ounces) unsalted butter, cut into large pieces

2 tablespoons granulated sugar

½ cup heavy cream

Pinch salt

1 teaspoon instant coffee or espresso powder

1 teaspoon vanilla extract

1 large egg

4 large egg yolks

Preheat the oven to 325°F. Spray a 13 × 9-inch baking pan with nonstick cooking spray.

To make the bottom layer, melt the butter and chocolate together in a double boiler or microwave. Whisk together until smooth and transfer to a large bowl. Stir in the vanilla, instant coffee and salt. Whisk in the sugar. Add the eggs one at a time, whisking well after each addition. Add the flour and stir briefly just until smooth. Then stir in the nuts, and scrape the batter into the prepared pan.

To make the top layer, melt the chocolate and butter together in a double boiler or microwave. Off the heat, whisk in the sugar, cream, salt, instant coffee and vanilla. Add the egg and egg yolks one at a time, whisking well after each addition. Stir until smooth. Pour over the bottom layer, using an offset spatula, if necessary, to spread evenly.

Bake for 25 to 30 minutes, or until the top has a dull cast and the edges are just pulling away from the pan's sides. A toothpick inserted in the center will have a bit of moist batter clinging to it. Do not overbake. Cool in the pan on a wire rack.

To serve, these must be thoroughly cooled. After cooling, they may be refrigerated for 30 minutes to 1 hour to facilitate cutting. Store at room temperature, or refrigerated, covered with plastic wrap. Best eaten within 2 days. May be served at room temperature or chilled.

continued

★ BAKE IT TO THE LIMIT

Perfect with coffee following a fancy dinner.

35 dark-chocolate-covered espresso beans (see Note)

You will need a 1½-inch round cookie cutter.

Cool the brownies to room temperature, then refrigerate for 1 hour. Cut out 35 rounds with the cookie cutter (rows of 5 across and 7 down). Place each round in a fluted cup, if desired, and top with a chocolate-covered espresso bean. Follow the storage and serving instructions above.

You'll be left with extra scraps of brownie. Fold them into vanilla ice cream for Truffle Brownie Ice Cream.

Note: Chocolate-covered espresso beans are real coffee beans, covered with dark chocolate. You can find them at better coffee stores and specialty food stores.

toffee fudgies

Here is a brownie recipe (you can never have too many) that gets its deep caramel flavor from dark brown sugar and toffee bits. Semisweet chocolate chips are thrown in for good measure.

Makes 24 brownies

1 cup (8 ounces) unsalted butter, cut into large pieces
5 ounces unsweetened chocolate, finely chopped
2 cups lightly packed dark brown sugar
1 tablespoon vanilla extract
4 large eggs

2 cups all-purpose flour
½ teaspoon baking powder
¼ teaspoon salt
6 ounces (about 1 cup) semisweet chocolate chips, or 6 ounces semisweet chocolate, cut into ¼-inch chunks
1¼ cups toffee bits (such as Skor)

Preheat the oven to 350°F. Spray a 13 × 9-inch baking pan with nonstick cooking spray.

Melt the butter and chocolate in a double boiler or microwave. Whisk together until smooth and transfer to a large bowl. Whisk in the brown sugar and vanilla. Add the eggs one at a time, whisking well after each addition.

In another bowl, stir together the flour, baking powder and salt. Add the dry ingredients to the wet mixture, stirring just until blended. Fold in the chocolate chips and 1 cup of the toffee chips.

Scrape the batter into the prepared pan. Bake for about 30 minutes. Sprinkle the remaining ¼ cup toffee bits over the top. Continue to bake for 5 to 10 minutes. The top should look dull and a bit puffed, and the edges should be barely coming away from the pan's sides. A toothpick inserted in the center will come out just clean.

Cool completely in the pan on a wire rack before cutting into bars. Store at room temperature, covered with plastic wrap. Best eaten within 24 hours.

fruity paradise bars

These are a naturally sweetened, fruit-filled bar further enhanced with whole wheat pastry flour. If you're looking for an alternative to chocolate-laced bars, this is it. They are a good lunch box addition. Light brown sugar may be substituted for the Sucanat, if desired.

Makes 9 bars

6 tablespoons (3 ounces) unsalted butter, at room temperature

¾ cup Sucanat (see Note) or lightly packed light brown sugar

2 teaspoons vanilla extract

1 large egg

½ cup all-purpose flour

½ cup whole wheat pastry flour

1 teaspoon baking powder

½ teaspoon salt

2 cups mixed dried fruit: equal amounts of diced pineapple, papaya, and dates, and whole cranberries or cherries

Preheat the oven to 350°F. Spray an 8 × 8-inch square baking pan with nonstick cooking spray.

In the bowl of a heavy-duty mixer, cream the butter and Sucanat with the flat paddle attachment on medium-high speed until light and fluffy, about 3 minutes. Beat in the vanilla, then add the egg, blending well.

In another bowl, stir the flours, baking powder and salt together. Add to the batter, mixing just until incorporated. Fold in the dried fruit. Scrape the batter into the prepared pan.

Bake for approximately 25 minutes. The top should be golden and a bit puffed, and the edges should be just coming away from the sides of the pan. An inserted toothpick will come out clean.

Cool completely in the pan on a wire rack before cutting into bars. Store at room temperature, covered with plastic wrap. Best eaten within 24 hours.

Note: Sucanat, which stands for SUgar CAne NATural, can be found at most natural-foods stores. It is granular like white sugar, but is a pale beige in color and has a slightly earthy, molasseslike flavor.

✦ BAKE IT TO THE LIMIT

Here's one of those super-easy, it's-almost-like-cheating techniques. Just reserve about a quarter of the dried fruit. After the batter has been spread in the pan, sprinkle the fruit over the top and press it in gently with your hand or with an offset spatula. The bars will bake up with the fruit looking as if it is bursting out of them, just waiting to be eaten.

blonde dates

I am a diehard brunette (my days of magenta hair are long over), but these are my favorite variety of blond. They are crunchy with nuts and very moist with dates.

Makes 24 bars

1 cup (8 ounces) unsalted butter, at room temperature

1¾ cups lightly packed dark brown sugar

Grated zest of 1 orange

1 teaspoon vanilla extract

2 large eggs

2 cups plus 2 tablespoons all-purpose flour

1 teaspoon baking powder

½ teaspoon salt

1 cup chopped pitted Medjool dates (about 12 dates)

2 ounces (about ½ cup) walnut halves, toasted (see page 152) and coarsely chopped

continued

Preheat the oven to 350°F. Spray a 13 × 9-inch baking pan with nonstick cooking spray.

In the bowl of a heavy-duty mixer, cream the butter at medium-high speed with the flat paddle attachment. Add the brown sugar gradually and beat on high speed until light and fluffy, 2 to 4 minutes. Beat in the zest and vanilla. Add the eggs one at a time, beating well after each addition and scraping down the bowl once or twice.

In another bowl, stir together the flour, baking powder and salt. Add to the wet mixture, pulsing the machine on and off just to begin to incorporate. There should still be streaks of flour remaining. Add the dates and nuts, mixing just until combined.

Scrape the batter into the prepared pan, smoothing the top with an offset spatula. Bake for 20 to 30 minutes, or until an inserted toothpick comes out clean. Cool completely in the pan on a wire rack before cutting into bars.

Store at room temperature, covered with plastic wrap. Best eaten within 3 days.

cocomac shortbread with lime curd

This bar consists of a buttery shortbread enriched with shredded coconut and finely chopped macadamias, topped with a layer of lime curd and toasted coconut flakes. A touch of the tropics.

Makes 24 bars

For the shortbread

1 cup (8 ounces) unsalted butter, at room temperature
½ cup granulated sugar

2 cups all-purpose flour
¼ cup unsweetened shredded coconut
2 ounces (about ½ cup) macadamias, toasted (see page 152) and finely chopped

For the topping

¾ cup unsweetened flaked coconut (large flakes)

For the lime curd

¾ cup granulated sugar
¼ cup freshly squeezed lime juice
2 large eggs
1 large egg yolk
6 tablespoons (3 ounces) unsalted butter, at room temperature, cut into chunks

Spray a 13 × 9-inch baking pan with nonstick cooking spray.

Make the shortbread. Place the butter in the bowl of a heavy-duty mixer and beat at medium-high speed with the flat paddle attachment until creamy. Add the sugar gradually and continue beating on high speed until very light and fluffy. This may take as long as 10 minutes. Do not rush this stage. The mixture should be almost white in color.

Gently stir in the flour, coconut and nuts by hand, just until incorporated. A light hand is necessary to retain the delicate texture of the shortbread.

Pat the shortbread into the prepared pan in an even layer, and refrigerate for at least 1 hour.

Fifteen minutes before the chilling time is done, preheat the oven to 325°F.

Bake the shortbread for 20 to 30 minutes, or until it is a pale golden brown. Place the pan on a wire rack and cool to room temperature.

While the crust is baking, make the topping. Spread the coconut flakes on a sheet pan and toast in

the oven for about 5 minutes, or until golden. Set aside.

Meanwhile, make the lime curd. Place the sugar, lime juice, eggs and egg yolk in the top of a double boiler. Whisk together just enough to break up the eggs and begin to combine the mixture. Add the butter. Fill the bottom of the double boiler with enough hot water to just touch the bottom of the insert. Set the double boiler over medium heat and bring the water to a simmer, whisking the mixture occasionally.

Cook for 20 to 30 minutes, whisking frequently, or until the mixture reaches 180°F when tested with an instant-read thermometer. The mixture will have thickened and should form a soft shape when a spoonful is dropped on top of the rest. Remove from the heat and let cool to room temperature.

Spread the cooled lime curd on top of the cooled shortbread. Refrigerate until the curd has completely firmed up, at least 1 hour. You may hold the bars overnight at this point. Store in the refrigerator for up to 1 day, with plastic wrap covering the pan but not touching the lime curd.

Sprinkle the top with the toasted coconut right before cutting and serving the bars.

sour cherry bars

Sour cherry season is brief, winking through around the end of July or the beginning of August. Pitting these cherries by hand will take an hour and is not fun. A manual cherry/olive pitter will make much quicker work of the job. I use mine only twice or maybe three times a year, but I feel the $20 gadget was well worth its cost. (You can, in a pinch, use canned cherries. The Thank You brand of water-packed sour cherries comes in 14½-ounce cans, which yield 1½ cups of cherries; so you would need 3 cans.)

Do not use sweet Bing cherries for this; they won't work.

Makes 20 bars

For the crust

1 cup (8 ounces) unsalted butter, at room temperature

4 ounces almond paste

½ cup granulated sugar

¼ teaspoon salt

1 large egg

1 large egg yolk

3 cups all-purpose flour

For the filling

1 quart sour cherries, pitted, or 3 cans sour cherries packed in water, drained

¾ cup granulated sugar

3 tablespoons instant tapioca

1 tablespoon plus 1 tablespoon unsalted butter

2 teaspoons almond extract

1 teaspoon freshly squeezed lemon juice

Spray a 13 × 9-inch baking pan with nonstick cooking spray.

Make the crust. Combine the butter, almond paste and sugar in the bowl of a heavy-duty mixer and beat with the flat paddle attachment on medium-high speed until light and creamy, about 3 minutes. Beat in the salt, egg and egg yolk. Add the flour and beat on low speed until the dough just begins to come together. Use your hands to gather it together; it will be sticky. Flatten the dough into a disc and divide in half. Wrap one half in plastic wrap. Pat the other half evenly over the bottom of the prepared pan, using floured fingertips. Refrigerate the pan and the wrapped dough for at least 2 hours, or overnight.

Meanwhile, make the filling. Combine the pitted cherries, sugar and tapioca in a medium-size saucepan. Bring to a boil over medium heat; then turn the heat down and simmer for 15 minutes, stirring frequently. The mixture should thicken appreciatively. Remove the pan from the heat and add the butter, almond extract and lemon juice. Cool to room temperature.

Preheat the oven to 375°F.

Bake the crust for 12 minutes, or until it is dry to the touch and just browning around the edges.

Meanwhile, on a floured surface, roll out the remaining dough and cut it into strips 13 inches long and ½ inch wide.

Remove the pan from the oven and spread the cherry filling over the crust. Lay the dough strips on top, first lengthwise about ½ inch apart, then diagonally about ½ inch apart, trimming to fit.

Bake for 30 to 35 minutes, or until the crust is just turning golden and the filling is bubbling.

Cool completely in the pan on a wire rack before cutting into bars. Store at room temperature, covered with plastic wrap. Best eaten within 24 hours.

Most bars are a simple eat-out-of-hand kind of affair, but these are a bit more substantial and are best served on a plate, maybe with the addition of some softly whipped cream.

✦ BAKE IT TO THE LIMIT

One simple twist can add a new dimension, literally, to these bars. When placing the lattice crust over the filling, simply twist the dough strips to make a loose spiral before laying them down on the fruit. This will give the bars a whole new look.

mousses, puddings and creams

White Chocolate Espresso Pot de Crème ∗ Amaretto Zabaglione with Fresh Apricots ∗ Banana Bourbon Brioche Bread Pudding ∗ Mocha Coeur à la Crème ∗ Crème Brûlée–Stuffed Apples ∗ White Chocolate Pear Mousse ∗ Cardamom Rice Pudding ∗ Citrus Pudding Cake ∗ Pumpkin Cobbler ∗ B&B Frozen Chocolate Mousse ∗ Three-Berry Mascarpone Gratin ∗ Earl Grey Tea Cream ∗ Hazelnut Espresso Crème Brûlée

This chapter includes a broad range of recipes—fruit and chocolate mousses, a pot de crème and a crème brûlée as well as a pudding cake, a creamy cobbler, a bread pudding, a gratin, a tea-flavored cream and a zabaglione. Texture plays an important role in dessert. If creamy and smooth is your idea of a good time, these recipes will satisfy.

white chocolate espresso pot de crème

A *pot de crème* is simply a very rich pudding. This version pairs sweet white chocolate with the bitter edge of espresso, a delightful combination.

Makes 5 servings

1 cup whole milk

1 cup heavy cream

¼ cup espresso beans, coarsely ground

3 ounces white chocolate, finely chopped

2 large eggs

2 large egg yolks

⅓ cup granulated sugar

Have ready 5 half-cup *pot de crème* cups or ramekins.

Bring the milk, cream and ground espresso beans to a boil in a heavy-bottomed saucepan over medium heat. Remove from the heat and add the chopped white chocolate, stirring until it melts and the mixture is smooth. Let steep for 30 minutes. Whisk gently, then reheat until just before the mixture starts to boil.

Meanwhile, preheat the oven to 300°F.

Whisk together the eggs, egg yolks and sugar in a heatproof bowl. To temper the egg mixture, pour a little bit of the hot cream mixture over the eggs and whisk well. Add the remaining hot cream and stir together well. Strain through a fine-mesh strainer into a large pitcher or measuring cup.

Pour the custard into cups or ramekins and set them in a larger pan. Fill the pan with hot water to reach halfway up the ramekins. Bake for 25 to 30 minutes or until set. The centers should still be wobbly; they will firm up upon chilling.

Chill the *pots de crème* for at least 4 hours before serving. They may be eaten the day they are made or refrigerated for up to a day, in which case they should be covered in plastic wrap.

⭐ BAKE IT TO THE LIMIT

These are fine as is, but with a sprinkling of dark chocolate they look more finished, and the slight textural interest is welcome.

1 ounce bittersweet chocolate, grated

Sprinkle the chocolate on the *pots de crème* before baking. The chocolate shavings will create a pretty speckling on top and will add a deep, dark chocolate bite.

amaretto zabaglione with fresh apricots

A *zabaglione* is a creamy yet frothy rich egg sauce. Here it is paired with fresh apricots and crunchy almond cookies.

Makes 6 servings

6 large (3-ounce) ripe fresh apricots

12 Amaretti di Saronno cookies
   (they are packaged in pairs) (see Note)

1 cup heavy cream

2 tablespoons granulated sugar

For the *zabaglione*

4 large egg yolks

¼ cup granulated sugar

2 tablespoons dry Marsala

2 tablespoons Amaretto liqueur

Have six 10-ounce (or larger) wine goblets or other individual dishes ready.

Pit the apricots and cut each fruit into 4 slices.

Crumble the cookies into a small bowl by hand, creating rough pieces; set aside.

Place the cream and sugar in the bowl of a heavy-duty mixer, and beat with the balloon whip attachment on medium speed until soft peaks form; set aside.

To make the *zabaglione*, place the egg yolks and sugar in the top of a double boiler set over simmering water. The bottom of the pan should not touch the water. Whisk until blended and creamy, about 3 to 5 minutes. Dribble the Marsala and Amaretto in slowly, beating all the while. Continue to whisk until the zabaglione is light, frothy and will coat a spoon, 1 to 3 minutes. Remove the top of the double boiler from the heat and immediately assemble the desserts as follows.

Place 4 apricot slices in each goblet. Top with some *zabaglione*, then some whipped cream, then some cookie crumbs. Repeat the sequence, ending with a layer of cookie crumbs on top. Repeat with the remaining goblets and ingredients; serve immediately.

Note: Amaretti di Saronno cookies are available in specialty stores and Italian markets.

banana bourbon brioche bread pudding

This is rich. Very rich. It starts with brioche, a very buttery French yeast bread that you can buy ready-made at any good bakery. The custard is rich with cream and eggs and is flavored with bourbon. The bananas add great flavor and an extra creaminess. The pudding is best served warm, so plan accordingly. Serve it with the bourbon sauce for maximum effect.

Makes 12 servings

1 pound brioche (to make 6 cups of 2-inch cubes)
2 medium-size (6- to 7-ounce) ripe bananas
2 cups whole milk
1 cup heavy cream
1 cup granulated sugar
⅓ cup bourbon
3 large eggs
1 teaspoon vanilla extract

Preheat the oven to 350°F. Butter a 2-quart oven-proof baking dish.

Cut the brioche into 2-inch cubes and place them in the prepared dish. Cut the bananas into ½-inch slices and toss with the cubes. Distribute evenly in the dish.

Whisk together the milk, cream, sugar, bourbon, eggs and vanilla in a large mixing bowl. Pour over the brioche, saturating the cubes evenly. Let sit for 10 minutes.

Bake for 30 to 40 minutes, or until the bread pudding is lightly golden and the custard is just set. A knife inserted into the custard will come out clean. Do not overbake, or the pudding will lose its creamy quality.

Let sit 5 minutes. Serve warm.

★ **BAKE IT TO THE LIMIT**

This bread pudding is flavorful as is, but the addition of a bourbon sauce caps it off gloriously. Make the sauce immediately before serving—it does not keep. Measure out the ingredients, take the pudding out of the oven, make the sauce and then serve.

1 large egg
½ cup granulated sugar
¼ cup (2 ounces) unsalted butter, melted
¼ cup bourbon

Whisk together the egg and sugar in the top of a double boiler. Set over simmering water and continue whisking until warmed and creamy, about 2 minutes. Dribble in the melted butter, then the bourbon, whisking continuously until light and fluffy, about 2 minutes more.

Spoon portions of the bread pudding onto serving dishes and top with some of the warm sauce, pooling some around the pudding as well.

mocha coeur à la crème

Traditional *coeur à la crème* is a lightly sweetened cream cheese that is often served with berries or a berry sauce. Here a coffee-flavored *coeur à la crème* is unmolded onto a chocolate shortbread cookie crust for a newfangled textural contrast. You will need a 3-cup *coeur à la crème* mold, which is a heart-shaped ceramic mold with drainage holes. They can be found in most cookware stores and catalogs. Note that you need to prepare the cream cheese mixture a day ahead.

Makes 6 to 8 servings

½ recipe Chocolate Espresso Shortbread dough (page 40)
1 pound cream cheese, at room temperature
6 tablespoons confectioner's sugar
¼ cup Kahlúa liqueur
2 tablespoons instant coffee or espresso powder
1 teaspoon vanilla extract
1¼ cups heavy cream

Line a sheet pan with parchment and spray with nonstick cooking spray.

Have the shortbread dough prepared and chilled. On a lightly floured surface, roll out the chilled shortbread dough to ½-inch thickness. Place the 3-cup *coeur à la crème* mold, open side down, on top of the dough. Use a sharp knife to trace and cut around the mold to make a large heart-shaped cookie. (You will have extra dough; cut out and make cookies, your choice of shape, for another use.) Transfer the dough to the prepared sheet pan and chill thoroughly while proceeding. Prepare the *coeur à la crème* mold by lining it with dampened cheesecloth, enough to overhang the edges by 4 inches all round.

In the bowl of a heavy-duty mixer, beat the cream cheese with the flat paddle attachment on medium-high speed until smooth and creamy. Add the confectioner's sugar gradually and beat until the mixture is light and fluffy, about 2 minutes.

Meanwhile, whisk together the Kahlúa, instant coffee and vanilla in a small bowl. Whisk until the coffee is dissolved; then beat into the cream cheese mixture.

In another bowl, use the balloon whip attachment to whip the cream until soft peaks form. Fold a quarter of the whipped cream into the cream cheese mixture to lighten it; then fold in the remaining whipped cream.

continued

Scrape the mixture into the prepared mold, smoothing the top. Fold the excess cheesecloth lightly over the mixture; it should cover the entire surface. Place the mold on a rimmed dish (to hold any liquid that drains out) and refrigerate overnight.

Preheat the oven to 325°F.

Bake the shortbread heart for about 35 to 40 minutes (the smaller cookies will take 20 to 25 minutes). These cookies are so dark that it is impossible to see if they are beginning to color. Use the time suggested and check to see if the edges and bottoms are completely dry. You should be able to lift a cookie up with a spatula to peek at the bottom; the cookie should be baked enough to remain stiff and not break. Set the sheet pan directly on a wire rack to cool for 10 minutes. Then remove the cookie(s) to a rack to cool completely.

Have ready a flat serving platter that is large enough to hold the *coeur à la crème* heart. Peel back the cheesecloth from the top of the mold, and place the heart-shaped cookie on top. Invert the platter over the mold and turn the whole thing over. Remove the mold and peel off the cheesecloth.

Serve immediately, or keep refrigerated, covered with plastic wrap, for up to 8 hours before serving. It is ideal if you can refrigerate the dessert for at least 1 hour—this allows the cookie to soften a little bit and facilitates serving.

✶ BAKE IT TO THE LIMIT

To make Broken Heart Coeur à la Crème, simply cover it with melted chocolate. The hardened glaze will crack upon serving—hence the romantic name. Dusting it with gold powder makes this a showstopper. The arrow is optional—but fun.

8 ounces bittersweet couverture chocolate, finely chopped (see page 166; Valrhona Caraque is excellent here)

Edible gold powder (see page 167; optional)

Before you unmold the *coeur à la crème*, cut out a cardboard heart the same size as the mold. Place the heart-shaped shortbread cookie on the *coeur à la crème*, then place the cardboard heart on the cookie. Invert, unmold, and place on a wire rack set over a sheet pan.

Melt the chocolate in a double boiler or microwave. Let it cool slightly. Then pour the melted chocolate over the *coeur à la crème*, covering it completely. If necessary, use a spatula to help distribute the chocolate. Place the heart on a serving platter, leaving the cardboard on, and refrigerate until the chocolate is hard and set, at least 30 minutes.

Serve immediately, or keep refrigerated for up to 8 hours before serving.

Immediately before serving, dust the chocolate with gold, if desired. Use a small dry, soft artist's paintbrush to brush gold powder on top of the chocolate. It will give it a soft burnished appearance—gorgeous.

crème brûlée–stuffed apples

This is a great fall dessert that manages to be homey and elegant at the same time. Cored apples are filled with a crème brûlée mixture and then baked along with the *crème*, making an edible shell.

One note: I made these in the fall with new apples and the recipe worked perfectly. Then, when I was retesting recipes the following summer, I had to use apples that had been in storage all year. It didn't work. The apples were watery and wreaked havoc with the filling. In fact, the apples themselves collapsed. Make this in the fall and winter only, when you know the apples are freshly picked.

Makes 4 servings

1 cup heavy cream

3 large egg yolks

½ cup lightly packed light brown sugar

Pinch salt

Four 8-ounce apples (I use Northern Spy or Ida Red)

Preheat the oven to 325°F. Have ready a 9½-inch deep-dish pie plate.

Bring the cream to a boil in a small saucepan over medium heat. Meanwhile, whisk together the egg yolks, ¼ cup of the brown sugar, and the salt in a heatproof bowl. Pour a little of the hot cream over the yolk mixture, whisking constantly, to temper the yolks. Then whisk in the remaining cream. Strain through a fine-mesh strainer back into the saucepan and cook over low heat, stirring constantly, for 1 minute. Do not let it boil.

Cut the top ¼ inch off each apple, and then peel a ½-inch-wide strip of skin from around the top of the apple. Core each apple, using a melon baller or a sharp spoon. You want to scrape out quite a bit of the apple while leaving an intact wall of flesh about ½ inch thick. It is very important that no cuts go through the skin.

Place the apples in the pie plate, and pour the *crème* mixture into the apples.

Bake for 30 to 35 minutes, or until the *crème* is puffed and a bit golden. Let cool to room temperature, or to a barely warm temperature.

Sift the remaining ¼ cup brown sugar over the *crème*, 1 tablespoon on top of each apple. Caramelize using a propane torch (see page 89), or place under the broiler until melted, 1 to 2 minutes. Serve immediately.

white chocolate pear mousse

I love chocolate, but white chocolate can often be too sweet for me. I prefer to balance it with other flavors. Here pears, both the fruit and the liqueur, add something to the chocolate mousse base.

Makes 6 servings

3 cups plus 2 tablespoons water

1 cup granulated sugar

1 vanilla bean, split

4 ripe pears (approximately 8 ounces each), such as Anjou or Comice, peeled

12 ounces white chocolate, finely chopped

3 tablespoons Poire William (pear liqueur)

1½ cups heavy cream

Have ready six 1-cup wine goblets or other individual serving dishes.

Place 3 cups of the water, the sugar and the vanilla bean in a medium-size saucepan over medium heat. Stir to dissolve the sugar. Then add the pears. Bring to a simmer and cook until the pears are tender to the core when pierced with a thin knife, 20 to 30 minutes. Remove from the heat and cool completely in the syrup.

continued

Remove the pears from the syrup, halve and core them; set 2 pears aside. Place the remaining 2 pears in a food processor fitted with the metal blade and process until smooth. Press through a fine-mesh strainer; reserve the puree. Dice the reserved 2 pears into ½-inch cubes; set aside.

Combine the chocolate, liqueur and remaining 2 tablespoons water in the top of a double boiler placed over simmering water. Stir until the chocolate has melted. Remove from the heat and cool to room temperature; the chocolate should remain liquid.

Using the balloon whip attachment, whip the cream in a heavy-duty mixer until soft peaks form. Fold in the cooled chocolate and the pear puree. Then fold in the diced pears.

Pour into goblets and refrigerate until set, at least 4 hours. Best served the day it is made.

✴ BAKE IT TO THE LIMIT

Garnishing this mousse with translucent pear chips gives it a professional finish.

2 firm but ripe pears
¼ cup granulated sugar

Preheat the oven to 200°F. Line 2 sheet pans with parchment and spray them with nonstick cooking spray.

Slice the pears, skin on and core intact, using a mandoline or a very sharp knife. The slices should be translucent, barely 1/16 inch thick. Whether you cut crosswise or lengthwise, there will be end pieces that must be discarded. Cutting crosswise might give you more usable slices, but cutting lengthwise will produce slices that have more of a pear shape. Your choice.

Arrange the pear slices in a single layer on the sheet pans and sprinkle evenly and lightly with the sugar.

Bake for 70 to 80 minutes, or until the pears are dry, almost crispy, but still with some moisture left in them. They should be stiff enough to hold their shape when picked up. They should not flop over, but they should also not brown. Timing is everything here.

Garnish each serving with a pear chip. They can be stored at room temperature for up to 1 day. Any extra chips make a great snack.

cardamom rice pudding

I have never been a huge fan of rice pudding, but Arborio rice (an Italian short-grain rice) yields such a creamy pudding, I am now a convert. The cardamom, cinnamon and raisins work well here, but there is room for experimentation. Try nutmeg and diced apple. Or add plumped dried tart cherries.

Makes 6 servings

2 cups water
1 cup Arborio rice
¼ teaspoon salt
4 cups whole milk
½ cup granulated sugar
½ cup raisins
¼ teaspoon ground cardamom
¼ teaspoon ground cinnamon

Have ready six 1-cup ramekins or goblets.

Combine the water, rice and salt in a large saucepan. Cover and bring to a boil over medium heat. Reduce the heat and simmer for 15 minutes, or until all the water has been absorbed.

Stir in the milk, sugar, raisins, cardamom and cinnamon. Bring to a boil, reduce the heat, and simmer for about 20 minutes, stirring often. The pudding should have the texture of a thick soup. Do not dry it out too much. It will firm up a lot upon cooling. If there is one mistake you can make in this recipe, it is cooking the pudding too much at this point.

Remove from the heat and cool to room temperature, stirring occasionally to release the heat. Scoop the pudding into serving dishes and refrigerate for at least 3 hours or until firm. Serve immediately or keep refrigerated for up to 1 day, covering the tops with plastic wrap.

✷ BAKE IT TO THE LIMIT

Simply top off the rice pudding with lightly sweetened whipped cream. Or layer it, parfait-style, in narrow glass goblets, alternating with thick homemade applesauce.

> ¾ cup heavy cream
> 1 tablespoon granulated sugar
> Ground cinnamon
> 3 cups homemade applesauce (optional)

Using the balloon whip attachment, whip the cream and sugar in a heavy-duty mixer until soft peaks form.

Immediately before serving, top the pudding with a dollop of whipped cream and a sprinkling of cinnamon.

If making a rice pudding applesauce parfait, simply alternate pudding and applesauce in the goblets, starting and ending with a layer of pudding. Top with a dollop of whipped cream and a sprinkling of cinnamon.

citrus pudding cake

Halfway between a pudding and a cake, this dessert appears in this chapter because of its creamy quality. Pudding cakes bake up with a pudding layer on the bottom and a cake layer on top. But only if served immediately. If allowed to sit, the pudding layer will begin to be absorbed. Luckily, this is a quick dessert to whip up.

I have to mention my new favorite kitchen tool here. The Microplane (which can be purchased from Cooking by the Book; see page 174) is an amazing citrus zester. It is so far superior to any other grater/zester that I consider it a necessary kitchen item. Your fruit will glide effortlessly over the Microplane, making copious amounts of zest with no bitter pith attached. Buy one now!

Makes 6 servings

> 1 cup whole milk, at room temperature
> 3 large eggs, separated
> ¼ cup (2 ounces) unsalted butter, melted
> 1 lemon
> 1 lime
> 1 orange
> ¾ cup granulated sugar
> ¼ cup all-purpose flour
> Pinch salt

Preheat the oven to 325°F. Spray a shallow 1-quart ovenproof baking dish with nonstick cooking spray.

Whisk together the milk, egg yolks and melted butter in a large bowl.

Grate the zest from half the lemon, half the lime and half the orange over the milk-egg mixture. Squeeze the juice from the entire lemon and half the lime into a measuring cup. (You need ¼ cup juice.) Pour over the milk-egg mixture. Save the orange for juicing or eating another time.

In another bowl, or over a piece of parchment paper, sift together the sugar, flour and salt. Fold into the egg yolk mixture.

Using the balloon whip attachment, in a heavy-duty mixer, whip the egg whites in a clean, grease-free bowl until soft peaks form. Fold them gently into the batter.

Scrape the batter into the prepared baking dish and place it in a larger pan. Fill the outer pan with hot water to reach halfway up the dish.

Bake for 20 to 30 minutes. (The center will be puffed and dry, but if you insert a toothpick, the bottom should be wet.) Let the pudding cake rest for just 5 minutes, and then serve by simply scooping out the cake and the pudding on the bottom. (It must be served immediately or this juicy part will be absorbed.) It does not look fancy on the plate, but it is a warm, comforting dessert for a weekday dinner.

pumpkin cobbler

The dominant texture of this cobbler is like a soft, creamy pumpkin pie. Not a classic cobbler, not a cake, not a pudding—it's sort of a combination of all three. The assembly technique is unconventional; just follow the directions. I first tasted this at my friend Mary McNamara's house; she had found the recipe in a now long-lost seed catalog.

Make this for a fall potluck or a Thanksgiving open house. A little bit of unsweetened or lightly sweetened whipped cream is a nice extra touch.

Makes 8 to 10 servings

For the base

½ cup (4 ounces) unsalted butter, melted

1 cup all-purpose flour

1 cup whole milk

½ cup granulated sugar

4 teaspoons baking powder

½ teaspoon salt

For the filling

One 29-ounce can (3½ cups) pumpkin puree

½ cup whole milk

½ cup heavy cream

½ cup granulated sugar

½ cup lightly packed dark brown sugar

2 large eggs

1 teaspoon ground cinnamon

½ teaspoon ground ginger

½ teaspoon salt

¼ teaspoon ground allspice

For the topping

¼ cup lightly packed dark brown sugar

2 ounces (scant ⅓ cup) pecan halves, toasted (see page 152) and chopped

1 tablespoon all-purpose flour

1 tablespoon (½ ounce) unsalted butter, melted

Preheat the oven to 350°F. Spray a 2-quart ovenproof baking dish with nonstick cooking spray.

To make the base, pour the melted butter into the prepared dish. In a small bowl, whisk together the flour, milk, sugar, baking powder and salt. Pour over the melted butter; set aside.

To make the filling, whisk together the pumpkin, milk, cream, sugar and brown sugar in a medium-size bowl. Whisk in the eggs one at a time, blending well after each addition. Stir in the spices. Pour the filling over the base. Do not stir together. The mixture will look mottled, with the base showing here and there. That's the way it should be.

To make the topping, combine the brown sugar, pecans, flour and melted butter in a small bowl. Stir together well and scatter over the cobbler.

Bake for 45 minutes, or until the cobbler is lightly golden and the edges are just coming away from the pan's sides. The center should still be slightly wobbly.

Set the baking dish directly on a wire rack to cool for 10 minutes. Serve warm. This should be served the day it is made and can be reheated. Store, lightly covered with foil, at room temperature.

b&b frozen chocolate mousse

This is an easy frozen chocolate dessert for mature palates. The B&B liqueur, which contains a blend of dozens of herbs and spices, gives it an elusive flavor. This mousse is rich, but it retains a slight icy quality that keeps it from being too rich. If you like, top the servings with lightly sweetened whipped cream.

Makes 8 to 10 servings

11 ounces semisweet chocolate, finely chopped

2 cups heavy cream

¼ cup B&B liqueur

4 large eggs, separated

Have ready a 6-cup soufflé dish fitted with a collar. (Simply take a strip of parchment and wrap it around the dish, extending above the edge by 2 inches. Hold in place with tape.)

Place the chocolate in a large heatproof bowl. Bring the cream to a boil in a medium-size saucepan over medium heat, and then pour it over the chocolate. Let sit a few minutes, then whisk to melt the chocolate. Stir in the liqueur. Whisk in the egg yolks, one at a time. Cool to room temperature, whisking occasionally.

Using the balloon whip attachment in a heavy-duty mixer, whip the egg whites in a clean, grease-free bowl on low speed until frothy. Increase the speed to high and whip until firm peaks form. Fold the whites into the mousse mixture, and pour into the prepared soufflé dish.

Freeze for 6 hours or overnight. Before serving, remove the soufflé from the freezer and let it sit at room temperature for 10 minutes. Remove the collar and scoop the soufflé directly out of the dish. It will have the texture of a firm ice cream. Present in glass bowls.

Note: The mousse can be made without the liqueur for a child-friendly treat.

★ BAKE IT TO THE LIMIT
B&B Frozen Fudge Pops

For this variation you need a frozen pop mold. I bought mine from Williams-Sonoma, and it makes pops that are shaped very similarly to commercial ones. The chocolatey, icy texture is just like the Fudgesicles kids love (and adults sometimes crave). Serve these at a fancy dinner with a white linen napkin wrapped around the stick.

Makes 8 pops

1 recipe B&B Frozen Chocolate Mousse
One 8-cup pop mold

continued

Follow the recipe as above, without preparing the soufflé dish. Divide the mousse mixture among the mold's cavities, put the top in place, and insert the wooden sticks.

Freeze overnight.

three-berry mascarpone gratin

This is super-easy and takes delicious advantage of summer's berry bounty. You can throw it together in 10 minutes. Mascarpone is a soft Italian cheese, similar to a cream cheese mixed with sour cream. Look for it in good cheese departments or specialty stores.

Makes 8 servings

1½ cups fresh raspberries
1½ cups fresh blueberries
1 pint fresh strawberries, hulled and halved
2 cups mascarpone
¼ cup whole milk
2 tablespoons granulated sugar
½ cup lightly packed light brown sugar

Toss the raspberries, blueberries and strawberries together in a 9½-inch deep-dish pie plate.

In a mixing bowl, stir together the mascarpone, milk and granulated sugar. Spread over the fruit, going all the way to the edges. Sprinkle the brown sugar evenly over the mascarpone.

Caramelize with a propane torch (see page 89), slowly waving the flame back and forth over the sugar. Alternatively, caramelize under a broiler, about 2 inches below the heat source. Serve immediately.

Note: You can assemble the fruit and mascarpone 6 hours beforehand. Just store, lightly covered with foil, in the refrigerator. Then sprinkle with the brown sugar and caramelize right before serving.

earl grey tea cream

This is an unusual gelatin dessert flavored with Earl Grey tea. It is light and cooling for the summer months, especially nice accompanied by freshly sliced strawberries and maybe a chocolate cookie or two. I first came across a cream like this in Richard Sax's *Classic Home Deserts*, a wonderful collection of comfort desserts.

Makes 4 servings

3 cups cold whole milk
1 tablespoon loose Earl Grey tea leaves
⅓ cup granulated sugar
3½ teaspoons gelatin

Have 4 small (1-cup) wine goblets ready.

Place 2¾ cups of the milk in a small saucepan and bring to a boil over medium heat. Remove from the heat and immediately stir in the tea leaves and sugar. Let steep for 5 minutes, stirring once or twice to dissolve the sugar.

Meanwhile, place the remaining ¼ cup cold milk in a measuring cup and sprinkle the gelatin over it. Stir to wet evenly; let sit 5 minutes to soften.

Add the softened gelatin to the warm tea mixture and stir well to incorporate. Make sure the gelatin dissolves. Strain the mixture through a fine-mesh sieve into a large measuring cup. Then pour it into the goblets.

Refrigerate for 3 hours, or until set.

Using a Propane Torch

A propane torch? Yes—an emphatic yes. This standard shop tool belongs in the kitchen. There are many uses for it.

To Caramelize, or "Brûlée": Some tarts and *crèmes* are finished off with a crackly sugar glaze. This can be accomplished under the broiler, but then the entire *crème* or tart will be exposed to the heat, which is not desirable. For instance, if you are making crème brûlée and place the ramekins under the broiler, the *crème* can overheat and begin to melt. You can place the ramekins in a larger pan and surround them with ice, but using a propane torch is easier, and fun.

I use a torch with an automatic ignition and an angled head. You simply open the main valve and press a button.

Hold the torch over the dessert with the tip of the flame just touching the sugar. Slowly wave the flame back and forth over the sugar until it melts and caramelizes. Do a small area at a time. It is better to go over an area repeatedly than to burn the sugar (it will turn black) or set it on fire. The sugar should melt, turn glassy, and become a dark golden brown. Be patient.

Unmolding: Propane torches can also be used to help remove desserts from their molds. Simply move the flame over the bottom and sides of the mold or pan, and the dessert will unmold easily.

⭐ **BAKE IT TO THE LIMIT**

This borders on being cutesy, but it is fun and delicious—and what more do you want out of a dessert? You will need a special egg-shaped mold, available through Jell-O (go to their Web site at www.kraftfoods.com, or call them at 800-431-1001). Perfect for Easter brunch.

1 recipe Earl Grey Tea Cream
One 6-egg gelatin mold
Fresh strawberries

Make the tea cream and pour it into the egg mold following the manufacturer's directions. Chill for 6 hours or overnight. Unmold and serve the "eggs" in a nest of sliced strawberries—maybe with a piece of shortbread alongside.

hazelnut espresso crème brûlée

MMM-mmm. This is creamy, dense, crunchy, sweet and satisfying. Two of my tasters declared it to be the best recipe in the book—so you've got to try it. The hazelnut paste, sometimes called praline paste, can be found in specialty food stores.

continued

2 cups heavy cream

3 tablespoons espresso beans, coarsely ground

2 tablespoons unsweetened hazelnut paste

4 large egg yolks

½ cup granulated sugar

3 tablespoons lightly packed light brown sugar

Place the cream and coffee beans in a medium-size saucepan and bring to a boil over medium heat. Remove from the heat and let steep for 15 minutes. Strain through a fine-mesh sieve and return to a clean saucepan. Reheat gently over low heat to just below a simmer, and whisk in the hazelnut paste.

Preheat the oven to 325°F. Have ready five ½-cup ramekins set in a larger pan.

Meanwhile, whisk the egg yolks and granulated sugar together in a small heatproof bowl. Dribble some of the hot cream mixture over the eggs to temper them, then whisk in the remaining cream. Strain through a fine-mesh sieve into a large measuring cup, then pour it into the ramekins.

Fill the large pan with hot water to reach halfway up the ramekins. Bake for 25 to 30 minutes, until the edges of the custard are set. The center should remain wobbly. It will firm up upon cooling. Remove the pan from the oven and remove the ramekins from the pan. Set the ramekins on a wire rack and let cool to room temperature. Refrigerate for at least 3 hours, or up to 2 days, in which case they should be covered with plastic wrap.

Immediately before serving, sift the brown sugar evenly over the tops of the custards. You want a thin, even layer—a veneer of brown sugar. Caramelize using a propane torch (see page 89) or under the broiler. If using the broiler, place the ramekins in a larger pan and fill that pan with ice and ice water to reach halfway up the sides of the ramekins. Place the pan 2 inches under the broiler and watch carefully. The caramelizing process can take as little as 30 seconds or as long as 2 minutes.

Serve immediately.

★ BAKE IT TO THE LIMIT
Hazelnut Mocha Crème Brûlée

This is one of those really simple but great ideas. A chocolate lattice or spiral, as in the photograph, is piped over the caramelized sugar, forming an additional luscious layer.

1½ ounces bittersweet chocolate, finely chopped

Melt the chocolate in a double boiler or microwave. Scrape into a parchment cone and snip a tiny opening from the point of the cone. Make a lattice pattern of melted chocolate over the caramelized brown sugar, leaving gaps so that you can see the sugar crust. Freeze for a minute or two to set the chocolate.

Serve immediately.

ice creams, sorbets and granitas

Making ice creams and other frozen desserts from scratch may seem above and beyond the call of duty, but if you own an ice cream maker, you know how truly simple it is and how satisfying the results can be.

All frozen dessert bases must be chilled before freezing in the machine, and I find that an extra-long chilling time—6 hours to overnight—improves the flavor and texture of the final product in many cases. Follow the individual recipe instructions. Also, although these desserts can be served when freshly churned, most manufacturers suggest a ripening period in the freezer to harden them fully, so plan your timing accordingly.

Know your ice cream maker's capacity. Many hold a quart of ice cream, some 6 cups. These recipes can be scaled directly up or down, if necessary, to fit your machine.

Frozen desserts will pick up odors from the freezer, so try to eat your creation within four days or less. And always store your frozen desserts in airtight containers. For maximum flavor and texture, let them soften for 5 to 10 minutes out of the freezer before serving.

vanilla ice cream

One Fourth of July I made five different vanilla ice creams and held a taste test. This version was favored by everyone, adult and child. Thank you to Mary and Wally, Annie and Steve, Claudia and Peter, Julie and Andy, Harry and all 13 kids for their input.

The combination of vanilla bean and extract makes for a particularly full, round flavor.

Makes 1½ quarts

2 cups whole milk
2 cups heavy cream
1 vanilla bean, split
6 large egg yolks
1 cup granulated sugar
½ teaspoon vanilla extract

In a medium-size heavy-bottomed, nonreactive saucepan, combine the milk and cream. Scrape the vanilla bean seeds into the mixture and then add the entire bean. Bring to a boil over medium-high heat. Immediately remove from the heat and let sit for 30 minutes to steep.

Meanwhile, whisk together the egg yolks and sugar in a medium-size heatproof bowl.

Reheat the milk mixture gently, and then slowly add a little bit to the egg mixture, whisking all the while, to temper the eggs. Add the remaining milk mixture, stirring until smooth.

Return the mixture to the saucepan and cook over medium heat, stirring constantly, until the custard has thickened slightly and coats the back of a spoon, about 5 minutes. Do not boil.

Strain into a bowl through a fine-mesh sieve. Discard the vanilla bean and stir in the vanilla extract. Cool almost to room temperature, stirring occasionally. Transfer to a storage container and refrigerate for 6 hours or overnight.

Pour into an ice cream maker and follow the manufacturer's instructions. Freeze the ice cream in an airtight container. Best eaten within 4 days.

✦ BAKE IT TO THE LIMIT
Meringue Nests with Vanilla Ice Cream and Roasted Fruits

A scoop of vanilla tucked inside a meringue nest and topped with roasted fruits makes a colorful and refreshing summertime treat.

Makes 6 servings

½ recipe (3 cups) Vanilla Ice Cream

For the meringue nests
4 large egg whites

Making Ice Cream

Many ice creams start with a custard base. This is accomplished by whisking egg yolks (sometimes whole eggs) with sugar, and then adding a tiny bit of heated milk or cream to temper the eggs. The remaining warm liquid is added and the whole whisked together well. This custard is stirred frequently while it is heated to approximately 170°F; it should not boil. Use a thermometer or go by visual cues: the mixture will thicken slightly, and a spoon drawn across the bottom of the pan will leave a small but distinct path. A little steam will also form. If you see tiny bubbles forming around the edges of the pan, remove it from the heat immediately, as it is about to boil. Boiling would overcook the eggs and result in a grainy texture. Straining the base mixture through a fine-mesh sieve yields the smoothest texture. Follow the instructions in the individual recipes.

½ teaspoon cream of tartar

1 cup granulated sugar

For the roasted fruit

2 large ripe (7-ounce) peaches

2 large ripe (4-ounce) purple-skinned plums

1 pint strawberries

¼ cup granulated sugar

¼ cup dry red wine (Merlot would be perfect)

Prepare the ice cream at least 4 hours in advance.

Preheat the oven to 225°F. Line a sheet pan with parchment and trace six 3-inch circles on the paper. Flip the paper over.

Make the meringue nests. Using the balloon whip attachment on a heavy-duty mixer, on low speed in a clean, grease-free bowl, whip the egg whites until frothy. Add the cream of tartar and continue to beat on high speed until soft peaks form. Add the sugar gradually, and beat until the meringue is stiff and glossy.

Scoop the meringue into a pastry bag fitted with a large open star tip, such as a Wilton 4B. Starting in the center of one of the traced circles, pipe concentric circles until the outline is filled in. Above the outside ring of the circle, pipe another ring. Pipe a third ring above the second, making a low wall of meringue. Repeat for all 6 circles.

Bake for about 1½ hours, or until completely dry and crisp to the touch. The nests should stay as white as possible, so don't overbake. Cool the pan directly on a wire rack. Store the nests in a covered container in a dry place for up to a week. (I keep mine in my turned-off gas oven with the pilot light on.)

Make the roasted fruit. Preheat the oven to 400°F. Pit the peaches and plums, and cut each fruit into 6 slices. Hull and halve the berries. Place all the fruit in an 8-cup ovenproof baking dish. Sprinkle the sugar over evenly, and pour the wine into the dish. Toss to coat.

Roast for 40 to 50 minutes, or until the fruit is very soft and there is a lot of thick, syrupy dark red juice. Cool to room temperature. The fruit may be stored in an airtight container in the refrigerator for up to 3 days. Reheat briefly on the stovetop or in the microwave before using.

Scoop the ice cream into the meringue nests, and top with the warm fruit. Serve immediately.

coconut ice cream

This velvety smooth ice cream is very quick to make. It may look like vanilla, but it has a pronounced coconut flavor accented with dark rum. Some canned cream of coconut separates and is not very smooth. I have had good luck with Coco Lopez.

Makes 1½ quarts

Two 15-ounce cans Coco Lopez cream of coconut
2 cups whole milk
2 cups heavy cream
¼ cup dark rum

Combine the cream of coconut, milk, cream and rum in a nonreactive bowl, whisking together well. Transfer to a storage container and refrigerate for at least 6 hours or overnight.

Pour into an ice cream maker and follow the manufacturer's instructions. Freeze the ice cream in an airtight container. Best eaten within 4 days.

⭐ **BAKE IT TO THE LIMIT**

Toasted Coconut Ice Cream in Chocolate Bowls

Here is a fun and easy presentation idea. Simply put, you blow up a balloon and dip the rounded end in melted chocolate. When the chocolate dries, you deflate the balloon and are left with a chocolate bowl to fill with ice cream.

These impressive edible bowls can be made with any flavor of chocolate. I like to use sausage-shaped balloons (about 3 to 4 inches in diameter, not the kind for making balloon animals), although a variety of shapes can be used for varied effects. If using a round balloon, blow it up just a little. The bowls are fun to make—just be sure your chocolate has cooled before dipping the balloons, or they will burst and there will be chocolate all over you and your kitchen! Believe me, I learned the hard way. (If you or your guests are allergic to latex, skip this embellishment.)

Makes 8 servings

10 balloons
10 paper clips
2 pounds semisweet or bittersweet chocolate, finely chopped
1 cup unsweetened flaked coconut (large flakes)
1 recipe Coconut Ice Cream

Line 2 sheet pans with parchment or aluminum foil. You will be placing the 10 balloons, spaced apart, on the sheets, so make sure you have enough room. Clear space in your refrigerator for the pans and balloons to fit.

Blow up the balloons halfway. Twist the ends well, fold them down, and secure with a paper clip. Do not tie them off; the chocolate will break if you try to pop tied balloons. Gently wash the balloons and dry them thoroughly.

Melt the chocolate in a double boiler or microwave. Cool until barely warm to the touch (this is important). Place 10 individual teaspoons of chocolate on the prepared pans, spacing them out well. These will form the bases of the bowls.

Pour the chocolate into a narrow bowl or other container to form a deep reservoir. Take a balloon by the clipped end and dip the rounded end about 3 inches deep into the chocolate. You may dip the balloon straight in or dip it three separate times, turning the balloon on an angle as you go, so each dip overlaps the other. This will make a petal shape. Set the balloon on one of the melted chocolate rounds. If the balloon needs help staying upright, assist it by using whatever you have on hand—peppermills, boxes of

food, etc. Repeat with the remaining balloons. Place the pans in the refrigerator until the chocolate is firm, about 15 minutes. Reserve any extra melted chocolate. You will have 2 extra bowls to experiment with.

When the chocolate is firm and there are no wet, shiny spots remaining, remove the paper clip from each balloon. The air should slowly emerge. The end of the balloon will be stuck to the inside bottom of the bowl. Carefully pull it out. You will need to tug a bit; that's okay. If there is a hole in the bottom, seal it with a dab of extra melted chocolate. Store the bowls in the refrigerator until needed for up to 2 days. (If you want to make them way ahead and be able to store them at room temperature, temper the chocolate first; see page 160.)

Preheat the oven to 350°F. Spread the coconut on a parchment-lined sheet pan and toast in the oven for 3 to 5 minutes, or until golden brown. Cool the pan on a wire rack.

To serve, simply place a scoop of Coconut Ice Cream in each chocolate bowl and top with toasted coconut. An extra drizzle of dark rum wouldn't hurt. Serve immediately.

Note: In the photograph, one perfect crystallized flower adorns the dessert. These can be ordered from Meadowsweets (see page 175) or you can make them yourself (see page 108).

pumpkin ice cream

Just like pumpkin pie—spicy, creamy, flavorful—but frozen.

Makes 4 cups

3 large egg yolks
½ cup granulated sugar
½ cup lightly packed light brown sugar
1¼ cups whole milk
1 cup heavy cream
¼ teaspoon ground cinnamon
¼ teaspoon ground ginger
¼ teaspoon ground nutmeg
Pinch ground cloves
1 cup canned pumpkin puree
1 teaspoon vanilla extract

Whisk together the egg yolks, sugar and brown sugar in a medium-size heatproof bowl. This mixture will be thick.

In a medium-size heavy-bottomed, nonreactive saucepan, combine the milk, cream, cinnamon, ginger, nutmeg and cloves. Bring the mixture to a boil over medium-high heat. Slowly add a little bit of the milk mixture to the egg mixture, whisking all the while, to temper the eggs. Then add the remaining milk mixture, stirring until smooth.

Return the mixture to the saucepan and cook over medium heat, stirring constantly, until the custard has thickened slightly and coats the back of a spoon, about 5 minutes. Do not boil.

With the pan off the heat, whisk in the pumpkin puree and vanilla. Strain into a bowl through a fine-mesh sieve. Cool almost to room temperature, stirring occasionally. Transfer to a storage container and refrigerate for 6 hours, or overnight.

Pour into an ice cream maker and follow the manufacturer's instructions. Freeze the ice cream in an airtight container. Best eaten within 4 days.

espresso kahlúa ice cream

This is a strongly flavored coffee ice cream with a very smooth, somewhat soft texture due to the liqueur. It is still firm enough to hold a scooped shape—just extra-velvety on the tongue.

Makes 5 cups

2 cups whole milk

2 cups heavy cream

¾ cup decaffeinated dark-roast coffee beans, coarsely ground

8 large egg yolks

1 cup granulated sugar

2 tablespoons Kahlúa or other coffee liqueur

Combine the milk, cream and ground coffee in a medium-size heavy-bottomed, nonreactive saucepan. Bring to a boil. Then remove from the heat and let sit for 15 minutes to steep. Strain into a bowl through a fine-mesh sieve.

Meanwhile, whisk the egg yolks with the sugar in a heatproof bowl. Add a little bit of warm cream mixture to the egg mixture, whisking all the while, to temper the eggs. Then add the remaining cream mixture, stirring until smooth.

Return the mixture to the saucepan and cook over medium heat, stirring constantly, until the custard has thickened slightly and coats the back of a spoon, about 5 minutes. Do not boil. Strain again through a fine-mesh strainer. Stir in the Kahlúa.

Cool almost to room temperature, stirring occasionally. Transfer to a storage container and refrigerate for 6 hours or overnight.

Pour into an ice cream maker and follow the man-ufacturer's instructions. Freeze the ice cream in an airtight container. Best eaten within 4 days.

✳ BAKE IT TO THE LIMIT

I have two Bake It to the Limit ideas for this coffee-flavored ice cream. I think this ice cream screams, yells and demands to be encased in chocolate *choux* pastry and topped with chocolate sauce. The second idea is really decadent: Just imagine coffee ice cream with chunks of espresso-soaked chocolate biscotti and a ripple of chocolate ganache.

Chocolate Espresso Cream Puffs

Makes 30 puffs, 8 servings

For the chocolate choux paste

1 cup water

6 tablespoons (3 ounces) unsalted butter, cut into large pieces.

¼ teaspoon salt

¾ cup plus 2 tablespoons all-purpose flour

2 tablespoons Dutch-process cocoa

4 large eggs

1 recipe Bittersweet Chocolate Sauce (page 147)

1 recipe Espresso Kahlúa Ice Cream

Preheat the oven to 400°F. Line 2 sheet pans with parchment.

Place the water, butter and salt in a heavy-bottomed saucepan and bring to a full boil over medium-high heat.

Meanwhile, whisk the flour and cocoa together in a bowl.

When the liquid boils, remove the pan from the heat and immediately add all the dry mixture. Stir it in quickly and vigorously with a wooden spoon. Place over low heat and stir until the paste has dried out a bit, 1 to 2 minutes. It should form a ball and come away from the sides of the saucepan.

Scoop the paste into the bowl of a heavy-duty mixer. Mixing on medium-low speed with the flat paddle attachment, add the eggs one at a time, beating well after each addition. Each egg should be completely absorbed. After all the eggs are added, the paste should be lighter in color and very smooth and sticky.

Scrape the mixture into a pastry bag fitted with a plain round ½-inch tip. Pipe 30 walnut-size balls onto the prepared pans. If they end up with a point on top, go back over them with a finger dipped in water to flatten and round off the top.

Bake for 20 minutes, then turn the oven down to 350°F and bake 5 minutes more. Pierce each puff on the side to let steam escape, and bake 5 more minutes. Watch the timing. The puffs should be puffed and dry to the touch, but not overbrowned on the bottom.

Place the pans directly on wire racks until the puffs are completely cooled. They may be used that day or stored, loosely covered with foil, at room temperature for 1 day. They may need to be recrisped in a 350°F oven for 5 minutes, then cooled.

Warm the chocolate sauce in a double boiler or microwave.

Split the puffs horizontally and place a scoop of ice cream on each bottom half. Replace the tops. Place 3 or 4 puffs together on a plate, and spoon the warmed sauce over and around them. Serve immediately.

Espresso Biscotti Ganache Ripple Ice Cream

Makes 8 servings

1 recipe Espresso Kahlúa Ice Cream

20 Chocolate Almond Biscotti made with chocolate-covered almonds (page 49)

¼ cup brewed espresso, at room temperature

⅔ cup Bittersweet Chocolate Ganache, cooled but pourable (page 154)

Have the ice cream churned but still soft.

Crumble the biscotti into 1-inch chunks in a small bowl. Sprinkle the espresso evenly over them and toss to coat.

Fold the biscotti into the ice cream. Then drizzle the ganache over the ice cream, and fold it in in a few broad strokes so that ribbons of chocolate remain.

Pack into a container and freeze until firm, about 4 hours, before serving.

ginger ice cream

Freshly grated ginger infuses this ice cream with its zingy flavor. When you buy fresh ginger, look for a firm, unblemished root. The skin should be smooth and taut, and the root should feel heavy for its size.

Makes 1 quart

3 ounces fresh ginger, peeled and finely chopped (about ⅔ cup)

1½ cups granulated sugar

1 cup water

2 cups heavy cream

1 cup whole milk

6 large egg yolks

Combine the ginger, sugar and water in a medium-size heavy-bottomed, nonreactive saucepan. Bring to a boil over medium-high heat. Turn the heat down and simmer for 5 minutes. Remove from the heat and let sit for 30 minutes to steep. Strain through a fine-mesh sieve, pressing down on the ginger, and return to the pan. Add the cream and milk and bring to a simmer.

Meanwhile, whisk the egg yolks in a medium-size heatproof bowl. Slowly add a little bit of the warmed cream mixture to the eggs, whisking all the while, to temper the eggs. Add the remaining cream mixture, stirring until smooth.

Return the mixture to the saucepan and cook over medium heat, stirring constantly, until the custard has thickened slightly and coats the back of a spoon, about 5 minutes. Do not boil. Remove from the heat.

Strain again through the strainer. Cool to room temperature, stirring occasionally. Transfer to a storage container and refrigerate for 6 hours, or overnight.

Pour into an ice cream maker and follow the manufacturer's instructions. Freeze the ice cream in an airtight container. Best eaten within 4 days.

✸ BAKE IT TO THE LIMIT

This refreshing ice cream pairs perfectly with a tangy plum compote. A Sesame Lace Cookie on the side adds crunch. Buy juicy ripe plums for this. Stick with the midsummer round plums; prune plums won't work here.

Makes 6 servings

For the Roasted Plum Compote (makes 2 cups)

1½ pounds (about 5) dark red or purple-skinned plums
½ cup granulated sugar
2 teaspoons freshly squeezed lemon juice

1 recipe Ginger Ice Cream
6 Sesame Lace Cookies (page 43)

Preheat the oven to 375°F. Have ready a 2-quart ovenproof baking dish.

Pit the plums and cut each one into 8 slices. Spread the slices in a single layer in the baking dish. Sprinkle with the sugar and lemon juice, and toss to mix.

Roast the fruit for 20 to 25 minutes, or until the slices are very soft and there is a lot of thick, syrupy, dark red juice.

The fruit may be used immediately, or cooled and stored in an airtight container in the refrigerator for 3 days. Reheat briefly on the stovetop or in a microwave before serving.

Scoop the Ginger Ice Cream into bowls, and top each serving with some warm Roasted Plum Compote. Wedge a Sesame Lace Cookie in the bowl, and serve immediately.

lemon velvet ice cream

Lemon oil, which is a specialty product, gives this ice cream its puckery, lemon-fresh flavor. You cannot make this ice cream without it.

Makes 1½ quarts

6 large egg yolks

1 cup granulated sugar

2 cups whole milk

2 cups heavy cream

¼ cup freshly squeezed lemon juice

1½ teaspoons lemon oil (see Note)

1½ teaspoons vanilla extract

Whisk together the egg yolks and sugar in a medium-size heatproof bowl.

In a medium-size heavy-bottomed, nonreactive saucepan, combine the milk and cream. Bring to a boil over medium-high heat. Slowly add a little bit of the milk mixture to the egg mixture, whisking all the while, to temper the eggs. Then add the remaining milk mixture, stirring until smooth.

Return the mixture to the saucepan and cook over medium heat, stirring constantly, until the custard has thickened slightly and coats the back of a spoon, about 5 minutes. Do not boil. Remove the saucepan from the heat and stir in the lemon juice, lemon oil and vanilla.

Strain into a bowl through a fine-mesh sieve. Cool almost to room temperature, stirring occasionally. Transfer to a storage container and refrigerate for 6 hours, or overnight.

Pour into an ice cream maker and follow the manufacturer's instructions. Freeze the ice cream in an airtight container. Best eaten within 4 days.

Note: Lemon oil, made by Boyajian, can be ordered from Williams-Sonoma or found at specialty food stores. It is the distillation of oils from lemon zest and has an incomparable flavor. Do not substitute lemon extract, which has an artificial taste, or lemon zest, which would ruin the texture here.

✴ BAKE IT TO THE LIMIT

This is great served with Macadamia Oat Crisps. Make a layered dessert using the cookies interspersed with the ice cream and accented with raspberries, whole and in a sauce. Use a luncheon-size plate for the presentation.

Makes 8 servings

1 quart Lemon Velvet Ice Cream

1 recipe Macadamia Oat Crisps (page 47)

½ pint fresh raspberries

1 cup Raspberry Coulis (page 147)

Soften the ice cream so that it is easy to scoop. Place a cookie on a flat individual serving plate and top it with a ¼-cup scoop of ice cream. Top with another cookie, another scoop of ice cream, and finally another cookie. Top the dessert with a perfect fresh raspberry, and use a squeeze bottle to squiggle Raspberry Coulis all over the plate. Scatter a few berries here and there. Repeat with the other servings and serve immediately.

white chocolate mint ice cream

This looks like vanilla ice cream, but one bite and the rich mint-accented white chocolate flavor explodes on your tongue. Peppermint oil, not extract, is key. You can find it in natural-foods stores and some pharmacies.

Makes 5 cups

6 ounces white chocolate, finely chopped

4 large egg yolks

¾ cup granulated sugar

2½ cups heavy cream

1½ cups whole milk

¼ teaspoon peppermint oil

Melt the white chocolate in a double boiler. Set aside, keeping warm.

Meanwhile, whisk together the egg yolks and sugar in a medium-size heatproof bowl.

In a medium-size heavy-bottomed, nonreactive saucepan, combine the cream and milk. Bring the mixture to a boil over medium-high heat. Slowly add a little of the hot cream mixture to the egg mixture, whisking all the while, to temper the eggs. Add the remaining cream mixture, stirring until smooth.

Return the mixture to the saucepan and cook over medium heat, stirring constantly, until the custard has thickened slightly and coats the back of a spoon, about 5 minutes. Do not boil.

With the pan off the heat, whisk in the warm melted chocolate and the peppermint oil. Strain into a bowl through a fine-mesh sieve. Cool almost to room temperature, stirring occasionally. Transfer to a storage container and refrigerate for 6 hours or overnight.

Pour into an ice cream maker and follow the manufacturer's instructions. Freeze the ice cream in an airtight container. Best eaten within 4 days.

✷ BAKE IT TO THE LIMIT
Polka-Dot Truffle White Chocolate Mint Ice Cream

Packed into a loaf pan with dark chocolate truffles buried inside, this ice cream turns into a graphic polka-dotted dessert when sliced. You can prepare this loaf up to 3 days ahead, which makes it a great company dish. Serve it on plates decorated with squiggles of the vivid green Mint Sauce.

Makes 12 slices

1 recipe White Chocolate Mint Ice Cream

1 recipe Mint Sauce (page 148)

For the chocolate truffles (makes 30)

4 ounces semisweet chocolate, finely chopped

1 cup heavy cream

Dutch-process cocoa

Prepare the ice cream and mint sauce in advance.

To prepare the truffles, place the chocolate in a heatproof bowl. Bring the cream to a boil in a small saucepan over medium heat, and pour it over the chocolate. Let sit a few minutes, then whisk until the chocolate has melted. Cool to room temperature. Freeze until firm, at least 4 hours.

Dust your hands lightly with cocoa, and roll the chilled truffle mixture into balls the size of large hazelnuts. Set aside in the refrigerator until needed.

To assemble the dessert, line a 6-cup, 8 × 4-inch straight-sided metal loaf pan with plastic wrap. Use one large, long piece and make sure the ends extend over the short sides, smoothing the rest down into the pan as well as you can.

continued

Pack half of the ice cream into the bottom of the loaf pan, making as even a layer as possible. Arrange the truffles here and there, embedding them in the ice cream, but not touching each other. Use as many as possible. (If there are leftover truffles, store them in an airtight container in the freezer and serve with espresso.) Pack in the remaining ice cream, smoothing the top. The truffles should be completely encased in ice cream. Cover with additional plastic wrap and freeze overnight.

To serve, have the mint sauce in a squeeze bottle. Unmold the ice cream right before serving. Cut it into 12 slices, using a thin-bladed sharp knife dipped in hot water. Place each slice on a serving plate, and squirt mint sauce over and around the slices in a free-form pattern. Serve immediately.

banana ice cream

Creamy, ripe bananas and banana liqueur flavor this custard-based ice cream. It has a subtle color and taste.

Makes 1 quart

3 large egg yolks
⅓ cup granulated sugar
1¼ cups whole milk
1¼ cups heavy cream
½ vanilla bean, split
2 ripe medium-size (6- to 7-ounce) bananas, peeled and sliced into 1-inch chunks
2 tablespoons banana liqueur (I use Leroux's Crème de Banana)

Whisk together the egg yolks and sugar in a medium-size heatproof bowl.

In a medium-size heavy-bottomed, nonreactive saucepan, combine the milk and cream. Scrape the vanilla bean seeds into the mixture, and then add the bean itself. Bring to a boil over medium-high heat. Slowly add a little bit of the milk mixture to the egg mixture, whisking all the while, to temper the eggs. Add the remaining milk mixture, stirring until smooth.

Return the mixture to a saucepan and cook over medium heat, stirring constantly, until the custard has thickened slightly and coats the back of a spoon, about 5 minutes. Do not boil.

Strain into a bowl through a fine-mesh sieve. Cool almost to room temperature, stirring occasionally.

Meanwhile, puree the bananas in a food processor fitted with the metal blade until completely smooth. Stir the puree and liqueur into the custard. Strain again, and transfer to a storage container. Refrigerate for 6 hours, or overnight.

Pour into an ice cream maker and follow the manufacturer's instructions. Freeze the ice cream in an airtight container. Best eaten within 4 days.

honey ice cream

The source of a batch of honey affects its flavor. Orange blossom and clover honey are common and have a fairly mild flavor. Lavender honey and buckwheat honey are quite distinctive, with the former having a floral taste, the latter a strong brown color and very pronounced flavor. Experiment to find your favorite.

Makes 6 cups

9 egg yolks

1½ cups honey

3 cups whole milk

3 cups heavy cream

1½ teaspoons vanilla extract

Whisk together the egg yolks and honey in a medium-size heatproof bowl.

In a medium-size heavy-bottomed, nonreactive saucepan, combine the milk and cream, and bring to a boil over medium heat. Slowly add a little bit of the hot cream mixture to the egg mixture, whisking all the while, to temper the eggs. Add the remaining cream mixture, stirring until smooth.

Return the mixture to the saucepan and cook over medium heat, stirring constantly, until the custard has thickened slightly and coats the back of a spoon, about 5 minutes. Do not boil. Remove the pan from the heat and stir in the vanilla.

Strain into a bowl through a fine-mesh sieve. Cool almost to room temperature, stirring occasionally. Transfer to a storage container and refrigerate for 6 hours, or overnight.

Pour into an ice cream maker and follow the manufacturer's instructions. Freeze the ice cream in an airtight container. Best eaten within 4 days.

✷ BAKE IT TO THE LIMIT
Blood Orange Honey Sundae

The light golden color and sweet, warm flavor of this ice cream look and taste great when complemented by a tart Blood Orange Sauce. Blood oranges are most easily found in February and have a short season, so plan accordingly. (Or make the sauce and freeze it for the day when you might desire a sunset-colored sauce.)

Makes 4 servings

½ recipe (3 cups) Honey Ice Cream

1 recipe Blood Orange Sauce (page 148)

Divide the ice cream among serving bowls and drizzle with the sauce. Serve immediately.

green tea ice cream

The first time I tasted pale green ice cream flavored with *matcha* was at Takashimaya in New York. The Tea Box, the restaurant in this Japanese store, serves wonderful bento boxed lunches, teas of all description and this delicious dessert. This is my version.

Matcha is a brightly colored green tea powder used in the traditional Japanese tea ceremony. You will probably find it only at select tea emporiums, or you can mail-order it from Takashimaya (see page 177).

Makes 4½ cups

2 cups whole milk

2 cups heavy cream

2 tablespoons matcha *(green tea powder)*

6 large egg yolks

1 cup granulated sugar

In a medium-size heavy-bottomed, nonreactive saucepan, combine the milk and cream. Bring to a boil over medium heat. Then, off the heat, stir in the tea powder. Whisk together well, then let steep for 15 minutes.

Whisk together the egg yolks and sugar in a medium-size heatproof bowl.

Reheat the cream mixture over low–medium heat. Slowly add a little bit to the egg mixture, whisking all the while, to temper the eggs. Add the remaining cream mixture, stirring until smooth.

Return the mixture to the saucepan and cook over medium heat, stirring constantly, until the custard has thickened slightly and coats the back of a spoon, about 5 minutes. Do not boil.

Strain into a bowl through a fine-mesh sieve. Cool almost to room temperature, stirring occasionally. Transfer to a storage container and refrigerate for 6 hours, or overnight.

Pour into an ice cream maker and follow the manufacturer's instructions. Freeze the ice cream in an airtight container. Best eaten within 4 days.

✦ BAKE IT TO THE LIMIT
Green Tea Jasmine Sorbet Coupe with Crystallized Flowers

This unusual ice cream doesn't need much to call attention to itself. However, to pull out all the stops, serve it with a scoop of Jasmine Tea Sorbet alongside and a crystallized flower on top. The combination of the gorgeous pale green of this ice cream with the frosty pastel colors of the sorbet and flowers makes for an extremely pretty presentation. Serve it in a crystal or glass dish, or one that is plain white or silver, so as not to distract from the dessert itself.

Make sure the flowers are edible and unsprayed. If egg safety is a problem in your area, or if you have a compromised immune system, use powdered egg whites and reconstitute them according to the manufacturer's instructions. (Just Whites is a brand available at many supermarkets and at N.Y. Cake and Baking Distributors; see page 176.)

If you prefer to purchase flowers already crystallized, call Meadowsweets (see page 175).

Makes 8 servings

½ recipe (2¼ cups) Green Tea Ice Cream
½ recipe (1½ cups) Jasmine Tea Sorbet (page 112)

For the crystallized flowers (makes 12 to 24 flowers, depending on size)
Edible flowers such as roses, pansies, violets, dianthus, lavender, lilac, marigolds or nasturtiums
1 cup superfine sugar
1 large egg white, whisked till frothy (or reconstituted powdered egg white)

Prepare the ice cream and sorbet in advance.

To crystallize the flowers, make sure that the blooms are dry and free of any loose pollen or dust. Have ready a shallow bowl filled with the superfine sugar, with a teaspoon set at its side. The bowl should be wide enough to accommodate the diameter of the largest flower. You'll also need a small bowl to hold the egg white, whisked just enough to break up its viscous nature. Two small soft paintbrushes are a necessity. One will remain dry to help separate petals, and one will be used to paint on the egg white. (Stiff ones will bruise and tear the petals.) Place a small-grid rack on a pan lined with parchment or aluminum foil (to catch any sugar that falls off). Tweezers help with some flowers, while your fingers will be fine for others.

Set up your work space as follows: On the left have your flowers. Then, moving to the right across the counter, have the bowl of egg whites, the sugar, then the rack, (all assuming you're right-handed). Using tweezers or your fingers, pick up one of the flowers by the base. Spread the petals apart gently with your fingers or with a dry brush to allow all surfaces to be exposed. Dip the other paintbrush in egg white and use it to paint all of the surfaces so that they are evenly coated. Now, holding the flower above the sugar bowl with one hand, scoop up some sugar with the spoon in the other hand and begin to sprinkle it over the flower. Keep rotating the flower so that all surfaces can be reached. If large unsugared petals flop over and stick to one another, use the tweezers or a toothpick to gently pry them apart. The tweezers can easily harm the petals, so be careful.

When the flower has been completely covered with sugar, place it on the rack to dry. If the sugar does not adhere to a part of the flower, it is probably because it was not coated with egg white. You can go back and patch with more egg white and sugar, but if you get egg white on parts already sugared, they will become thick and unsightly. Practice makes perfect. Do not start with the flower you like the best. Practice on a few imperfect blooms until you get the hang of it. You may crystallize edible leaves, such as mint leaves, as well.

Now the flowers must be dried completely. Try placing the rack, with a pan underneath, in a gas oven. The pilot light provides a dry, warm environment. Some flowers will dry this way overnight; others take 48 hours.

To store, place the crystallized flowers on top of parchment paper inside a large flat airtight container. A single layer is best. They will last for months at room temperature.

To serve, place scoops of ice cream and sorbet side by side in serving dishes, and top off with 1 to 3 crystallized flowers. Serve immediately.

triple vanilla ice milk

This frosty ice milk is a lightened version of vanilla ice cream, but by no means is it a mere substitute. It stands on its own as a refreshing frozen dessert. The blend of vanilla extract and two kinds of vanilla beans produces the fullest, roundest vanilla flavor possible.

Makes 5 cups

4 cups whole milk
1 cup granulated sugar
2 vanilla beans, split (preferably one Bourbon and
*   one Tahitian; see page 167)*
2 teaspoons vanilla extract

Place the milk and sugar in a medium-size saucepan and stir to wet the sugar. Scrape the vanilla bean seeds into the mixture, and add the entire beans. Bring to a boil over medium heat. Remove from the heat and let sit for 30 minutes to steep.

Stir in the vanilla, and strain into a bowl through a fine-mesh sieve. Cool almost to room temperature, stirring occasionally. Transfer to a storage container and refrigerate for 6 hours, or overnight.

Pour into an ice cream maker and follow the manufacturer's instructions. Freeze the ice milk in an airtight container. Best eaten within 4 days.

lemon ice milk

This is creamy and icily refreshing at the same time. You must churn as soon as the lemon juice has been added to the milk mixture, or it may curdle, which will ruin the texture.

Makes 6 cups

4 cups whole milk
1½ cups granulated sugar
1 cup freshly squeezed lemon juice

Place the milk and sugar in a medium-size nonreactive saucepan and stir to wet the sugar. Bring to a boil over medium heat and stir to dissolve the sugar. Remove from the heat and cool to room temperature, stirring occasionally. Transfer to a storage container and refrigerate for 6 hours or overnight.

Add the lemon juice and whisk together well. Strain through a fine-mesh sieve. Pour into an ice cream maker and follow the manufacturer's instructions. Freeze the ice milk in an airtight container. Best eaten within 4 days.

bittersweet chocolate sorbet, two ways

I love chocolate, both light and rich. The first sorbet here is so rich, you can eat only a tiny bit, but it certainly satisfies a chocolate craving. The second version was preferred by some of my recipe testers and deemed the better choice when you want to sit down with a big bowl of sorbet. You choose; the technique is the same for both.

Try Valrhona cocoa and their Manjari, Caraibe or Caraque chocolate for this sorbet.

Makes 1 scant quart

Rich Bittersweet Chocolate Sorbet

3 cups water
1 cup granulated sugar
9 ounces bittersweet or semisweet chocolate, finely chopped
½ cup (2 ounces) Dutch-process cocoa, such as Valrhona

Lighter Bittersweet Chocolate Sorbet

3 cups water
1 cup granulated sugar
6 ounces bittersweet or semisweet chocolate, finely chopped
¼ cup (1 ounce) Dutch-process cocoa, such as Valrhona

Combine the water, sugar, and chocolate in a medium-size heavy-bottomed, nonreactive saucepan. Sift the cocoa and add to the mixture. Whisk the ingredients together.

Bring to a boil over medium-high heat. Turn the heat down and simmer for 1 minute, whisking a few times.

Remove from the heat and strain into a bowl through a fine-mesh sieve. Cool almost to room temperature, stirring occasionally. Transfer to a storage container and refrigerate for 6 hours, or overnight.

Pour into an ice cream maker and follow the manufacturer's instructions. Freeze the sorbet in an airtight container. Best eaten within 4 days.

⭐ **BAKE IT TO THE LIMIT**
Skinny Black and White Frappe

This sorbet is good by itself, but a scoop alongside a scoop of Triple Vanilla Ice Milk is a great combo. Or for a low-fat treat, make a Skinny Black and White Frappe. You need a blender and tall clear glasses. And long slender ice cream spoons are useful too. Most blenders can make two frappes at a time.

Makes 2 servings

1 cup skim milk

¾ cup Triple Vanilla Ice Milk (page 109)

½ cup Bittersweet Chocolate Sorbet, either version

Place the milk and Triple Vanilla Ice Milk in a blender. Process until thick and smooth. Pour into two 12- to 14-ounce glasses and add a ¼-cup scoop of Bittersweet Chocolate Sorbet to each glass. Serve immediately.

pear and red wine sorbet

Have you ever had pears poached in red wine? This is the frozen version. The pureed pears give this sorbet a rich texture.

Makes 1 quart

5 firm, ripe 7-ounce pears (Comice are excellent)

1⅓ cups granulated sugar

1⅓ cups water

1½ cups dry red wine (any table wine is fine)

1½ teaspoons freshly squeezed lemon juice

Peel, halve and core the pears; set aside.

Put the sugar and water in a large saucepan, stir to wet the sugar, and bring to a boil over medium-high heat. Add the pears along with the red wine. Bring back to a boil. Then reduce the heat and simmer for

10 to 15 minutes, or until the pears are tender when pierced with a knife. Remove from the heat and let cool to room temperature.

Puree the pears and any liquid in a blender, in batches if necessary. Then pass the mixture through a fine-mesh strainer. Add the lemon juice and stir to combine. Transfer to a storage container and refrigerate for 6 hours, or overnight.

Pour into an ice cream maker and follow the manufacturer's instructions. Freeze the sorbet in an airtight container. Best eaten within 4 days.

crème fraîche sorbet

My palate first reveled in crème fraîche sorbet at Hawthorn Lane in San Francisco, where Nicole Plue, the pastry chef, presented some to me as part of a sorbet assortment. They were all great, but this one captured my attention.

Makes 5 cups

1⅔ cups water

⅔ cup granulated sugar

1 vanilla bean, split

4 cups crème fraîche (page 150)

2 tablespoons freshly squeezed lemon juice

Combine the water and sugar in a medium-size saucepan. Stir to wet the sugar. Scrape the vanilla bean seeds into the pan and add the bean as well. Bring to a boil over medium heat. Turn the heat down and simmer for 1 minute. Remove from the heat and cool almost to room temperature.

Remove the vanilla bean. Whisk in the crème fraîche and lemon juice. Strain into a bowl through a fine-mesh strainer. Transfer to a storage container and refrigerate for 6 hours, or overnight.

Pour into an ice cream maker and follow the manufacturer's instructions. Freeze the sorbet in an airtight container. Best eaten within 4 days.

egg whites and reconstitute according to the manufacturer's instructions. (Just Whites is a brand available at many supermarkets and at N.Y. Cake and Baking Distributors; see page 176.)

jasmine tea sorbet

This tea-flavored sorbet can be made with any black tea. Jasmine has a very floral taste, which you will really like or really not. Try a rose-scented tea or an Earl Grey for variations.

Makes 3 cups

2¾ cups water

3 tablespoons loose jasmine tea (approximately ½ ounce)

⅔ cup superfine sugar

2 tablespoons light corn syrup

1 large egg white, lightly beaten (see Note)

Cold-brew the tea by combining the water and tea leaves in a glass jar or bowl. Whisk, cover with plastic wrap, and let sit overnight at room temperature. Strain out the leaves. (Do not hot-brew the tea, or the sorbet will be bitter.)

Add the sugar and corn syrup to the tea, and blend well until the sweeteners have dissolved.

Whisk in the egg white. Refrigerate for 6 hours, or overnight.

Pour into an ice cream maker and follow the manufacturer's instructions. Freeze the sorbet in an airtight container. Best eaten within 4 days.

Note: If egg safety is a problem in your area, or if you have a compromised immune system, use powdered

minted honeydew sorbet with lime

Many orange-fleshed melons give off a delicious aroma when ripe. Honeydews are harder to gauge; the stem end should yield to slight pressure. You must have a ripe melon for the flavor of this sorbet to work.

Makes 1 quart

1 large or 2 small ripe honeydew melons

½ cup fresh mint leaves, rinsed

1½ cups water

1⅓ cups granulated sugar

¼ cup freshly squeezed lime juice

Seed the melon and cut it into ½-inch cubes to make 5 cups. Place the melon and mint in a food processor fitted with the metal blade, and process until smooth.

Meanwhile, combine the water and sugar in a saucepan, and stir to wet the sugar. Bring to a boil over medium heat. Turn the heat down and simmer for 1 minute. Pour this sugar syrup down the feed tube of the processor, along with the lime juice, and pulse the machine on and off to incorporate. (The heat of the sugar syrup helps to release the mint's essential oils and flavor.)

Strain through a fine-mesh sieve and chill overnight in an airtight container for the flavors to develop. This will help the mint to permeate the sorbet.

Pour into an ice cream maker and follow the manufacturer's instructions. Freeze the sorbet in an airtight container. Best eaten within 4 days.

BAKE IT TO THE LIMIT

I don't believe in using mint leaves as a garnish where they do not belong. They do belong here. The mint in the sorbet can be echoed with a crystallized mint leaf garnish. See the instructions for crystallizing flowers on page 108. Mint leaves are easy to crystallize and make a beautiful frosted green adornment for this sorbet, as well as adding a slight crunch. Crystallize a small mint sprig for each serving.

merlot cinnamon granita

A fruity Merlot simmered with cinnamon makes up this wine-flavored granita. This packs a wine-flavored punch, so serve it to your favorite adult guests.

Makes 3½ cups

1 cup water

½ cup granulated sugar

2 cinnamon sticks (about 4 inches long), each broken in half

2 cups Merlot

1 tablespoon freshly squeezed lemon juice

Combine the water, sugar and cinnamon sticks in a saucepan, and stir to wet the sugar. Place over medium-high heat and bring to a boil. Turn the heat down and add the Merlot. Simmer for 2 minutes. Remove from the heat and stir in the lemon juice. Steep the mixture for 30 minutes, then strain it through a fine-mesh strainer.

Pour the granita mixture into a freezer-safe container, preferably a shallow stainless-steel dish. (The nonreactive metal will quick-chill the granita effectively.) Freeze overnight.

Immediately before serving, rake the tines of a fork over the surface of the granita. It will fluff up into icy flakes. Scoop them up and mound lightly into serving dishes. Serve immediately.

plum wine granita

Japanese plum wine has a sweet-tart flavor that makes this granita a dessert and aperitif in one. Serve it for an unusual treat after a midsummer Asian-inspired meal, or use it as an intermezzo between courses of a lengthy, rich meal.

Makes 3 cups

2½ cups water

⅓ cup granulated sugar

¾ cup Japanese plum wine (umeshu)

Combine the water and sugar in a saucepan, and stir to wet the sugar. Bring to a boil over medium heat. Turn down the heat and simmer for 1 minute. Cool to room temperature. Add the plum wine. Then pour the granita mixture into a freezer-safe container, preferably a shallow stainless-steel dish. (The nonreactive metal will quick-chill the granita effectively.) Freeze overnight.

Immediately before serving, rake the tines of a fork over the surface of the granita. It will fluff up into icy flakes. Scoop them up and mound lightly into serving dishes. Serve immediately.

cakes

Marzipan Chocolate Pound Cake with Cognac Apricots ✳ Crème Fraîche Cheesecake in a Walnut Crust ✳ Chocolate Sour Cherry Bûche de Noël ✳ Caramel Devil's Food Cake ✳ Chocolate Raspberry Mousse Cake ✳ Molten Chocolate Cake ✳ Strawberry Almond Genoise ✳ Mocha Almond Dacquoise ✳ Gingerbread Roll with Sautéed Apples

Some of the most complex, dramatic desserts are special-occasion cakes. In this chapter you'll find some simple cakes and some showstoppers as well. Don't let the length of some of these recipes turn you off. Many are made up of components that can be prepared way ahead, simplifying the process. If you make a lot of special-occasion cakes, or want a more thorough resource for your creations in this area, please refer to my first book, *The Wedding Cake Book*. Although it is about wedding cakes, any of the recipes can be adapted for large celebration cakes.

As with all desserts, pay attention to the serving temperature. Many of these cakes have so much butter in them, as well as in their buttercreams, that if they are served cold, the texture and taste suffer greatly. Follow the serving suggestions.

Also, please read Decorating Cakes (see page 126) for more in-depth information on finishing your cakes.

Making Chocolate and Marzipan
Roses and Leaves

It is helpful to have cutters in the shape of a large rose petal (about 2 inches across, teardrop-shaped) as well as 2 sizes of rose leaves. If you do not have them, you can use round cookie cutters for the petals and cut the leaves free-form. Also, a very small rolling pin, sold for use with gum paste, is handy. All of these items can be purchased at a cake decorating store.

The instructions are the same for both chocolate plastic (white, milk or dark chocolate; see page 153) and marzipan. Marzipan is used here as an example.

Dust your work surface liberally with confectioner's sugar. Roll out the marzipan to approximately ⅛ inch thick. Cut out 3 to 7 rose petals with an appropriate cutter, or simply cut out 2-inch rounds. For each flower you should use the same size cutter. Remove the excess marzipan from around the petals. Keep any extra marzipan tightly covered in plastic wrap. Loosen the petals from the work surface with a spatula. Dust the surface with more confectioner's sugar if necessary. Using a small rolling pin, thin out the broad edges of the petals. They should be thin and delicate to give a realistic look. Or just thin out one side of a cut-out circle.

Cutting out a rose petal

Thinning the petal edges with a small rolling pin

For each rose, you need to mold a center. Take a piece of marzipan and roll it into a cone shape. The height of the cone should be approximately the same as the length of the petals. The diameter of the base should be half that of the height. Set the cone on the work surface with the point up.

Take one of the petals, and using the point on the narrow end as a guide, fold it in half lengthwise while still keeping the petal open. Pinch the bottom together. Gently flare out the top edge in a tight outward furl. Some asymmetry is permissible and even desired. Real roses are not perfect. Real petals have tiny cuts and a combination of loosely curled and tightly curled shapes.

Place one petal against the cone base with the pinched end down. Somewhat flatten one broad side against the cone, leaving the other side open and away from the cone. This will allow another petal to be tucked beneath it in an overlapping manner, just like a real rose. Repeat with a second petal, starting in the middle of the first petal. The third petal will be tucked under the first. These three petals create a rosebud. You may add more petals, each beginning in the middle of the one underneath. As you add more petals, they should be more and more open and not as tightly fixed as the initial rows.

*One petal with the bottom
pinched together*

*A center forming the base,
with 1 petal attached*

Two petals added

Three petals added

A full rose with 6 petals

At this point the base may be quite wide and clunky. Release the entire rose from the work surface by sliding an offset spatula or a thin, sharp knife beneath the flower. Trim any excess marzipan with a sharp paring knife. Roll the bottom back and forth between your fingers to create a rounded shape. When you are done, use a broad, soft brush to dust off any extra confectioner's sugar that remains.

The rose may be made a couple of days ahead and stored in an airtight container at room temperature.

To make leaves out of marzipan, I use purchased leaf-shaped cutters and veiners. Leaf veiners are plastic or silicone mats that come in almost as many shapes as do the cutters. You simply press a cut-out marzipan leaf against the raised vein pattern on the veiner. You can also make veins individually, using the blunt edge of a knife.

Marzipan leaves should be made close to the time that you need to use them. They dry out a bit during storage, which makes it difficult to bend or manipulate them into the shapes you need when applying to your cake. (Roses are not bent or manipulated after they are made, so they can be made ahead.)

Roll out your marzipan to ⅛-inch thickness and cut out the number of leaves desired. Remove the excess marzipan from around the leaves. Loosen the leaves with a spatula, and press them against the veiner to create realistic veins. Curve the leaves gently by draping them over bottles, cardboard tubes or rolling pins. Let them sit for up to 1 hour to develop their shape. Then apply them directly to the cake. (Alternatively, the leaves can be shaped and applied directly to the cake if time is tight.)

When ready to serve the cake, place the rose in the center (without confectioner's sugar) and surround it with some leaves. Roll a bit of marzipan into a long thin rope, about ¼ inch in diameter, and place coils here and there, tucked below the rose and leaves, to mimic stems.

marzipan chocolate pound cake with cognac apricots

For this pound cake, almond paste is added to the batter, along with shaved chocolate and cognac-soaked apricots. It tastes fantastic and remains moist for days.

Makes one 8-inch cake, 10 to 12 servings

7 ounces (1 cup) dried apricots, chopped

½ cup cognac

¾ cup plus 1 tablespoon all-purpose flour

5 ounces (1⅔ cups) sliced blanched almonds,
  lightly toasted (see page 152)

¼ teaspoon salt

2 ounces semisweet chocolate (do not use chips)

10 tablespoons (5 ounces) unsalted butter,
  at room temperature

6½ ounces almond paste

¾ cup granulated sugar

1 teaspoon vanilla extract

1 teaspoon almond extract

5 large eggs

Confectioner's sugar

Combine the apricots and cognac in a nonreactive bowl, cover with plastic wrap and soak for 4 hours, or overnight, at room temperature. Or, microwave on high for 1 to 2 minutes. The apricots will absorb most or all of the cognac. If there is extra, just fold it into the batter along with the apricots.

Preheat the oven to 325°F. Spray an 8 × 2-inch round cake pan with nonstick cooking spray, and line the bottom with parchment.

Place the flour, almonds and salt in a food processor fitted with the metal blade, and process until the almonds are ground to a fine meal. This is best accomplished by pulsing on and off initially to get the mixture going, then leaving the machine on for about 15 seconds. Set aside.

Using the largest holes on a hand greater, grate the chocolate onto a piece of parchment. Try not to touch the grated chocolate or it may melt from the warmth of your hands. Alternatively, shave the chocolate off a block with a large chef's knife.

In the bowl of a heavy-duty mixer, cream the butter with the flat paddle attachment on medium speed until smooth. Add the almond paste and beat until lightened. Add the sugar gradually and continue to beat at medium-high speed until the mixture is very light and fluffy, about 5 minutes. Beat in the vanilla and almond extracts. Add the eggs one at a time, beating well after each addition and scraping down the sides of the bowl once or twice. Beat in the flour mixture by pulsing the mixer on and off, taking care not to overmix. Fold in the apricots.

Pick up the parchment with the chocolate on it, and pour the chocolate over the batter. Fold it in with a large spatula in a few broad strokes.

Scrape the batter into the prepared pan and smooth the top with a small offset spatula. Bake for 65 to 75 minutes, until the cake is lightly golden and the edges are coming away from the pan's sides. An inserted toothpick should come out clean. Place the pan on a wire rack to cool for 10 minutes. Then unmold the cake and set it on the rack to cool completely. Serve sprinkled with confectioner's sugar.

Store the cake at room temperature, wrapped in plastic wrap, for up to 3 days.

Crowned with a beautiful marzipan rose, this cake is dressed up enough for any special occasion.

6 ounces marzipan (page 152)

Make 1 large marzipan rose and several leaves (see page 116). Dust the cake with confectioner's sugar, if desired. Then arrange the marzipan rose and leaves on top of the cake.

crème fraîche cheesecake in a walnut crust

Cheesecakes seemed to hit their zenith in the 1970s, but they still appear on dessert menus from coast to coast. This one has the added tang of crème fraîche, and the walnuts contribute texture to the crust.

Makes one 9-inch cheesecake, 12 servings

For the crust

7½ ounces (1½ cups) walnut halves, toasted
  (see page 152)
½ cup all-purpose flour
2 tablespoons granulated sugar
¼ cup (2 ounces) unsalted butter, melted

For the cheesecake

2 pounds cream cheese, at room temperature
1¼ cups granulated sugar

2 large eggs
1 tablespoon freshly squeezed lemon juice
2 teaspoons grated lemon zest
½ teaspoon vanilla extract
1 cup crème fraîche (page 150), or ½ cup sour cream
  and ½ cup plain yogurt

Preheat the oven to 350°F. Spray a 9 × 3-inch round cake pan with nonstick cooking spray, and line the bottom with parchment. Have ready two 9-inch cardboard rounds.

To make the crust, place the walnuts, flour and sugar in a food processor fitted with the metal blade and process until the nuts are reduced to a fine meal. Add the melted butter and pulse on and off a couple of times to incorporate.

Press the walnut crust into the prepared pan, evenly covering the bottom and going ½ inch up the sides. Use a flat-bottomed glass to facilitate pressing the crumbs along the bottom and to help with the edges. Keeping the glass flat, move toward the edges; it will press the crumbs along the sides, creating an even layer all around.

Bake the crust for 10 to 12 minutes, or until it is just beginning to turn a light brown. Remove the pan from the oven and place it on a wire rack until needed.

Meanwhile, make the cheesecake. In the bowl of a heavy-duty mixer, beat the cream cheese until smooth with the flat paddle attachment on medium-high speed. Add the sugar gradually and continue beating until the mixture is lightened and completely smooth, about 2 minutes. Add the eggs one at a time, beating well after each addition and scraping down the bowl once or twice. Beat in the lemon juice, zest and vanilla. Stir in the crème fraîche by hand until completely incorporated. Pour over the crust.

continued

Place the cake pan in a larger pan, and fill the larger pan with hot water to reach halfway up the cake pan.

Bake for 1 hour, until the top is beginning to just be tinged with golden brown and looks dry and smooth. Turn the oven off and let the cake remain in the oven for 1 more hour. Then remove the pan from the water bath and refrigerate the cake overnight, covered with plastic wrap, before unmolding.

To unmold the cheesecake, have the two cardboard rounds ready. Cover one round with plastic wrap.

Run hot water over the bottom of the cake pan. (Don't worry—the cheesecake will not fall out.) Warm a spatula under hot water and blot it dry. Run the spatula around the sides of the cake, pressing outward toward the sides of the pan. The warmth will loosen the cake from the sides and bottom of the pan. Take the plastic wrap–covered cardboard round and place it on top of the cake. With your fingertips on the cardboard and your thumbs on the bottom of the cake pan, flip the pan upside down. Make a few quick twisting motions and you should feel the cake begin to slip out. If it doesn't, turn the cake pan right side up and repeat the warm water step. When it starts to slide down and out of the pan, lower the cake to the table and gently lift off the pan completely. Peel off the parchment paper if it has stuck to the crust. Place the other cardboard round on top. Slip one hand under the bottom cardboard round, and with the other hand on the top cardboard, flip the cake over and place it on a serving platter. Remove the cardboard that is now on the top of the cheesecake. The surface should hardly be marred at all—the plastic wrap should have minimized any damage. If the top is badly marked, smooth it with a spatula that has been warmed in hot water and wiped dry.

Keep refrigerated up to 2 days, covered with plastic wrap. Serve cold. Cheesecakes are best sliced with a thin-bladed knife that is dipped in hot water between cuts.

This cake is excellent served with fresh strawberries, raspberries or blackberries.

BAKE IT TO THE LIMIT
Pansies Under Glass

This makes a perfect Mother's Day dessert or a great cake for a bridal shower—any time you want something really pretty. The cheesecake is covered with a white chocolate cream cheese frosting. Then the top is decorated with pressed pansies and/or rose petals and covered with an apple jelly glaze. The flowers look like little jewels under glass. Plan ahead: the flowers must be pressed for at least 3 days, and may be done up to a week ahead. Make sure the flowers are unsprayed.

For the pressed flowers
> *6 pansies*
> *Petals of 1 fully opened rose*

For the white chocolate cream cheese frosting
> *15 ounces white chocolate, finely chopped*
> *1 pound cream cheese, at room temperature*
> *14 tablespoons (7 ounces) unsalted butter,*
>   *at room temperature*
> *1 teaspoon vanilla extract*

For the glaze
> *½ cup apple jelly*
> *4 teaspoons water*

To press the flowers, use a flower press or a large, heavy book, and press the pansies and rose petals between pieces of clean white paper. Do this 3 days to a week ahead.

continued

Make the frosting. Melt the chocolate in the top of a double boiler. Stir until completely smooth. Cool to slightly warm room temperature.

Meanwhile, in the bowl of a heavy-duty mixer, beat the cream cheese and butter until smooth with the flat paddle attachment on medium-high speed. Beat in the vanilla. Place a strainer over the bowl and scrape the melted chocolate into the strainer. Press it through, using a rubber spatula. Beat the chocolate in until it is completely incorporated and the frosting is smooth. If the texture seems grainy or separated, refrigerate until completely firm (this will bring all the ingredients to the same temperature), then soften by warming carefully in the microwave; whip again until smooth.

Place the cheesecake, on its cardboard base, on a cake decorator's turntable or a lazy susan. Place a good quantity of frosting on top of the cake and smooth it over the top. Then spread the excess down around the sides. The cheesecake is firm and will allow you to exert some pressure when spreading the frosting around (see page 127). Pipe a shell border of frosting around the top and bottom edges using a #18 star tip (see page 141). You may make any design you like—just make sure that the edges are completely covered because this decoration also functions to keep the glaze from dripping down the cake's sides. Refrigerate until firm, about 1 hour.

Place the pressed pansies and rose petals on the cake top, pressing them lightly onto the frosting so they adhere.

Make the glaze. Heat the jelly and water in a small saucepan on low heat until melted. Pour the glaze through a fine-mesh strainer into a measuring cup with a pouring spout. Press the glaze through the strainer to remove any lumps. Immediately pour the warm glaze slowly over the top of the cake. You want to completely cover the space within the decorative border. Tilt the cake around to facilitate this. If there are any uncovered spots, use a spoon to gently pour glaze and fill them in. Refrigerate the cake to set the glaze, about 30 minutes. The cake may be held overnight at this point. Serve chilled. Cut the cheesecake with a thin-bladed knife that is run under hot water between slices.

chocolate sour cherry bûche de noël

This Christmas log consists of a cocoa cake roll filled with chocolate whipped cream and tart cherries, topped with a dark, rich chocolate ganache. In its Bake It to the Limit version, the cake becomes a three-dimensional chocolate wonder guaranteed to elicit gasps of appreciation from your lucky guests. And that's before they even taste it.

This is very rich—for die-hard dark chocolate fans only. The recipe is long and has many components, but some can be done ahead and the results are well worth it. You'll probably make this traditional French Christmas dessert only once a year anyway, so enjoy the process.

Assemble the *bûche* the day before or on the day of serving. The Bittersweet Chocolate Ganache can be made up to a month ahead and frozen; the optional chocolate decorations can be made a week ahead; and the Whipped Chocolate Ganache Filling, Cherry Filling, and Cocoa Roulade should be made the day before serving.

Makes one 12-inch log, 12 servings

1 recipe Bittersweet Chocolate Ganache (page 154)

1 recipe Whipped Chocolate Ganache (page 154)

For the cherry filling

One 14½-ounce can water-packed tart cherries

   (I use Thank You brand, available nationwide)

2 tablespoons granulated sugar

2 tablespoons Kirschwasser (cherry liqueur)

For the cocoa roulade

¼ cup whole milk

2 tablespoons (1 ounce) unsalted butter

½ cup cake flour

¼ cup Dutch-process cocoa

1 teaspoon baking powder

¼ teaspoon salt

3 large eggs

3 large egg yolks

1 cup granulated sugar

For decoration

Confectioner's sugar

Pine boughs

Have the Bittersweet Chocolate Ganache and Whipped Chocolate Ganache made. Both should be chilled, the latter held prior to its final whipping.

To make the cherry filling, drain the cherries, reserving the liquid. Place the cherries in a small mixing bowl; set aside. Combine the sugar and 2 tablespoons of the reserved cherry juice in a small saucepan. Bring to a boil over medium-high heat, stirring to dissolve the sugar. Remove from the heat and add the Kirschwasser. Pour over the cherries and marinate for least 1 hour, or until needed.

To make the cocoa roulade, preheat the oven to

350°F. Spray a sheet pan with nonstick cooking spray, line it with parchment, and spray again.

Place the milk and butter in a saucepan and warm over medium heat to melt the butter, or melt together in a microwave. Set aside, keeping warm.

Into a bowl, sift together the cake flour, cocoa, baking powder and salt; set aside.

In the bowl of a heavy-duty mixer, beat the eggs, egg yolks and sugar with the balloon whip attachment on high speed until light and fluffy, about 2 minutes. A ribbon should form when you lift the whip from the mixture.

Resift the dry ingredients over the egg mixture, adding them in 3 batches. After each addition, stir with a whisk and then finish off with a spatula.

Dribble the warmed milk mixture over the batter a little at a time, folding all the while. (If you add the liquid too quickly, it will sink and create a rubbery layer in your cake.)

Pour the batter onto the prepared sheet pan, using an offset spatula to spread it evenly. The cake will be thin.

Bake for 10 to 12 minutes, rotating the pan front to back once during the baking time. The cake should be puffed and lightly golden brown, and an inserted toothpick should come out clean. Do not overbake or it will lose its flexibility.

Place the pan on a wire rack to cool. Use the cake as soon as it has cooled, or wrap it, still on the pan, in plastic wrap and store it at room temperature for up to 24 hours.

Assembly

Begin assembly the day before serving, or very early in the day of serving. Have ready a large flat serving platter. It must be at least 18 inches long, at least 6 inches wide, and able to fit in your refrigerator.

Unmold the cake, using a knife tip to loosen the edges. Lay a clean piece of parchment on your work surface and invert the cake onto it. Remove the pan and very gently peel off the baked-on parchment. Arrange the clean parchment so the long sides of the cake are horizontal in front of you.

Dip a pastry brush into the cherry marinade to saturate the brush with liquid. Dab the liquid all over the surface of the cake.

In the mixer bowl, whip the Whipped Chocolate Ganache with the balloon whip attachment on medium-high speed until firm peaks form (a little stiffer than soft peaks).

Using an offset spatula, spread the Whipped Chocolate Ganache evenly over the cake, going all the way to the short edges but leaving a ¼-inch border along the top long edge. Scatter the cherries evenly over the filling. Press them into the filling slightly by running the spatula over them.

Using the parchment to help, roll the cake, starting with the long side nearest you. Roll firmly, separating the parchment from the cake as you go so that it doesn't get rolled up inside. Carefully transfer the roll to the serving platter, cover with plastic wrap, and refrigerate for at least 1 hour or until the filling has firmed up. (If you are working in a cool room, you may be able to proceed immediately without this cooling step. Just make sure the filling is firm enough so that the pressure from applying the Bittersweet Chocolate Ganache will not make the filling seep out.)

Remove the cake from the refrigerator. Trim one end on an angle (snack on the scrap). Cut off the other end on an angle about 4 inches down the log. Take this piece and lay it a third of the way down the side of the log, nestling the angled end against the log. This creates a "branch."

Check to see that the Bittersweet Chocolate Ganache is at spreading consistency. Spread it all over the log, using an icing spatula. A small offset spatula might help to get at the corners and the edges that are resting on the platter. Cover the ends with ganache as well. If serving as is, use a small, narrow icing spatula to make long ridges in the ganache to simulate bark. Use a fork to make concentric rings on the ends. (If making the Bake It to the Limit version, stop here and proceed with those assembly directions.) Refrigerate for 6 hours, or overnight. Let the cake sit at room temperature for 30 minutes before serving. Arrange pine boughs around the cake, and dust the cake and the boughs with confectioner's sugar to mimic snow.

✦ BAKE IT TO THE LIMIT

This deluxe version adds tempered chocolate pieces to create a three-dimensional bark effect. The chocolate pieces can be made up to a week ahead. The acetate makes the chocolate super-shiny, which is a great effect.

1 pound bittersweet couverture chocolate (such as Valrhona Manjari or Caraque; see page 166), finely chopped
One 20 × 20-inch piece clear plastic acetate (available at art supply stores) or aluminum foil

Temper the chocolate (see page 160). Using an offset spatula, spread a thin layer of chocolate over the acetate. Let the chocolate harden at room temperature, about 10 minutes. When the Bûche de Noël has been filled, rolled and spread with Bittersweet Chocolate Ganache, break off pieces of tempered chocolate in long, irregular pieces, about the length of the log and about 2 inches wide. Nestle them into the ganache on a slight angle, overlapping each row over the previous one. Finish the cake off as above, with pine boughs and confectioner's sugar.

caramel devil's food cake

This layer cake pairs good old-fashioned devil's food cake layers with a sophisticated chocolate caramel buttercream. It's a perfect birthday cake for any chocolate-loving member of the family. Use Magi-Cake Strips (see page 163) for all layer cakes. The layers will rise more evenly, making your decorating job easier.

Makes one 8-inch layer cake, 10 servings

1¾ cups cake flour

1 teaspoon baking soda

¼ teaspoon salt

½ cup (4 ounces) unsalted butter, at room temperature

1 cup granulated sugar

1 cup lightly packed light brown sugar

1 teaspoon vanilla extract

2 large eggs

1 cup hot water

½ cup natural cocoa (such as Hershey's)

½ cup buttermilk, at room temperature

1 recipe Italian Meringue Buttercream, chocolate
  caramel variation (page 157)

1 cup Chocolate Curls (page 160)

Preheat the oven to 350°F. Spray two 8 × 2-inch round cake pans with nonstick cooking spray and line the bottoms with parchment. Have ready one 8-inch cardboard round.

Sift the cake flour, baking soda and salt into a mixing bowl; set aside.

In the bowl of a heavy-duty mixer, beat the butter with the flat paddle attachment on medium-high speed until light and creamy, about 2 minutes. Add the sugar and brown sugar, and continue beating until light and fluffy, about 3 minutes. Beat in the vanilla. Add the eggs one at a time, beating well and scraping down the bowl after each addition.

In another bowl, whisk together the hot water, cocoa and buttermilk.

Add the dry and liquid ingredients to the butter mixture alternately in 3 batches, pulsing the machine on and off on low speed, scraping down the bowl once or twice. Beat until the ingredients are well combined and the batter is smooth, about 30 seconds after all the ingredients have been added.

Divide the batter between the 2 prepared pans, and wrap with Magi-Cake Strips (see page 163). Bake for 45 minutes, or until an inserted toothpick comes out clean. Cool the pans on wire racks for 10 minutes, then unmold the cakes onto the racks and cool completely.

The cake may be filled and frosted the day it is baked, or the layers may sit at room temperature, wrapped well with plastic wrap, overnight. You may also freeze them for up to a month; double-wrap in plastic and foil, and bring to room temperature while still wrapped.

Assembly

Have the buttercream and chocolate curls ready and see page 126 for general directions on decorating cakes before you start to assemble this cake. Trim the cake layers so that they are level, if necessary. Place

Decorating Cakes

There are certain techniques that should be followed if you want your cake to look as professional as possible. If you make a lot of large cakes, refer to my first book, *The Wedding Cake Book*. Although wedding cakes are the focus, the techniques can be applied to any large cake, such as a birthday, anniversary, baby shower or graduation cake. Here is a synopsis of the basic tips.

First, have the right equipment. A decorator's turntable is absolutely necessary. You can use an inexpensive lazy susan, but in any case you need a flat rotating surface. An assortment of straight and offset spatulas, large and small, with varying degrees of flexibility, is also de rigueur. Purchased cardboard rounds (from cake decorating stores) the same size as your cake are invaluable. An assortment of pastry bags and tips and a coupler will make it a breeze to apply the finishing touches.

And you need time. You cannot rush this process.

Leveling: Once your cake layers have cooled, they must first be leveled. Often the top will be peaked (using Magi-Cake Strips will alleviate this; see page 163). Use a sharp slicing knife to level the layers. Serrated knife blades can work well, but they dredge up crumbs, the bane of the cake decorator's existence. One caveat: Make sure your worktable is level, or your cuts won't be.

Torting: Torting a cake is the process of horizontally slicing a single layer. Occasionally you will want to make one layer into two (or more), and this is how you do it. Place the solid cake tier on a cardboard round and set it on your turntable. Using a small sharp knife, scribe a vertical line from top to bottom. (This will help you to realign the layers later.) Decide how many layers you want. Divide the height of the cake by that number of layers. If you have a 2-inch cake and would like 4 layers, then you come up with a figure of ½ inch. This means that you should mark off your layers in ½-inch increments by making small cuts with the tip of the knife on the side of the cake. Make sure that you place the ruler on top of the cardboard round so that you are truly measuring from the bottom of the cake.

To make the horizontal cuts level, place a few toothpicks into the cake at the heights you have marked off. This will help you guide the knife across at the same level. The bottom layer should be left on the cardboard on the turntable in front of you.

At this point, some recipes have sugar syrup brushed onto the layers to add flavor and moistness. The best way to do this is with a pastry brush dipped into the sugar syrup; dab and press the syrup all over the cake layers. Actually brushing back and forth will create crumbs—dabbing is better. Then you are ready to fill the layers.

Place whatever filling or buttercream you have chosen on top of the bottom cake layer. Spread it evenly to the desired thickness. Offset spatulas work well for this step. Take the next cake layer and find the small incision on its side. Line it up with the cut on the bottom layer. This way the layers are positioned on top of one another (with filling in between) as they were initially. This will create the most even shape. Repeat with any remaining filling and cake layers. Then proceed with the crumb coat.

Applying the Crumb Coat: The first layer of buttercream you apply is called the crumb coat. It is a very thin veneer of buttercream that seals in any crumbs that remain on the cake's surface. Have your cake in front of you on the turntable. Place a good amount of buttercream on top of the cake and smooth it over the top, spreading the excess toward the sides. Don't worry if crumbs come up and stick within the buttercream. They will not visually or texturally mar the final coating. Spread the buttercream over onto the sides of the cake. Now hold the spatula vertically, with the tip facing straight down and resting against the outside of the cardboard for guidance. The flat part of the spatula should rest almost flat against the cake; just angle it out slightly. Rotate the turntable as you smooth the buttercream along the sides. Some chefs find a straight-edge spatula is easiest to work with; others prefer an offset. Use whichever is best for you. You will see much of the cake through the thin layer. This is fine. Even off the top, square off the edges, and chill thoroughly 2 to 4 hours.

Applying the Final Coat of Buttercream: When the crumb coat has firmed up in the refrigerator, you are ready to proceed with the final coat. Place the cake on your turntable, and put a good amount of buttercream on top of the cake. Spread a thick layer over the top. Manipulate your spatula so that it glides above the coat of new buttercream, pushing it out from the center. Do not let your spatula touch the crumb coat—always have a buffer of the final buttercream layer between your spatula and the crumb coat. This will prevent any crumbs from being lifted off the surface. The final coat will go on more smoothly than the first, as the crumb coat provides a more inviting surface upon which to work. When it comes to smoothing the sides, the cardboard will help you achieve a smooth surface. The perfect shape of the cardboard provides a smooth guide for you to follow with your spatula. Feel your way along the edge of the cardboard, bridging your spatula vertically between it and the upper edge of the cake. By keeping the spatula perfectly vertical and rotating the turntable simultaneously, you will be able to create smooth sides. No matter what amount of decoration you are planning to eventually place on the cake, a smooth final buttercream coating will present the best canvas.

Here is a professional tip that can help you achieve a super-smooth look. Run your spatula under the hottest tap water. Wipe it dry and use the warmed tool to smooth the final coat of buttercream. The warmth of the spatula will slightly melt the uppermost layer of buttercream, creating an ultra-smooth texture. I use this technique for practically every cake I make. Some pastry chefs use a spray bottle to apply a fine mist of warm water to the cake's surface, then smooth out any imperfections with a spatula. Any droplets of remaining moisture on the cake's surface will evaporate on their own.

Covering the Buttercream with Other Toppings: To cover the sides, parts of the sides, or the entire cake with crumbled dacquoise, cake crumbs, chopped nuts, coconut or anything similar, follow these instructions. Nuts are used as the example.

While the final coat of buttercream is still soft, apply the nuts. Hold the cake, on its cardboard, in your left hand. Scoop up the nuts with your right hand and press them against the sides of the cake. Rotate the cake in your left palm as you go along. The nuts that do not stick will fall back down onto your work surface. It is best to do this over a piece of parchment so that you can keep scooping up the nuts easily as you need them. Repeat the procedure until you have covered as much of the surface as you want. (Reverse hands for lefties.)

Using Pastry Bags, Couplers and Decorating Tips: The baker has dozens of decorating tips at his or her disposal and should take advantage of them. Most cost less than a dollar, and the tiniest bit of difference in the tip can make a big difference in how your icing will look when it is piped out of a bag.

A coupler is a plastic piece that fits in your pastry bag (which, if new, will have to have its opening cut larger) and extends beyond the opening. A tip is fitted onto the coupler, and the collar piece of the coupler screws on, keeping the tip in place. This allows you to change tips while icing is in the bag.

Make a batch of buttercream and practice. You can practice on a sheet of parchment and just pick it up and throw it away when you are done.

Fill the bag about a third of the way with the desired filling and twist the top closed. For right-handers, place your left hand on the coupler. This hand will guide the tip. The right hand should hold the twisted part down in place. This pressure will force the icing out. Do not squeeze the middle of the bag.

Practice, practice, practice.

one cake layer on an 8-inch cardboard round and set it on a cake decorator's turntable or a lazy susan. Spread the top with a layer of buttercream. Top with the second cake layer. Apply a thin layer of buttercream to the top and sides of the cake to form the crumb coat. Refrigerate for 3 hours or until the buttercream is firm. Apply a final coat of buttercream and place the cake on a serving dish. Pipe a reverse shell border around the top and bottom, if desired, using a #18 tip (see page 141).

Refrigerate until the buttercream is firm, at least 1 hour or overnight. Let the cake come to room temperature before serving, about 30 minutes to 1 hour. Top with chocolate curls and serve.

✳ BAKE IT TO THE LIMIT
Praline Chocolate Cake with Chocolate Roses

Turn the basic cake into a stunner with this variation, in which it is brushed with hazelnut liqueur and filled and frosted with a praline buttercream. The roses on top are made of chocolate plastic, which is a combination of chocolate and corn syrup. This makes a great birthday cake; you can make the same number of roses as guests so that they all get one. (Remember when you were little and the birthday boy or girl always got a rose and the rest were doled out through some strange hierarchy? Let's put an end to that!)

continued

1 recipe Devil's Food Cake, layers baked and cooled

½ recipe Sugar Syrup, strongly flavored with hazelnut liqueur, such as Frangelico (page 151)

1 recipe Italian Meringue Buttercream, praline variation (page 157)

1 recipe Chocolate Plastic (page 153)

Assemble the cake as described above, brushing the layers with the hazelnut sugar syrup and filling and frosting with praline Italian Meringue Buttercream.

Make 10 chocolate roses of various sizes out of Chocolate Plastic, following the directions on page 116. The roses in the photograph are made from both semisweet and milk chocolates.

After the frosted cake has chilled, apply a simple top and bottom buttercream border, using a #8 tip to make a loose reverse spiral (see page 141). Right before serving, place the chocolate roses and leaves here and there (see the photo for ideas). The cake may be refrigerated, unadorned, for 24 hours.

Store and serve as described above.

chocolate raspberry mousse cake

This cake consists of a thin vanilla sponge shell filled with a hot-pink raspberry mousse. The entire cake is surrounded by a crisp marbled chocolate band and topped with whipped cream. It is elaborate looking but relatively easy to make, and the process can be broken down into stages. The sponge cake, which is incredibly flexible, is almost exactly the same as Alice

Medrich's in her book *Cocolat*, which every dessert-lover should own. Making the chocolate band takes patience but is not difficult.

Makes one 8-inch cake, 10 servings

For the vanilla sponge cake

¼ cup whole milk

2 tablespoons (1 ounce) unsalted butter, at room temperature

¾ cup cake flour

1 teaspoon baking powder

3 large eggs, at room temperature

3 large egg yolks, at room temperature

¾ cup granulated sugar

1 teaspoon vanilla extract

For the raspberry mousse filling

One 12-ounce package frozen unsweetened raspberries, defrosted (I use Red Valley brand, available nationwide)

¾ cup cold water or cranberry-raspberry juice

1 tablespoon unflavored gelatin

¼ cup granulated sugar

1½ cups heavy cream

For the chocolate band

2 ounces white chocolate, finely chopped

2 ounces semisweet chocolate, finely chopped

For the topping

2 cups heavy cream

⅓ cup granulated sugar

1 pint fresh raspberries

To make the cake, preheat the oven to 375°F. Spray a sheet pan with nonstick cooking spray, line it

with parchment, and spray again. Also have ready an 8-inch-diameter, 3-inch-deep springform pan and an 8-inch cardboard round.

Measure out the milk in a microwaveable measuring cup. Add the butter and microwave on full power until the butter is melted. (Alternatively, melt the butter with the milk in a saucepan on the stovetop.) Set aside, keeping warm.

Meanwhile, sift the cake flour and baking powder onto a piece of parchment.

Place the eggs, egg yolks and sugar in the bowl of a heavy-duty mixer and whip with the balloon whip attachment on high speed until the mixture is light and fluffy and has tripled in volume, about 5 minutes. A ribbon should form when the whip is lifted from the mixture. Beat in the vanilla.

Resift the dry mixture over the egg mixture in 3 batches, folding in each batch thoroughly with a large whisk. Be gentle and retain as much volume as possible. Finish the folding with a large rubber spatula.

When all of the dry mixture is incorporated, dribble in the warm milk mixture a little at a time, folding slowly and carefully. The liquid is heavier than the batter, and if you do not fold it in so that it is suspended in the batter, it will sink and create a rubbery layer in your sponge.

Spread the batter into the prepared pan, using an offset spatula to spread it evenly. It will be thin.

Bake for 10 minutes, rotating the pan front to back once during the baking time. The cake should spring back to the touch and be just beginning to turn golden; an inserted toothpick should come out clean. Do not let it overbrown or it will lose its flexibility.

Place the pan on a wire rack to cool. Use immediately after cooling, or wrap it in plastic wrap, still in the pan, and store at room temperature for 24 hours.

To make the mousse, pour the defrosted raspberries and any juice into a food processor fitted with the metal blade. Process until the berries are pureed and the fruit is completely smooth. This may take as long as 1 to 2 minutes. The metal blade will chop up many of the seeds, so it is not necessary to strain the puree. Pour into a large bowl.

Pour $1/2$ cup of the water or juice into a large microwaveable measuring cup, sprinkle the gelatin over the liquid, and stir to combine. Let sit to soften for 5 minutes. Add the remaining $1/4$ cup liquid and the sugar. Heat in the microwave until the gelatin has melted and the sugar has dissolved, stirring once or twice. (Alternatively, heat in a small saucepan on the stovetop.) Add the gelatin mixture to the raspberry puree.

Place the bowl with the puree over another bowl filled with ice and cold water, and stir often until the puree is as thick as raw egg white, 20 to 40 minutes.

Meanwhile, unmold the cake. Use a knife tip to loosen the edges. Lay a clean piece of parchment on your work surface and invert the cake onto it. Remove the pan and very gently peel off the baked-on parchment. Line the prepared springform pan with sponge cake as follows: cut out two 8-inch rounds, as close to one long side of the cake as possible. Cut the remaining cake into 2½-inch strips running the length of the cake. Place one round in the bottom of the springform pan. Arrange the strips around the sides, cutting to fit. The ends should fit snugly, but don't worry too much because the mousse will eventually hold it all together. Reserve the second round.

In the mixer, using the balloon whip attachment on medium-high speed, whip the cream until soft peaks form. Fold the whipped cream thoroughly into the cooled raspberry puree.

Pour the mousse into the sponge shell, and top with the remaining cake round. Wrap with plastic wrap and refrigerate for at least 4 hours, until the mousse is set, or overnight.

Open the springform pan, unmold the cake, and place it on an 8-inch cardboard round. Refrigerate until needed.

To make the chocolate band, have ready an acetate strip measuring 26½ × 2½ inches (see Note). Melt the white and semisweet chocolates separately in a double boiler or microwave. Scrape each into a parchment cone. Snip a medium-size opening (about ¼ inch) from each cone. First pipe with the white chocolate, making large free-form loopy patterns all along the acetate strip. Repeat with the semisweet chocolate. Using a small offset spatula and starting at one short end, spread the chocolates over the acetate to cover it. The effect will be a mottled dark-and-white chocolate pattern.

Remove the cake from the refrigerator and place it on a flat serving plate. Pick up the acetate strip from both short ends. Place the center of the strip, chocolate side in, at the center rear of the cake. Make sure the bottom of the strip is aligned with the base of the cake. Bring the two ends of the acetate toward you, wrapping the circumference of the cake. The wet chocolate will "glue" the strip to the cake. One short end should lie flat against the cake. The other short end should be left sticking out by about ½ inch. Refrigerate until the chocolate is set, at least 30 minutes.

Starting with the end that is sticking out, peel off the acetate. Then gently press the chocolate that is sticking out against the cake to seal the band. The warmth of your hands should make it flexible enough, or just wait a few minutes for the chocolate to soften at room temperature.

To make the topping, place the cream and sugar in a mixer bowl, and using the balloon whip attachment on medium-high speed, whip until medium-stiff peaks form. Place the whipped cream in a pastry bag fitted with a large star tip, and pipe large rosettes all over the surface of the cake. Refrigerate until ready to serve, at least 30 minutes or up to 6 hours. Immediately before serving, scatter the fresh berries on top of the whipped cream.

The cake looks as if it will be hard to cut, but it isn't. Just use a thin-bladed, very sharp knife and cut it into wedges.

Note: Clear plastic acetate can be purchased at art supply stores. It is a great material for chocolate work because it leaves an extremely shiny surface.

molten chocolate cake

This is not so much a cake as a luscious liquid-centered soufflé. Save this for impressing friends (or a special loved one) or for when you don't mind being in the kitchen for the last-minute preparations. The recipe may be halved.

Makes 10 servings

For the truffle centers

6 ounces bittersweet couverture chocolate (I use Valrhona Caraque; see page 166), finely chopped

½ cup plus 1 tablespoon heavy cream

For the soufflé

1 cup (8 ounces) unsalted butter, cut into large pieces

10 ounces bittersweet couverture chocolate, finely chopped

4 large eggs

4 large egg yolks

½ cup granulated sugar

2 tablespoons all-purpose flour

1 teaspoon instant espresso powder

3⅓ cups Triple Vanilla Ice Milk (page 109)

To make the truffle centers, place the chopped chocolate in a heatproof bowl. In a small saucepan, bring the cream just to a boil. Immediately pour it over the chocolate. Let sit for a few minutes, then whisk to combine. Cool to room temperature. Then freeze until firm, at least 6 hours, or overnight.

Scoop out balls of the truffle mixture with a teaspoon and make 10 small, round, marble-shaped truffles. Flatten them into fat discs. Keep in the refrigerator until needed or these can be made a month ahead and stored, wrapped airtight, in the freezer.

To make the soufflé, preheat the oven to 425°F. Butter and flour ten ½-cup ceramic ramekins very thoroughly. There should be no bare spots.

Melt the butter and chocolate together in a double boiler or microwave. Whisk to combine. Set aside to cool slightly.

In the bowl of a heavy-duty mixer, whip the eggs, egg yolks and sugar with the balloon whip attachment on high speed until light and fluffy, about 2 minutes.

Fold the chocolate mixture into the egg mixture. Sift the flour and espresso over the mixture, and fold in gently.

Fill the ramekins halfway. Nestle a truffle in the center of each one, and top with the remaining soufflé mixture. (They can be refrigerated at this point for up to 6 hours; just bring to room temperature before proceeding.)

Bake for 8 to 9 minutes. The edges will be dry and coming away from the sides of the ramekins, but the center will be soft. Remove from the oven and let sit for 2 minutes.

Carefully loosen the edges of each cake and quickly invert the ramekins onto serving dishes. Serve immediately, with a ⅓-cup scoop of Triple Vanilla Ice Milk next to each soufflé.

strawberry almond genoise

Almond genoise, Amaretto, vanilla buttercream and fresh strawberries. Make this in June and July when the strawberries are at their best.

Makes one 9-inch layer cake, 12 to 14 servings

For the almond genoise

⅓ cup (2⅔ ounces) clarified butter (page 150), warmed

1 teaspoon vanilla extract

9 ounces (scant 2 cups) whole blanched almonds, toasted (see page 152)

1 cup cake flour

8 large eggs, separated

1⅓ cups sugar

1 cup Sugar Syrup flavored with Amaretto (page 151)

For the filling

1 recipe Italian Meringue Buttercream, vanilla variation (page 157)

1 pint strawberries, hulled and thinly sliced, reserving the nicest berry whole

Preheat the oven to 350°F. Spray two 9 × 2-inch round cake pans with nonstick cooking spray, and line the bottoms with parchment. Have ready a 9-inch cardboard round.

Combine the clarified butter and vanilla in a small bowl. The mixture should be at warm room temperature.

Place the nuts and cake flour in a food processor fitted with the metal blade. Pulse on and off about 5 times, then leave the processor running for approximately 10 seconds. Pulse again to fluff the mixture. The nuts should be very finely ground, but should not form a paste.

In the bowl of a heavy-duty mixer, whip the egg yolks with 1 cup of the sugar, using the balloon whip attachment on high speed, until a thick ribbon forms when the whip is lifted from the mixture, about 3 minutes.

In a clean, grease-free bowl, whip the egg whites with the balloon whip attachment on low speed until frothy. Increase the speed to high and continue beating until soft peaks form. Add the remaining ⅓ cup sugar gradually and whip until the peaks are stiff but not dry.

In a large mixing bowl, fold the egg yolk and egg white mixtures together. Sprinkle the dry mixture over the eggs in 3 batches, folding in with a large whisk. Cut the whisk down into the batter, bringing it up and folding over, retaining the volume of the batter at all times.

Sprinkle the clarified butter mixture, 1 tablespoon at a time, over the batter. Use the whisk to fold it in, finishing off with a few broad strokes of a rubber spatula.

Pour the batter into the prepared pans and bake for 30 to 40 minutes, until the cake is light brown and an inserted toothpick comes out clean. Cool the pans on a wire rack for 5 minutes, then unmold the cakes onto the rack and cool completely.

Assembly

Before you begin, read about decorating cakes on page 126. Horizontally split each cake layer so that you have four even layers. (If the tops are peaked, you'll have to trim them to flatten.)

Place one layer on the 9-inch cardboard round, and set it on a decorating turntable or a lazy susan. Brush with some of the Amaretto syrup, spread with some vanilla buttercream, and top with a single layer of strawberry slices. Top with another cake layer and repeat the sequence, using all of the cake layers and finishing with the last cake layer. *continued*

Spread a thin layer of buttercream all over the top and sides to make a crumb coat. Refrigerate the cake until the buttercream is firm, about 2 hours.

Apply the final coat of buttercream. Place the cake on a serving platter and pipe decorative borders around the top and bottom, using your favorite decorating tip (a #67 leaf tip gives a nice look). Pipe a nest of buttercream "leaves" in the center of the cake. Place that one perfect strawberry in the middle of the leaves, and store the cake in the refrigerator for up to 1 day.

Let the cake come to room temperature before serving, at least 30 minutes to 1 hour.

★ BAKE IT TO THE LIMIT
Strawberry Marzipan Dome

This is a showstopper. I use food coloring sparingly in my cake decorating, but here it is employed to great effect. The almond genoise is baked in a dome shape and completely covered in a violet-colored marzipan accented by green marzipan leaves. Crowned with a real full-blown red rose, this makes a stunning celebration cake. I first made it for my friend Kathy Stier's birthday.

1 recipe Almond Genoise batter

1 cup Sugar Syrup flavored with Amaretto (page 151)

1 recipe Italian Meringue Buttercream, vanilla variation (page 157)

1 pint strawberries, hulled and thinly sliced, reserving the nicest berry whole

1 recipe Marzipan (page 152), 4 ounces tinted green with moss green paste food coloring, the remaining tinted violet with violet paste food coloring

1 fully opened dark red rose

Preheat the oven to 350°F. Butter and flour a large rounded ovenproof bowl (I use my KitchenAid mixer bowl, which is 8 inches in diameter and about 8 inches deep). Have ready an 8-inch-diameter, 3-inch-high cake pan that has been sprayed with nonstick cooking spray, the bottom lined with parchment, plus one 8-inch cardboard round.

Pour half of the almond genoise batter into the cake pan, and the other half into the prepared bowl. Bake the round cake layer for 30 minutes, or until an inserted toothpick comes out clean. At the same time, bake the dome (the batter in the bowl) for 35 to 40 minutes; turn the oven down to 325°F and continue cooking the dome for 5 to 10 more minutes, or until an inserted toothpick comes out clean. Let both layers cool in their pans on wire racks for 10 minutes. Then unmold and cool completely on the racks.

Cut the dome in half horizontally.

Proceed as for the basic cake, placing the 8-inch round layer on an 8-inch cardboard round and using Amaretto syrup, vanilla buttercream and strawberries. End with the rounded section of the cake dome.

Cover with a thick crumb coating of buttercream and refrigerate.

Meanwhile, roll out the violet marzipan ¼ inch thick and at least 20 inches in diameter on a work surface that has been sprinkled with confectioner's sugar.

Place the cake on a flat serving platter and set it in front of you. Pick up the violet marzipan and drape it over the dome. Use your palms to smooth the marzipan down the sides. Don't worry too much if there are a few folds—just try to keep them small and down toward the cardboard.

Roll out the green marzipan and cut out free-form leaf shapes (see photo), making a vein pattern with the back of a knife blade. Moisten the backs of the leaves with a tiny bit of water and arrange them here and there over the cake. Press gently so they adhere to the violet marzipan. This is your chance to cover any imperfections, so place the leaves accordingly.

continued

Refrigerate the cake for up to 24 hours. Let sit at room temperature for at least 1 hour before serving. Right before serving, cut the rose's stem down to 1 inch and stick it into the top center of the cake.

Serve the cake in large wedges.

mocha almond dacquoise

This cake has it all: crisp almond-studded dacquoise coated with bittersweet chocolate, almond genoise moistened with Kahlúa, all bound together with espresso buttercream. It's crunchy, creamy and sweet with a bitter espresso edge.

Makes one 8-inch layer cake, 10 to 12 servings

1 cup Sugar Syrup flavored with Kahlúa (page 151)
6 cups Italian Meringue Buttercream, espresso
variation (page 157)

For the dacquoise
2½ ounces (about ½ cup) whole blanched almonds,
toasted (see page 152)
1 tablespoon all-purpose flour
5 large egg whites
½ teaspoon cream of tartar
1¼ cups granulated sugar
1 teaspoon almond extract

For the Almond Genoise
3 tablespoons (1½ ounces) clarified butter (page 150),
warmed
½ teaspoon vanilla extract

4½ ounces (scant 1 cup) whole blanched almonds,
toasted (see page 152)
½ cup cake flour
4 large eggs, separated
½ cup plus 3 tablespoons sugar
6 ounces bittersweet chocolate, finely chopped

Have the sugar syrup and Italian Meringue Buttercream ready before you begin. Also, have ready one 8-inch cardboard round.

To make the dacquoise, preheat the oven to 250°F. Line 2 sheet pans with parchment and trace one 8-inch round on each parchment. Flip the parchment over; you should be able to see the traced circle.

Place the nuts and flour in a food processor fitted with the metal blade. Pulse on and off about 5 times, then leave the processor running for approximately 10 seconds. Pulse again to fluff the mixture. The nuts should be very finely ground but should not form a paste.

Meanwhile, in the bowl of a heavy-duty mixer, whip the egg whites with the balloon whip attachment on low speed until frothy. Add the cream of tartar, increase the speed to high, and continue whipping until soft peaks form. Add the sugar gradually and continue to whip on high speed until stiff but not dry peaks form. Beat in the almond extract. Fold in the ground nuts.

Place the mixture in a pastry bag fitted with a ½-inch plain round tip and pipe concentric circles, beginning in the center, inside each traced circle. (Or, alternatively, spread an even layer of dacquoise using an offset icing spatula.) There should be extra dacquoise. Pipe or spread random shapes here and there around the circles; these will be crushed to apply to the sides of the cake during assembly.

continued

Bake for 1½ hours, or until very dry and crisp. It may color a little bit—that's okay.

Store the dacquoise in an airtight container until needed. It may be made 3 weeks ahead, but only if stored sealed away from any moisture.

To make the genoise, preheat the oven to 350°F. Spray an 8-inch round cake pan with nonstick cooking spray and line the bottom with parchment.

Combine the clarified butter and vanilla in a small bowl and set aside. The mixture should be at warm room temperature.

Place the nuts and cake flour in a food processor fitted with the metal blade. Pulse on and off about 5 times, then leave the processor running for approximately 10 seconds. Pulse again to fluff the mixture. The nuts should be very finely ground but should not form a paste.

In the bowl of a heavy-duty mixer, whip the egg yolks with ½ cup of the sugar, using the balloon whip attachment on high speed. Whip until a thick ribbon forms when the whip is lifted from the mixture, about 3 minutes.

In a clean, grease-free bowl, whip the egg whites with the balloon whip attachment on low speed until frothy. Increase the speed to high and continue beating until soft peaks form. Add the remaining 3 tablespoons sugar gradually, and whip until the peaks are stiff but not dry.

In a large bowl, fold the egg yolk and egg white mixtures together. Sprinkle the dry mixture over the batter in thirds, folding it in with a large whisk. Cut the whisk down into the batter, bringing it up and folding over, retaining the volume of the batter at all times.

Sprinkle the clarified butter mixture, 1 tablespoon at a time, over the batter. Use the whisk to fold it in, finishing off with a few broad strokes of a rubber spatula.

Pour the batter into the prepared pan and bake for 25 to 35 minutes. The cake should be light brown, and an inserted toothpick should come out clean. Cool on a wire rack for 5 minutes, then unmold the cake onto the rack and cool completely.

Assembly

Before you begin, read about cake decorating on page 126. Melt the chocolate in a double boiler or microwave. Spread the chocolate on the smooth side (underside) of each dacquoise round, using an offset spatula. Refrigerate briefly, chocolate side up, for the chocolate to harden, about 5 minutes.

Cut the genoise in half horizontally. (If the top was peaked, you'll have to trim that too.)

Place one genoise half, cut side up, on an 8-inch cardboard round, and set it on a cake decorator's turntable or a lazy susan. Brush with some Kahlúa syrup, then spread with a thin layer of espresso buttercream. Top with a dacquoise, chocolate side down. Then spread with a layer of buttercream and add the second dacquoise, chocolate side down. Spread more buttercream on top of the second dacquoise. Brush the cut side of the other genoise half with more syrup. Place it on top of the cake, cut side down. If any of the dacquoise is poking out of the sides, trim it with a sharp serrated knife. Spread a thin layer of buttercream over the top and sides of the cake, making a crumb coat. Refrigerate the cake until the buttercream is firm, about 3 hours.

Then apply the final coat of buttercream, making sure the top is smooth. Crumble the extra pieces of dacquoise and apply the crumbs to the sides of the cake. Place the cake on a serving platter and refrigerate for at least 3 hours to firm up. You may pipe a top or bottom border around the cake with extra buttercream, if desired. A simple shell with a #18 tip would work well.

Let the cake sit at room temperature for at least 1 hour before serving, to soften the buttercream.

Decorative Piped Borders

Using a pastry bag and decorator's tips to make buttercream borders on cakes is a learned skill. But anyone can do it, with enough practice. You can make elaborate decorations and spend a lot of time perfecting your technique, but even very simple borders can finish off a cake with a flourish.

For all decorative work, fill the pastry bag about one-third full with buttercream. Twist the top shut, holding it closed with the right hand. The left hand will guide the tip (reverse for lefties). Apply pressure with the right hand; do not squeeze from the middle. Here are some basic techniques.

Shell Border: Using an open star tip (such as #16 to #18), hold the bag at a 45° angle and squeeze out some buttercream. A ridged portion will emerge. If you draw the bag away from it and let up on the pressure at the same time, a tail will form. This makes one "shell." By experimenting with the angle and the pressure you can vary the size and shape of the "shell." You can make a different kind of shell by holding the bag at a 45° angle and beginning with a swirl, then continuing with the tail. A reverse shell can be made by alternating the angles and swirls of every other shell.

Bead Border: To make a bead border, use a plain round tip (such as a #2 for a tiny dot, or a #11 for a bead about the size of a pea). If you hold the bag at a 45° angle as you press out the buttercream, and cease pressure when a round bead has emerged, the bead may have a slightly elongated shape. If you hold the bag straight down, the bead may have a little pointed cap. You can use a wet finger to press down on the tip, rounding it out, if desired.

Rope Border: This is accomplished with plain round tips. Simply make a tight spiral with the buttercream, which will look like a rope.

Loose Reverse Spiral: This is made like the rope border above, but the loops are spaced apart and in alternating directions.

Leaf Border: Leaf tips #66 to #68 make leaves with a ridge in the middle. Hold them so that the broad side of the tip is parallel to the cake. Holding the bag at a 45° angle, press some buttercream out to make the base of the leaf. Reduce the pressure and pull the tip away to make the pointed end of the leaf. Where the buttercream breaks off, the leaf tip may be split; use 2 wet fingers to pinch it together.

Tips #350 to #352 make a different-looking leaf. Hold these tips so that the V-shaped opening is perpendicular to the cake surface, and use the same action with the bag as above.

gingerbread roll with sautéed apples

This fragrant, spongy gingerbread is wrapped around whipped cream and sautéed apples. The molasses and spices in the cake, rich cream and buttery, caramelized apples make a memorable combination.

Makes one 16-inch roll, 12 servings

For the roll

¾ cup cake flour

1 teaspoon baking powder

1 teaspoon ground cinnamon

1 teaspoon ground ginger

1 teaspoon ground allspice

3 large eggs

3 large egg yolks

⅔ cup granulated sugar

2 tablespoons unsulfured molasses

¼ cup whole milk

2 tablespoons (1 ounce) unsalted butter, melted

For the filling

7 apples (2 pounds), such as Golden Delicious or Northern Spy

2 tablespoons (1 ounce) unsalted butter, cut into large pieces

⅔ cup granulated sugar

1½ cups heavy cream

Confectioner's sugar

To make the cake, preheat the oven to 375°F. Spray a sheet pan with nonstick cooking spray, line it with parchment, and spray again.

Into a mixing bowl, sift the flour, baking powder, cinnamon, ginger and allspice; set aside.

Place the eggs, egg yolks and sugar in the bowl of a heavy-duty mixer and whip with the balloon whip attachment on high speed until the mixture is light and fluffy and has tripled in volume, about 5 minutes. A ribbon should form when you lift the whip from the mixture. Beat in the molasses.

Meanwhile, measure out the milk in a microwaveable measuring cup. Add the butter and microwave on full power until the butter has melted. (Alternatively, melt the butter and milk in a small saucepan on the stovetop.) Set aside, keeping warm.

Resift the dry mixture over the egg mixture in 3 batches, folding each one in thoroughly using a large whisk. Be gentle and retain as much volume as possible.

When all of the dry mixture is incorporated, dribble in the warm milk mixture a little at a time, folding it in. Do this step carefully. The liquid is heavier than the batter, and if it is not suspended in the batter, it will sink and create a rubbery layer in your sponge.

Spread the batter into the prepared pan, using an offset spatula to spread it evenly. It will be thin.

Bake for 10 minutes, rotating the pan front to back once during the baking time. The cake should spring back to the touch, and it will be just beginning to turn golden. An inserted toothpick should come out clean. Do not let it overbake, or it will lose its flexibility.

Place the pan on a wire rack to cool. Use immediately after cooling, or wrap the cake, still in the pan, in plastic wrap and store at room temperature for 24 hours.

To make the filling, peel the apples and slice them into ¼-inch slices. Melt the butter in a large saucepan; stir in the sugar and apples. Toss to coat.

continued

Cook over medium-low heat until the apples soften, about 5 minutes. The apples should be fork-tender and lightly caramelized. There will be some syrup thrown off by the fruit. Remove from the heat and drain, reserving the liquid. Cool completely.

Using the balloon whip attachment on medium-high speed, whip the cream with 2 tablespoons of the reserved syrup (if there is any) until medium-stiff peaks form.

Have a large flat platter ready; it must be at least 18 inches long and 6 inches wide to accommodate the roll. If you do not own such a platter, you can use a cutting board or cover a piece of heavy cardboard with foil.

To unmold the cake, use a knife tip to loosen the edges. Lay a clean piece of parchment on your work surface and invert the cake onto it. Remove the pan and very gently peel off the baked-on parchment. Arrange the parchment so the long sides of the cake are horizontal in front of you. Spread the whipped cream evenly over the cake, leaving an uncovered ¼-inch border along the upper long edge. Then scatter the apples over the cream. Using the parchment to help, roll up the cake as tightly as possible, starting with the near long side. Transfer the cake to the platter. You can facilitate this process by slipping a long offset spatula beneath the roll to help lift it up. Cover the platter with plastic wrap and refrigerate for at least 30 minutes, or up to 6 hours, before serving.

When ready to serve, sift some confectioner's sugar over the top of the cake. This is easiest if it is in a dredger. If you have placed the cake on foil-covered cardboard, mask the foil with greenery such as pine boughs or lemon leaves. Slice the cake with a serrated knife and serve immediately.

✶ BAKE IT TO THE LIMIT

If you have a real sweet tooth, try serving this cake with Caramel Sauce.

1 recipe Caramel Sauce (page 146)

Have the sauce warmed and in a squeeze bottle. Place slices of cake on serving dishes and squirt Caramel Sauce over and around each slice right before serving.

sauces

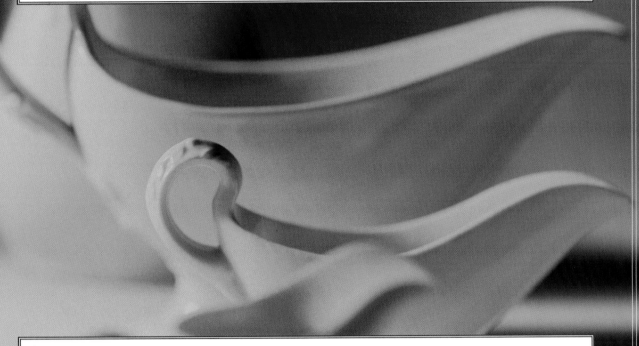

Crème Anglaise ✶ *Caramel Sauce* ✶ *Raspberry Coulis* ✶ *Bittersweet Chocolate Sauce* ✶ *Mint Sauce* ✶ *Blood Orange Sauce*

Sauces can add the final touch, raising a basic recipe to a higher level of elegance. They also add a moist component to a dessert. Be creative, and purchase a few plastic squeeze bottles with needle-nose spouts (easily found in the hair-coloring section of the drugstore or at a cake-decorating supply store). They dispense any of the sauces with ease. You can store the sauces in them, and when ready, use the bottles to help you pool, splatter, dot and squiggle to your heart's content.

crème anglaise

This classic custard sauce is used frequently as an accompaniment to cakes, tarts and other desserts. The basic recipe is flavored with vanilla, and you may add your choice of liqueur for variation.

Makes 3 cups

2 cups whole milk
½ vanilla bean, split
½ cup granulated sugar
6 large egg yolks

Combine the milk and vanilla bean in a nonreactive saucepan, and bring to a boil over medium heat. Remove from the heat and let sit for 10 minutes to allow the bean to steep. Cover the pan to keep warm.

Meanwhile, whisk the sugar and egg yolks in a heatproof mixing bowl until creamy. Slowly pour some of the hot milk over the yolk mixture, stirring constantly; this will temper the eggs. Then stir in the remaining milk and return the mixture to the saucepan, whisking all together well.

Cook the mixture over medium-low heat, stirring frequently. You need to watch out for two things: the mixture can burn on the bottom, and the sauce can boil over. To prevent this, keep whisking and watch carefully. If tiny bubbles appear around the edges of the sauce, remove the pan from the heat immediately. Use an instant-read thermometer and cook the sauce to 175°F—no higher. Do not let it boil.

Strain the custard through a fine-mesh sieve. The bean will be left in the strainer. If desired, scrape the seeds right into the sauce using a blunt knife tip or the tip of a spoon. The seeds will be in sticky little clumps; whisk well to disperse them. Cool to warm room temperature, stirring occasionally to release the heat.

Store the sauce in an airtight container in the refrigerator. May be made up to 4 days ahead.

VARIATION

To add a liqueur flavor, stir in 2 tablespoons of the liqueur of your choice at the very end—Kahlúa, rum, cognac, hazelnut liqueur and Grand Marnier are wonderful flavors to add. Experiment with your favorite, taking into consideration the dessert it will be accompanying.

caramel sauce

This is a delicious sauce that keeps particularly well. It may be made 1 month ahead and stored, refrigerated, in an airtight container. To make any caramel preparation, whether a candy or a sauce, the color of the caramel is the key to the resulting flavor. If the caramel is light, the taste will be too. Conversely, if the caramel is allowed to darken too much, the final product will taste burnt. You don't necessarily need a thermometer—just go by color. The caramel should be a rich, nutty, amber brown. This sauce is featured in the photograph of Gingerbread Roll with Sautéed Apples on page 142.

Makes 2¾ cups

2 cups heavy cream
2 cups granulated sugar
1 cup water
2 teaspoons vanilla extract

Bring the cream to a boil in a saucepan over medium heat and set aside, keeping warm.

Place the sugar and water in a large (at least 6-quart) heavy-bottomed pot. Stir to moisten the sugar, and then cook over medium-low heat, without stirring, until the syrup begins to color. Wash down the sides of the pot once or twice with a damp pastry brush if necessary. When the syrup is a medium amber color, remove the pot from the heat and carefully pour in the warm cream. The mixture may bubble up furiously. Whisk until smooth. If the cream is too cool, it will cause the caramel to seize. Just place the pot back over low heat and stir until the sauce liquefies. When done, stir in the vanilla off the heat. If the sauce remains too thick, simply thin it with a little warm cream.

Store, refrigerated, in an airtight container for up to 1 month. Reheat in a double boiler or microwave before using.

raspberry coulis

This puree of raspberries complements desserts with its fresh taste as well as its gorgeous color. It may be made a month ahead and frozen, or 3 days ahead and refrigerated. Fresh raspberries can be very expensive, but the IQF (individually quick frozen) berries work perfectly.

Makes 2 cups

Two 12-ounce bags unsweetened frozen raspberries (I use Red Valley Brand, available nationwide)
⅓ cup superfine sugar
1 teaspoon freshly squeezed lemon juice

Defrost the berries completely overnight in the refrigerator or at room temperature for a few hours. (Do not defrost in the microwave because the heat will cook the fruit and you will lose some of the fresh color and flavor.) Pour off and reserve any liquid.

Puree the berries in a blender or food processor fitted with the metal blade. Pour the puree into a strainer set over a large bowl. Press the puree through the strainer. Discard the seeds. Stir half the sugar and all of the lemon juice into the strained puree. Taste, and adjust the sweetness if desired. If the puree is too thick, add some of the reserved juice. You do want it to have some body, so be careful not to overthin it.

Store in an airtight container in the refrigerator or freezer.

bittersweet chocolate sauce

This dark, shiny, silky chocolate sauce is perfect for such desserts as Chocolate Espresso Cream Puffs (page 99). The recipe can be made a month ahead and frozen, or made a week ahead and stored in the refrigerator in an airtight container.

Makes 2½ cups

6 ounces unsweetened chocolate, finely chopped
1½ cups heavy cream
¾ cup granulated sugar
2 tablespoons (1 ounce) unsalted butter, cut into large pieces
Pinch salt
1 teaspoon vanilla extract

Place the chocolate, cream, sugar, butter and salt in a heavy-bottomed pot. Stir frequently over medium heat, taking care not to scorch the chocolate. Heat until the chocolate is melted and the sugar has dissolved; you should have a shiny, smooth sauce. Remove from the heat and stir in the vanilla.

Store in an airtight container in the refrigerator. Warm briefly in a double boiler or microwave before using.

mint sauce

This fresh mint sauce explodes on the tongue, and its clear shiny green color makes a vibrant addition to a dish. You must have a high-quality blender, such as Waring brand, to make this sauce. Inferior blenders will not chop the mint fine enough, and the sauce will have a grainy texture.

Makes scant 1 cup

¾ cup granulated sugar
½ cup water
2 cups lightly packed mint leaves

Combine the sugar and water in a small saucepan. Stir to wet the sugar, then bring to a boil over medium heat. Make sure that the sugar has dissolved. Remove from the heat and cool for 5 minutes.

Wash and dry the mint. Combine the sugar syrup and mint in a blender and puree. Cool to room temperature, pour into a squeeze bottle, and refrigerate until needed. Use within 1 day.

blood orange sauce

This sweet/tart sunset-colored sauce is served with Honey Ice Cream (page 106), but you will think of other uses for it too. Blood oranges are available in February; make some sauce then to freeze for future use.

Makes ¾ cup

6 blood oranges
¼ cup granulated sugar

Juice the oranges; you need 1½ cups of juice. Strain the juice and pour it into a saucepan. Add the sugar and bring to a boil over medium heat, stirring to dissolve the sugar. Turn down the heat and simmer for 5 minutes, or until the sauce has reduced and is syrupy. You should end up with about ¾ cup of sauce.

Cool to room temperature. Store in an airtight container and refrigerate for up to 1 week or freeze for up to 6 months.

basic recipes

This chapter contains building-block formulas for many of the recipes found throughout

the book. Familiarize yourself with these and you'll have a good head start on the rest.

clarified butter

Start with 25% more unsalted butter than you need to have of clarified butter, because the process reduces the volume.

Melt the butter slowly in a saucepan without stirring. A foam may appear on the surface as it melts; simply remove it by skimming it off with a spoon. Be careful not to stir up the mixture. When the butter looks clear, watch carefully. The milk solids, which are white, will fall to the bottom of the pan. Remove the pan from the heat and gently pour off the clarified butter, leaving all of the milk solids behind. You may find it easier to skim the clarified butter off the top using a ladle. Discard the solids.

Store the clarified butter, refrigerated, in a covered container. It will keep for a month. It will turn solid in the refrigerator, so heat it gently to restore fluidity.

crème fraîche

Makes approximately 2¼ cups

2 cups heavy cream
¼ cup buttermilk

Combine the cream and buttermilk in a saucepan and heat over medium heat to 110°F. Pour into a clean glass container, cover loosely with aluminum foil, and store in a warm place for at least 6 to 8 hours, or until thickened. If it sits too long, it will turn overly sour. I put mine in my gas oven with the pilot light on.

Once it has thickened, cover the crème fraîche airtight and refrigerate it for at least 3 hours. It will thicken further. Crème fraîche keeps for up to 3 weeks.

pastry cream

Pastry cream is a basic component of fruit tarts and cream puffs. The amount of flour varies because sometimes you want a thicker pastry cream and sometimes you want a more delicate version. For large tarts that will be cut into individual servings, the thicker pastry cream will give you cleaner slices that hold up. For individual tarts or cream puffs, a lighter, thinner pastry cream is preferable.

Makes 3 cups

2 cups whole milk
7 large egg yolks
½ cup granulated sugar
⅓ to ½ cup all-purpose flour
Pinch salt
2 tablespoons (1 ounce) unsalted butter, at room
  temperature

Bring the milk to a boil in a medium-size nonreactive saucepan over medium heat. Set aside and keep warm.

Meanwhile, whisk together the egg yolks, sugar, flour and salt in a medium-size nonreactive heatproof bowl.

Dribble the warm milk over the egg mixture, starting with just a few tablespoons to temper the eggs, whisking together well. Then whisk in the remaining milk. Return the mixture to the saucepan and bring to a simmer over medium-low heat. Stirring continuously, simmer for 1 to 2 minutes to remove the raw flour taste. Immediately strain through a fine-mesh sieve into a storage container, and stir in the butter. Stir occasionally until it comes to a cool room temperature, then press a piece of plastic wrap directly onto the surface to prevent a skin from forming. Refrigerate until chilled, at least 4 hours, before using. May be stored for 4 days.

VARIATIONS

Vanilla Pastry Cream

Add 1 split vanilla bean to the milk while heating. Let the milk and vanilla bean sit off the heat to steep for 30 minutes. Remove the bean, reheat the milk, and proceed with the basic recipe.

Liqueur-Flavored Pastry Cream

Whisk in 1 tablespoon to ¼ cup liqueur of choice along with the butter.

sugar syrup

Sugar syrup traditionally is made with equal amounts of sugar and water. This version is a medium-bodied sugar syrup, used to moisten cake layers.

The recipe may be scaled up or down directly, if desired.

Makes 1¼ cups

1 cup water
½ cup granulated sugar

Combine the water and sugar in a small saucepan. Stir to wet the sugar thoroughly. Place over medium heat and bring to a simmer. Cook for 1 minute. Remove from the heat, cool to room temperature, and store in an airtight container in the refrigerator for up to 1 month.

VARIATION

Liqueur-Flavored Syrup

The amount of liqueur added will depend on the strength of the alcohol and the flavor desired. A good starting point is to add ¼ cup liqueur to the basic mixture (1¼ cups syrup). Add the liqueur after the syrup has cooled. Stir to combine. Store as suggested above.

nuts: peeled and toasted

Nuts contain perishable oils that can go rancid, so taste and smell them before you buy them. They should have a distinct flavor, unique to the particular nut, but with no musty aftertaste. Buy in the quantity that you need, from a vendor with a high turnover. If you have any extra left over, store them in an airtight container in the freezer.

The flavor of nuts is greatly improved by toasting, and most of the recipes require this step. If they are toasted before freezing, you will want to refresh them: reheat lightly in a 325°F oven for 3 to 7 minutes, or until the nuts are warmed through and any moisture retained from the freezer has been removed.

Once they are toasted and/or peeled, nuts may be stored in an airtight container in the freezer for up to a month.

To Peel Nuts:

Hazelnuts: Shelled hazelnuts have a papery skin that must be peeled off. You have to toast them first, in order to peel them. Spread the hazelnuts in a single layer on a sheet pan and toast in a 325°F oven for 5 to 12 minutes. Shake the pan once or twice during toasting to encourage even browning. They are done when you start to smell them and they are a golden brown color. Remove from the oven and cool slightly. Then take clean kitchen towels and rub the nuts vigorously between them. With a little work, most of the skins will come off. My hazelnuts usually retain a tiny bit of skin on them—that's fine. Hazelnuts can be purchased peeled, at an added expense.

Almonds: Shelled almonds are sold whole, sliced and slivered, either blanched (peeled) or natural (skin on). You cannot peel the sliced or slivered shapes, so buy them the way you need them. If you care to spend the extra money on blanched almonds, go ahead—it will save you time. If you need to peel whole ones yourself, follow these instructions: Drop them in boiling water and blanch for 1 minute, then drain. You should be able to slip the skins right off by pinching the nuts with your fingers.

Walnuts, pecans and macadamias: These nuts must be shelled, of course, but they do not need to be peeled.

To Toast Nuts:

Your hazelnuts will probably be toasted enough during the peeling process. Place walnuts, pecans, almonds or macadamias in a single layer on a sheet pan. Toast them in a 325°F oven until golden brown and fragrant, 5 to 12 minutes. Shake the pan once or twice during toasting to encourage even browning. The timing will vary depending on the quantity of nuts as well as the oil content in the nuts. High-oil-content nuts, such as macadamias, will toast more quickly. Always cool nuts before chopping. The oils, which will have been brought to the surface by the heat, must be reabsorbed or the nuts could turn pasty.

marzipan

Almond paste can be purchased from cake decorating stores, specialty food stores, even your supermarket. Some marzipan has raw egg white added. For health reasons, I offer a version moistened with corn syrup.

Makes approximately 2½ pounds

21 ounces almond paste
3¾ cups (1 pound) confectioner's sugar, sifted, plus extra for kneading
6 tablespoons light corn syrup

Place the almond paste in the bowl of a heavy-duty mixer. Using the flat paddle attachment, turn the machine on and off to break up the paste. Turn the machine off, add the confectioner's sugar, and pulse on and off briefly to incorporate. Once the paste and sugar have begun to blend, run the machine on medium speed. The mixture will look like finely ground nuts or large-grained sand; it will not come together in the bowl.

Add the corn syrup to the mixture and continue to beat until it begins to clump together. Do not process too long, or the oils from the almonds will begin to ooze through to the surface and create a greasy layer.

Remove from the machine and knead briefly by hand, dusting your hands and the work surface with a veil of confectioner's sugar. Form the marzipan into a ball and cover it well with plastic wrap. Let sit overnight at room temperature. The resting time allows the oils to distribute evenly and will make the marzipan easier to work with.

Keep the marzipan refrigerated, well wrapped in plastic in an airtight container. It can be stored for months. It should be kneaded again before using to ensure smoothness.

chocolate plastic

Chocolate plastic, or modeling chocolate, is simply a combination of melted chocolate and light corn syrup. But the sum is greater than its parts because these two ingredients make a wonderful, malleable chocolate "clay" that can be rolled out and molded into a variety of shapes. You may make the plastic out of bittersweet, semisweet, milk or white chocolate.

Chocolate plastic may be made 1 week ahead if it is wrapped tightly with several layers of plastic and then placed in an airtight container and stored at room temperature. Just make sure it does not dry out. It will harden as it sits, regardless, and will require kneading before using.

Makes 2¼ pounds

28 ounces bittersweet, semisweet, milk or white
   chocolate, finely chopped
1 cup light corn syrup

Melt the chocolate in a double boiler or microwave. Stir the corn syrup into the melted chocolate until the mixture comes together. At first the chocolate might look grainy and as though it were about to seize. Keep stirring until blended, but don't worry if it doesn't look completely smooth. Pour out onto a large piece of plastic wrap and wrap up well. It will look like a large thick puddle.

Let the mixture sit at cool room temperature for at least 1 hour, or until it has completely firmed up. Then divide it into manageable pieces. Knead each piece before using. The warmth of your hands will soften it up and make it easy to manipulate. It is now ready to roll out and be made into flowers, leaves, or whatever you like. For those instructions, see page 116.

Chocolate plastic flowers can be made weeks ahead if stored in an airtight container. Leaves, which are often shaped right before placing on a dessert for a more realistic look, have a tendency to crack. If they are very fresh, this problem is minimized. If they have been made way ahead, just make sure to bring them to warm room temperature before shaping.

Store flowers in an airtight container. Flat leaves may be wrapped in plastic wrap and placed in an airtight container.

bittersweet chocolate ganache

A basic ganache is made up of equal quantities of chocolate and cream. This one has a slightly larger proportion of chocolate, which I feel gives a better texture. The recipe can be scaled up or down directly.

Makes 2½ cups

12 ounces bittersweet or semisweet chocolate,
* finely chopped*
1¼ cups (10 ounces) heavy cream

Place the chocolate in a heatproof bowl. Heat the cream in a heavy-bottomed pot over medium heat until it comes to a simmer. Immediately pour the hot cream over the chocolate. Let sit for a few minutes, then whisk to melt the chocolate.

For pourable ganache, you may use it immediately. A temperature of 90°F is perfect for glazing.

For piping ganache, the mixture must be cooled. Let it sit at room temperature until thick enough to pipe, or stir over a bowl of ice water until thickened.

All ganache may be stored in an airtight container in the refrigerator for up to 4 days, or frozen for up to 1 month.

To melt the ganache after chilling, warm it in a microwave at low power, checking and stirring frequently, or melt it in a double boiler.

Note: I like my ganache to be bittersweet. You can improve many semisweet chocolates by substituting a small amount of unsweetened chocolate; try combining 11 ounces semisweet with 1 ounce unsweetened. Or you may choose to start with a bittersweet chocolate.

whipped chocolate ganache

A whipped ganache is a mixture of chocolate and heavy cream, with a larger proportion of cream than in the Bittersweet Chocolate Ganache. Notice that this recipe has much more cream than chocolate. You can scale it up or down accordingly.

This is like a very rich chocolate whipped cream and is simple to make; the trick is not to overwhip the ganache. When overwhipped, it will become grainy. If worst comes to worst, it can be gently remelted, chilled and rebeaten. Whip it immediately before using.

Makes 8 cups

1 pound semisweet or bittersweet chocolate,
* finely chopped*
4 cups (32 ounces) heavy cream

Place the chocolate in a bowl that is large enough to hold the cream as well. (The bowl of a 5-quart KitchenAid mixer is perfect.) Bring the cream to a boil in a medium-size saucepan and immediately pour it over the chocolate. Stir until the chocolate has melted and the mixture is smooth. If many unmelted chocolate pieces remain, let sit for 10 to 15 minutes, stirring occasionally; the residual heat will melt them.

Cover the mixture with plastic wrap, placing the wrap directly on the surface of the ganache to prevent a skin from forming. Refrigerate for at least 6 hours, preferably overnight.

Mix the chilled ganache (it will look quite thick) in a heavy-duty mixer, using the balloon whip attachment on medium-high speed, until it just starts to thicken. At this point watch the ganache constantly and whip just until soft peaks form. If you prefer, stop the mixer as soon as the mixture thickens and finish it off by hand with a large whisk. Do not overbeat.

The ganache is now ready to use. It firms up quickly, so have your cakes and other components prepared and ready to receive the ganache.

italian meringue buttercream

Italian Meringue Buttercream has a sublime, silky texture and is not cloyingly sweet. It is a very traditional preparation: An Italian meringue, by classic definition, is made up of whipped egg whites that are sweetened and stabilized with a cooked sugar syrup. For a buttercream, unsalted butter is added as well.

This buttercream can be made ahead and refrigerated for almost a week, even frozen for up to a month. The instructions are long, but if you read through them once, the process will flow quickly when you actually make the buttercream.

Most of the recipes in this book can be prepared with an ordinary hand mixer. This recipe is meant to take advantage of the size of a standing 5-quart mixer, and the directions are written for using such a machine.

Makes 7 cups

1¼ cups plus ⅓ cup granulated sugar

½ cup water

8 large egg whites, at room temperature

1 teaspoon cream of tartar

3 cups (1½ pounds) unsalted butter, at room
temperature, cut into small pieces

Have a candy thermometer handy. If you are not using a thermometer, see below for visual cues to assess the syrup's doneness.

Place 1¼ cups of the sugar and the water in a small saucepan. Stir quickly to wet all of the sugar, but do not stir again during boiling or you will encourage sugar crystals to form. Bring to a boil over medium heat. As the mixture begins to heat up, use a pastry brush dipped in cold water to brush any sugar crystals down from the sides of the pot. Turn the heat down to a simmer.

Meanwhile, place the egg whites in a clean, grease-free mixer bowl, and using the balloon whip attachment on low speed, whip until frothy. Add the cream of tartar and continue to whip on high speed. When soft peaks form, add the remaining ⅓ cup sugar gradually. Continue whipping until stiff peaks appear. This is the meringue part of the buttercream. Turn the mixer down to a slow speed to keep the meringue moving until the sugar syrup is ready.

Increase the heat under the sugar/water mixture and bring to a rapid boil. You will need to cook it for approximately 5 minutes to get it to the desired temperature, between 248° and 250°F. The trick here is to have the syrup ready at the same time as the meringue. If the meringue is done before the syrup, turn the speed down to low so that the whites are continuously moving but not highly agitated, which might overwhip them. If the syrup is done first, add a bit of hot water to lower the temperature and continue to cook until the meringue catches up.

As the syrup cooks at a rapid boil, there are many visual clues to look for. It starts out thin, with many small bubbles over the entire surface. As it cooks, the water evaporates and the mixture becomes thicker. The bubbles get larger and don't bubble up so rapidly.

continued

The bubbles will be thick and sticky and will pop open more slowly. At this point the syrup definitely looks thickened, but it has not yet begun to color, which would result in caramel. It is right before this caramelization stage that the syrup will be ready. This is called the firm ball stage. If you drop a bit of the syrup into a glass of cold water, it will harden into a ball. When you squeeze the ball between your fingertips, it will appear firm.

When the syrup is ready, turn off the mixer very briefly and quickly pour about ½ cup of the syrup into the meringue. Immediately turn the machine on to high, and continue to pour in the syrup in a steady stream, without getting any on the rotating whisk. (If it does, it will harden and cling and not make it into the meringue mixture.) Turn off the machine to add the syrup if you find it easier. You just don't want to let the meringue sit still for longer than a few seconds.

The meringue must be whipped constantly until it cools, which may take as long as 15 minutes, depending on the ambient temperature. Occasionally touch the outside bottom of the bowl—you will be able to feel it cooling down. When the bowl is no longer warm, stop the machine and touch the surface of the meringue with your finger to double-check that it is indeed cooled. (If you add the butter while the meringue is warm, the butter will melt and will ruin the texture. It will also decrease the volume of the final product.)

Turn the machine back on at medium speed and begin to add the butter, bit by bit. I usually add it in 2-tablespoon chunks (this can be done by eye—no measuring). The butter will immediately become incorporated and the mixture will become creamy. Continue to whip the buttercream while you add the remaining butter. Keep mixing until the mixture is homogenous and smooth. If at any time the mixture looks lumpy or separated, just continue to beat; it will come together.

Temperature is everything with this buttercream. If the ingredients are warm or hot when combined, it will become soupy and greasy. If they are cold, the mixture will be lumpy and too firm. Following the directions carefully should eliminate these problems. If you do end up with a loose buttercream, simply chill it slightly by placing the bottom of the bowl in a larger bowl filled with ice. Chill for a few minutes before proceeding. If the mixture is too lumpy because cold butter has created pockets of solid fat, just keep whipping. It will smooth out. Or, if you prefer, aim a hot hair dryer at the outside of the bowl; it will warm up the buttercream quickly.

Your buttercream is now ready to use, and any flavorings can be added at this point. Any extra can be frozen for later use. Or refrigerate it for 4 days, well sealed in an airtight container.

To reconstitute chilled buttercream: If the buttercream has been refrigerated and has become completely firm, follow these instructions to reconstitute it. If it is frozen, defrost it in the refrigerator overnight and then follow the same instructions.

One method is to take the container it is stored in and, if it is microwaveable, place the container in the microwave and heat the buttercream on very low power in 15-second spurts, assessing the softness each time. You want it to be brought to room temperature uniformly, without melting the butter. This technique will depend on your familiarity with your microwave and your ability to control its power and defrosting times.

The technique I usually employ is to place a quantity of cold buttercream in the stainless-steel bowl of my mixer and set it over extremely low heat on top of the stove. Holding the bowl with one hand, constantly stir the chunks of buttercream, folding the pieces over each other so that no one piece stays on the bottom, receiving too much heat. You want to warm the buttercream but not melt the butter. Be careful.

Another technique is to place a quantity of buttercream in your mixer bowl and, as mentioned above, heat it with a warm hair dryer. Use the hair dryer to blow warmth directly on top of the buttercream as well as to the underside and sides of the bowl.

After you have warmed up your buttercream, whip it with the balloon whip attachment until it is smooth and creamy. Heat it again if it is still lumpy; chill if too soupy. It is better to be conservative and heat it slowly than to melt the butter and end up with sweet soup.

VARIATIONS

Vanilla

And 1 tablespoon vanilla extract to 7 cups buttercream. Whip well to incorporate.

Chocolate Caramel Buttercream

Follow the basic recipe, but allow the sugar/water mixture to caramelize, turning a nice dark golden brown. Then proceed. After you have added the butter, add 2 ounces of cooled melted unsweetened chocolate, and beat in until smooth.

Liqueur-Accented Buttercream

Add approximately ⅓ cup of the liqueur of your choice to 7 cups buttercream. Adjust the quantity as needed. Some of the more potent liqueurs will require less; some more. The texture of the buttercream will guide you; you do not want it to get too liquidy.

Chocolate Buttercream

Add 12 ounces of white, milk, semisweet or bittersweet chocolate that has been melted and cooled to room temperature. If the chocolate is too warm, it will melt the butter. Whip until the chocolate is thoroughly incorporated.

Praline Buttercream

Add ½ to ¾ cup unsweetened hazelnut paste to 7 cups buttercream. Whip until smooth.

Espresso Buttercream

Dissolve ¼ cup instant espresso powder or instant coffee powder in 2 tablespoons hot water or in 2 tablespoons Kahlúa liqueur. Add to 7 cups buttercream and whip until smooth.

basic pie crust

I don't think I ever had a cookie or cake baked by my nana, but her pies were legendary. She used orange juice in the crust, which she felt gave it the best flavor and texture. Try it as a variation and see if you agree.

Make sure your butter, shortening and water or orange juice come straight from the refrigerator. For a complete treatise on pies and crusts, check out Rose Levy Beranbaum's *Pie and Pastry Bible* and Carole Walter's *Great Pies and Tarts*.

Makes 1 double crust for a 9½-inch deep-dish pie

2½ cups all-purpose flour

1 teaspoon salt

10 tablespoons (5 ounces) unsalted butter, chilled and cut into large pieces

3 ounces (6 tablespoons) shortening, chilled

3 to 4 tablespoons ice water or chilled orange juice

Measure the flour and salt into a mixing bowl and place in the freezer for 15 minutes. (This chilling is optional, but it will go a long way toward helping your crust be perfectly flaky.)

Cut the butter and shortening into tablespoon-size pieces and scatter over the dry ingredients. Cut in, using a pastry blender or 2 butter knives, until the fats are the size of large flat raisins.

Sprinkle the water or orange juice over the mixture. Toss it with 2 forks or your fingertips until the dough begins to come together. Do not overwork the dough, or the heat of your hands will melt the fat, yielding a mealy crust.

Place the dough on a lightly floured work surface and knead it briefly, just enough to bring it together into a ball. Divide it into 2 pieces, form them into balls, and flatten. Wrap both dough discs in plastic wrap and refrigerate for at least 2 hours, or overnight, to relax the gluten in the flour. The dough may also be frozen for a week and defrosted in the refrigerator overnight.

To roll out, lightly flour your work surface and rolling pin. Place one of the discs of dough on the work surface and begin to apply pressure, starting at the center of the dough and rolling toward the top of the circle. Then pick up your pin, place it in the center again, and roll it toward the bottom. Do the same for the sides and all the in-between angles. Check to see that the dough is not sticking to the work surface by spinning it in quarter turns and reflouring the surface. Keep rolling until the desired size and thickness are reached. A ¼-inch thickness is standard, if not specified otherwise. Repeat with the other disc of dough.

Follow individual recipes for baking specifics.

chocolate pie crust

This makes a lightly sweetened chocolate pie crust that is used in the Chocolate Banana Pecan Pie (page 10), but I put the recipe here in the Basics section in the hope that you'll find many uses for it.

Makes 1 single pie crust for a 9½-inch deep-dish pie

1¼ cups all-purpose flour

¼ cup Dutch-process cocoa

¼ cup granulated sugar

¼ teaspoon salt

½ cup (4 ounces) unsalted butter, chilled and cut into large pieces

1 large egg yolk

3 tablespoons ice water

Place the flour, cocoa, sugar and salt in the bowl of a heavy-duty mixer. Using the flat paddle attachment at low speed, pulse the mixer on and off a few times to blend the ingredients. Scatter the cold butter over the dry mixture. Mix the ingredients on low speed until the butter is the size of raisins. Add the egg yolk and ice water, and pulse the mixer on and off to blend until the egg and water disappear into the dry mixture. You may also mix this by hand, as described for Basic Pie Crust (page 158), but I find that it is easier to make this dough by machine. The cocoa will be more evenly distributed.

Knead briefly on a lightly floured work surface until the dough comes together and gathers into a ball. Flatten the ball, wrap it in plastic wrap, and chill for at least 2 hours before rolling, to relax the gluten in the flour. The crust may also be frozen for up to a week and defrosted in the refrigerator overnight.

See page 10 for the Chocolate Banana Pecan Pie recipe, which uses this crust as a base. Or use the Chocolate Pie Crust in your favorite recipe.

sweet tart dough

Tart dough is a tad sweeter and a bit sturdier than Basic Pie Crust. The fat is cut into smaller pieces, which makes the crust less flaky while giving it structure, and still keeps it just as tender.

Makes two 11-inch tart crusts

3 cups all-purpose flour
¼ cup granulated sugar
¼ teaspoon salt
1 cup (8 ounces) unsalted butter, chilled and
* cut into large pieces*

2 large egg yolks
¼ cup heavy cream, chilled

Measure the flour, sugar and salt into a mixing bowl.

Scatter the butter in tablespoon-size pieces over the dry ingredients. Cut the butter in, using a pastry blender or 2 butter knives, until the mixture resembles a coarse cornmeal or finely ground nuts. The fat is cut into much smaller pieces than with pie dough, and the tart dough is more uniform at this stage.

In another bowl, whisk together the egg yolks and cream. Drizzle this over the dry ingredients and toss it in with 2 forks or your fingertips until the dough begins to come together.

Scrape the dough onto a lightly floured work surface and knead it briefly, just enough to bring it together into a ball. Divide it into 2 pieces, form them into balls, and flatten. Wrap both discs in plastic wrap and refrigerate for at least 2 hours, or overnight, to relax the gluten in the flour. The crust may also be frozen for a week and defrosted in the refrigerator overnight.

Refer to the various tart recipes in the Pies and Tarts chapter for specific applications of this tasty sweet crust.

tempered chocolate

You will need a chocolate thermometer, a marble slab and a long offset spatula in addition to the chocolate.

1 pound couverture chocolate (see page 166),
finely chopped

Place the chocolate in the top of a double boiler and set it over hot, not simmering, water. Do not let the hot water touch the bottom of the top pan. Stir constantly until the chocolate is melted. Insert the thermometer in the middle of the pan; do not let the chocolate exceed 120°F.

Remove the top pan from the double boiler and wipe the bottom dry. (You do not want to chance any water droplets getting into the chocolate, which will make it seize.) Begin to cool the chocolate by stirring it gently. When the temperature has cooled to 100°F, pour about two thirds of it out onto the marble slab. Begin to work it back and forth with the offset spatula by spreading it thin and then gathering it up and spreading it out again. Work the chocolate until it begins to thicken. The thermometer should register about 75°F to 80°F.

Scrape the chocolate back into the top of the double boiler, off the heat, and stir to blend it with the remaining melted chocolate. Test with the thermometer: The temperature should be 88° to 91°F for bittersweet and semisweet chocolates, 85° to 88°F for milk chocolate, 84° to 87°F for white chocolate. If the temperature is lower, replace the pan over the hot water. Stir continuously until the proper temperature is reached. If the chocolate goes above its range, it will lose its temper.

The chocolate is now ready to use. To maintain the correct temperature while you are working with it, place the pot on a warming tray or set it back over a pot of warm water. Keep track of the chocolate's temperature, and keep it within the proper range while working with it. The chocolate will have a tendency to firm up and harden around the edges of the pan, where it cools first. Stir constantly to prevent this.

After you have made your curls, shapes, etc., they should be stored in an airtight container in the refrigerator or freezer.

chocolate curls

To make simple chocolate curls, warm a block of chocolate in your hands for a minute or two, then shave off curls with a sharp vegetable peeler.

For more formal-looking chocolate curls, spread tempered chocolate on a clean sheet pan. Refrigerate until firm. Then, using a triangular scraper, make the curls as follows: starting at an edge of the chocolate and holding the scraper at a 45° angle, push the scraper away from you, forming curls. If the chocolate splinters, it is too cold. If the curls fail to form, it is too warm. Temperature is everything when making curls. Play with the temperature and the angle of the scraper, and you can make the curls large or small, tight or unfurled.

Store all curls in an airtight container in the refrigerator for up to 1 month, or in the freezer for up to 2 months.

equipment,
ingredients and
techniques

equipment

Cardboard Rounds

I cannot stress enough the importance of using precut cardboard rounds. They come in diameters from 4 inches to 18 inches, and can be purchased from cake decorating stores or mail-ordered from Wilton Industries or N.Y. Cake and Baking Distributors for a few cents apiece (see pages 177 and 176). The cardboards are used as guides for your icing spatula to help make smooth, clean sides for your cakes. They also make it easier to move cakes onto serving platters.

Chocolate Chipper

This is a heavy-gauge fork that makes quick work of chopping chocolate. It will save your knives and is indispensable if you often bake with chocolate. They can be ordered from Sweet Celebrations (see page 176).

Decorating Turntable

You can frost a cake without a turntable, but it will not come close to looking like one frosted with the aid of one. A free-wheeling turntable will aid in creating ultra-smooth coatings of buttercream or glaze. You can purchase an inexpensive plastic lazy susan, or invest in a heavy-duty turntable with a cast-iron bottom and a stainless-steel top if you are going to do a lot of cake decorating.

Dredger

These are small metal containers, usually about 8 ounces in size, that come with perforated tops—sometimes mesh, sometimes pierced metal. They also come with various size meshes or holes to allow more or less of the contents to flow. Some come with a plastic cover, which keeps the contents dry and free-flowing.

Filled with flour, confectioner's sugar, cornstarch, cocoa or cinnamon, they can be used in various ways when a dusting of that ingredient is desired. I use them most often to shake sweet ingredients over desserts and plates for decoration, or with flour or confectioner's sugar to dust my work surface.

Grater/Zester

There is a tool called the Microplane that will make quick work out of any zesting job. It does a better job than any other zester on the market, removing citrus zest effortlessly and leaving behind all the bitter white pith. This is a must-have kitchen tool. It's available from Cooking by the Book (see page 174).

Heavy-Duty Mixer vs. Handheld Mixer

Where a mixer is required, I use a free-standing 5-quart KitchenAid and suggest that you use the same or a similar machine. The KitchenAid not only has a large capacity, it also has a powerful motor, is well built, and will last a lifetime.

The KitchenAid comes with a stainless-steel bowl, a balloon whip, a flat paddle and a dough hook. The balloon whip incorporates air into whipped cream, buttercream and eggs; the flat paddle creams butter, cream cheese and most cake batters. The dough hook is used with yeast doughs.

It is handy to have an extra stainless-steel bowl (which can be purchased separately), especially when a recipe calls for creaming butter and egg yolks and then requires a clean, grease-free bowl for whipping egg whites.

If you are using a handheld mixer, the mixing times will be longer and you should be prepared to hold the mixer over the bowl for extended periods of time in certain instances.

Icing Spatulas

Having an assortment of large and small, offset and straight, icing spatulas will aid you immensely when making desserts. They all have their own specific functions and can make the difference between a dessert that looks homemade and one that looks professional. I also have a broad spackling knife, purchased from the hardware store, that I use to smooth my cake icings. Experiment.

Leaf Veiners

These are soft, flexible mats (often silicone or other plastic) that come in various leaf shapes. The vein pattern particular to that leaf appears as raised lines on the mat. Soft chocolate plastic or marzipan is pressed onto the mats and the vein pattern is transferred.

Magi-Cake Strips

These are aluminum fabric strips that are soaked in water and wrapped around the sides of cake pans before baking. They keep the edges of cakes moist by helping them to bake more slowly than the center, yielding a more uniformly baked cake. Just as important, the cakes will rise evenly without peaking in the center. This makes your job easier when it comes to leveling the layers and decorating the cakes. Magi-Cake Strips can be found in cake decorating stores and through certain mail-order sources (see page 173).

You can make your own disposable strips. Take a strip of aluminum foil that is long enough to go around your cake pan. Dampen a similar length of paper towels, fold them into a narrow strip, and place them on the foil strip. Completely fold the foil around the wet towels. Wrap the foil strip around the outside of the pan and fix into place with a paper clip.

Microwave Oven

It is hard to standardize recipes using microwave ovens because the ovens come in various wattages. My Sharp oven is 900 watts, which is considered a powerful oven. I have given approximate levels of power for microwave usage, but for specific information, follow the manufacturer's directions.

Ovens and Oven Thermometers

Ovens have different capacities. If you have a large oven, you may be able to have two racks in the oven at once, creating a top and bottom level. All of the recipes in this book were tested on the single middle rack of an oven. If you choose to bake on two levels at once, to save time, know that the heat will not be the same on both racks. In some ovens the top level is hotter, in others the bottom. Shift the pans around halfway through the baking time to equalize the heat.

Also, make sure your floor and oven are level, or your baked goods will be off-kilter. Literally.

These recipes were tested on both gas and electric home ranges, and the baking times have taken this into consideration. Internal oven temperatures can vary from the dial temperatures by as much as 25 to 50 degrees. Because of this I strongly suggest you use an oven thermometer and adjust your oven accordingly.

Parchment Paper

Parchment is available in rolls, like aluminum foil, from kitchenware stores and mail-order sources. Most professional chefs use parchment to provide a nonstick surface upon which to bake. Cut out parchment circles to fit pan bottoms, and use it to line sheet pans. When parchment is used in conjunction with a greased pan, your baked goods will release effortlessly.

Parchment can also be cut into triangles to make

paper cones. I use these for writing on or decorating cakes with melted chocolate (see page 14).

Pastry Bags and Decorating Tips

Some of these recipes require pastry bags, coupled with various tips, for applying decorative buttercreams and frostings. Fabric bags are available, but I prefer the polyester type made by Wilton. They are called Featherweight Decorating Bags and come in sizes ranging from 8 inches to 18 inches (in 2-inch increments). The opening is trimmed to allow a large decorating tube to fit—or to fit a coupler, which allows you to change small tips easily. I use the 14-inch size most often.

Decorating tips are quite inexpensive (usually less than a dollar), and owning a variety will allow you to experiment with different looks. Equip yourself with a basic set, which should include a range of round tips, closed and open star tips, leaf tips, petal tips and a tip for basket weave.

Plastic Squeeze Bottles with Needle-Nosed Tops

These bottles can be purchased in drugstores or from cake decorating supply stores. Fill one with a sauce, cut a small hole in the tip, if necessary, and use it to squeeze sauces decoratively onto plates.

Pots, Nonreactive

Aluminum pots are found in many kitchens, but this metal will react with acidic foods. If you cook pastry cream, for instance, in aluminum, it may develop a metallic taste and turn gray. Some nonreactive materials are stainless steel, Pyrex, and enamel.

Scales

Professional bakers measure by weight because it is more accurate than volume measurement.

The choice of a scale is important. Electronic scales are the most accurate, and I recommend that you purchase one. It may represent a high initial outlay ($50 and up), but precise measurements will yield the best baked goods.

Sheet Pans and Cookie Sheets

Most cookie sheets are flimsy, are likely to warp, and encourage burning. I use high-quality aluminum or stainless-steel sheet pans whenever I need a flat baking surface.

A standard half-sheet pan, which I refer to as a sheet pan throughout, measures 16½ inches by 11¾ inches, is rimmed and is what I use for baking cookies or whenever I need a flat baking surface, such as for dacquoise or baking tarts in open rings.

Strainer

A regular round strainer with a medium-size mesh and a long handle, so it fits over a bowl, is fine for sifting dry ingredients. I prefer not to use a traditional flour sifter. They are small and not efficient for large amounts of dry ingredients.

I use a very fine mesh strainer for straining ice cream bases, crème Anglaise, etc.

Tart Pans and Tart Rings

Most of the tart recipes in this book use loose-bottomed fluted tart pans. Tart rings have no bottom. They are simply open metal rings that must be placed on a sheet pan, which supports the bottom of the tart. These two types of pans can be used interchangeably.

Thermometers

An *instant-read thermometer* can be used when assessing the doneness of sugar syrups, melting chocolates, etc.

An *oven thermometer* should live in your oven, and you should check it frequently and make adjustments when needed. (See Ovens, above.)

A *chocolate thermometer* is used during tempering. This type of thermometer has one-degree increments, allowing you to precisely determine the temperature of the chocolate, which is crucial during this procedure.

ingredients

Almond Extract

Almond extract, like vanilla extract, comes in artificial and pure varieties. Use pure only.

Butter

Always use unsalted (sweet) butter. Salted butter has a higher moisture content, is salty, and has a longer shelf life. Unfortunately, this also means that it may not be as fresh.

I refrigerate what I need and freeze the rest. It will keep frozen for months. Always keep it well wrapped, or it will pick up strong flavors and odors from other foods.

Chocolate and Cocoa

Unsweetened Chocolate: This chocolate is also referred to as chocolate liquor, bitter chocolate or baking chocolate. It is quite bitter tasting, being made up of approximately 45% chocolate liquor and 55% cocoa butter, with no added sugar. Do not substitute unsweetened chocolate for semisweet or bittersweet chocolate.

Bittersweet and Semisweet Chocolates: These must, by law, contain at least 27% cocoa butter and no less than 35% chocolate liquor. The difference between the two is that the semisweet has more sugar added. They can, however, be used interchangeably in most recipes.

The recipes calling for semisweet chocolate were tested with Mercken's Yucatan Vanilla, which is my favorite all-purpose chocolate. It has vanilla topnotes (hence its name) and, to my palate, a taste somewhere between regular semisweet and bittersweet. Your favorite semisweet can be substituted. Mercken's can be purchased through The Baker's Catalogue (see page 173). I buy 10-pound blocks and large drops. The drops are easy to weigh and melt, but the blocks offer versatility. For instance, if you are going to grate or shave the chocolate, you will want a block to work with.

A note on supermarket semisweet chocolate chips: the standard chocolate chips, which you have probably bought to use in cookies, are formulated to hold their shape when exposed to heat. They do not make good melting chocolate. For these recipes, it is best to search out bulk chocolate.

Valrhona chocolates, a fine French brand, were used in some of the recipes and are mentioned where appropriate.

Milk and White Chocolates: Milk chocolate contains milk solids and usually has a higher sugar content than semisweet. White chocolate is not actually chocolate at all, according to the FDA, because it does not contain any of the essential chocolate liquor. High-quality white chocolate contains cocoa butter, however, and is the only type that I use. Lesser-quality white chocolate contains other types of fats that are not indigenous to chocolate, such as cottonseed oil or palm kernel oil. It is the cocoa butter in the higher-quality brands that gives white chocolate a chocolatey aroma and taste.

Both of these chocolates can be temperamental during melting. In general, melt slowly and do not heat above 110°F. Use an instant-read thermometer or a chocolate thermometer for best results. I prefer to melt these chocolates over hot water, not in the microwave, because it allows me more control over the temperature and I can keep a careful eye on the melting process.

I use Mercken's Marquis Milk, Callebaut Milk and Callebaut White chocolates.

Couverture: These chocolates (which can be white, milk or dark) have a high cocoa butter content—at least 32%. This makes the chocolate more fluid when melted. Couverture is the coating of choice of professional chocolatiers. It must be tempered before use in order to get a shiny, beautiful end product (see page 160). Use it for making perfect curls and other chocolate shapes. Couverture chocolates can be found at cake decorating stores and some specialty food stores.

Cocoa: There are many unsweetened cocoas on the market, both imported and domestic. All of them fall into one of two categories: regular (sometimes called natural) or Dutch-process. Dutch-process means that the cocoa beans, or one of their by-products, are exposed to an alkaline solution. This reduces the acidity of the cocoa, making its flavor more mellow, yet the color darker and richer. Just as important, the solubility of the cocoa is increased as well. Do not sub-stitute one for the other. The specific cocoa is listed in the recipes.

I use Valrhona and Bensdorp Dutch-process cocoas, and Hershey's natural cocoa.

Cream of Tartar

This acidic white powder is a by-product of the wine-making process. It is used in small amounts to help stabilize whipped egg whites and to help prevent crystallization in sugar syrups.

Crème Fraîche

I make my own crème fraîche, which is like a tangy sour cream (page 150). You may also purchase crème fraîche at specialty stores.

Flours

The two flours used most often in this book are cake flour and all-purpose flour. Purchase regular cake flour, not cake flour that is labeled "self-rising," which contains leavening and salt. Cake flour is very finely milled and can easily attract moisture, so proper storage is crucial. I keep mine in an airtight plastic container at room temperature because I go through it so quickly. Store yours in the refrigerator if you plan to keep it for an extended time.

Fruit Oils

I do not like lemon and orange extracts and will not use them. I use fresh zest and juice or oil.

Lemon, orange and lime oil are made by Boyajian and are available from Williams-Sonoma (see page 177). They are actual oils distilled from the zest of the fruits. They are pure-tasting and impart a wonderfully fresh taste to baked goods.

Gold Leaf, and Powdered Gold and Silver

Gold leaf is edible if it is at least 23 karats. It is an inert substance that has no flavor, but it adds an unusual beauty to your creations. It comes in packages of small square sheets (about 3 by 3 inches) and can be found in art supply stores and some cake decorating stores. The thin sheet of gold, the same gold that sign painters use, is very flimsy and requires deft handling.

The static electricity provided by a dry paintbrush will pull bits off so you can apply them to your dish. Tweezers can work as well.

Dry gold and silver powders, found in cake decorating stores, can be mixed with a small amount of vodka to form a metallic paint that is then brushed on desserts (see Chocolate Espresso Shortbread, page 40).

Leaveners

Baking soda and baking powder are the common leavening agents used in this book. Leaveners, like other ingredients, must be measured accurately to maximize their usefulness. When the correct amounts are added, they help to lighten the batter and create height.

Baking powder is made up of acid, an acid-reacting salt and bicarbonate of soda. The type used in these recipes is double-acting baking powder—the standard type sold in supermarkets. It is called "double-acting" because it works in two stages: first when exposed to moisture, and a second time when exposed to heat.

In a pinch you can make your own baking powder by combining 2 parts cream of tartar and 1 part baking soda; this is for immediate use only and will not store well.

Baking soda, or bicarbonate of soda, is used in bat-ters that have an acid component, such as buttermilk, honey or chocolate. Its addition helps to neutralize the acid as it releases carbon dioxide gas. Foods that are leavened only with baking soda must be baked immediately because the reaction will begin as soon as the acid in the batter and the baking soda are combined.

Mascarpone

This is an Italian product, sort of a cross between cream cheese and sour cream. There is no substitute, and I suggest you search it out for the Three-Berry Mascarpone Gratin (page 88). It can be purchased in cheese shops, specialty food stores, some supermarkets, and in the cheese departments of some health food stores.

Vanilla Beans, Extract and Powder

There are various kinds of vanilla beans on the market. Bourbon-type beans, which come from Mexico or Madagascar, are the basic vanilla bean from the *Vanilla planifolia* plant. Tahitian vanilla beans, which have a stronger, more floral taste, come from *Vanilla tahitensis.* Try both, alone or in combination, in recipes to see which you prefer. Any kind of vanilla bean that you use should be plump, pliable and soft.

To use vanilla beans, split them lengthwise, and then scrape out the seeds if required in the recipe or simply use the split bean.

For extract, use pure vanilla extract only. Neilsen-Massey brand is a good brand.

One teaspoon extract is roughly equivalent to 1 whole (6-inch) bean.

Vanilla powder is a beige, slightly granular powder made from the essence of the vanilla bean. Use it in the same amounts as vanilla extract.

techniques

Measuring Ingredients

Dry ingredients should be measured with cups specifically calibrated for them. Stir flours to aerate them before measuring. Then "dip and sweep": Dip the correct-size measuring cup into the container and then, using the blunt edge of a straight knife or an icing spatula, sweep the excess off the top, back into the container. If you shake or tap the measuring cup before leveling it off, the dry ingredient will settle, becoming denser and heavier, and therefore skew your results. I also "dip and sweep" when using measuring spoons in containers of baking powder and baking soda. Baking soda often clumps; sift it occasionally to prevent this.

Liquids, such as honey, oil, liqueurs, water and lemon juice, should be measured in liquid measuring cups. The commonplace Pyrex cups with spouts, which you can find in most supermarkets and hardware stores, are meant for this purpose. Place your measuring cup on a level surface and pour the ingredient up to the line that indicates the amount needed. Use appropriate-size cups. Do not try to measure ¼ cup liquid in a 4-cup measurer; it will not be as accurate as measuring it in a 1-cup measurer. When measuring sticky ingredients, like honey or corn syrup, lightly spray your measuring cup with nonstick cooking spray; the honey will slip right out of the measurer.

Other ingredients, such as butter and chocolate, are easier to weigh than to measure by volume, so I have given weights for these. You will need a scale to make these recipes. Most professional pastry chefs weigh everything—dry goods, liquids, dried fruit, whatever. However, this book is meant to address the needs of home bakers, so I have adopted this blend of approaches.

Preparing Pans

A cake that releases easily will have beautiful sides, with its crust intact. I use a vegetable oil–based nonstick cooking spray most often for my cakes, brownies, and so on. PAM, which is available everywhere, is fine. But only use the unflavored kind. For cakes, I lightly spray the pan's sides and bottom, cut out a parchment piece to fit the bottom of the pan, insert it, and them lightly spray the top of the parchment. Brownie pans are usually just sprayed. Cookie sheets are usually covered with a piece of parchment, cut to fit. Check individual recipes for any special pan treatments.

Creaming Fat and Sugar

Creaming fat and sugar together maximizes the amount of air that is added to your batter and yields a high volume, which in turn gives you the light, tender baked goods you want.

Start with room-temperature ingredients. Put the fat (butter, shortening) in your mixer's bowl. Using the paddle attachment, cream on medium-high speed until smooth and creamy. Add the sugar(s) gradually, and continue creaming until light and fluffy before adding the dry and/or liquid ingredients.

Separating Eggs and Whipping Egg Whites

Cold eggs separate most easily. The white is stiffer and more viscous, and the yolk is less prone to break. However, in general, eggs should be at room temperature when they are actually incorporated into other ingredients or when the whites or yolks are whipped.

Room-temperature eggs will give you maximum volume. (Note, though, that sanitation codes suggest not letting eggs stay at room temperature for more than 1 hour.)

Many dessert recipes call for egg whites to be whipped separately from the yolks. Folding whipped whites into a batter lightens the texture by adding the air provided by the whipped whites. A bit of cream of tartar can be added for increased stability in the egg white foam. This acid affects the protein strands in the whites and makes for a more stabilized foam. Any grease will prohibit proper whipping, so make sure that absolutely no trace of yolk gets into your mixture and always use scrupulously clean bowls and beaters.

Begin by beating the whites with the balloon whip attachment on low speed. When the mixture is frothy, add cream of tartar, if using. Increase the speed to medium-high and beat until soft peaks form. Then add sugar gradually, if called for in the recipe. Soft peaks are reached when the whites form peaks that still fold over on themselves a bit. Stiff peaks will stand up straight, and the meringue will take on a glossy sheen. Do not overbeat, or you will get grainy, lumpy whites.

When beating whites without sugar, the stages are similar. There will be a frothy stage and a soft peak stage. The stiff peak stage will come next, and at this point you must be very careful not to overwhip the whites. They can easily become dry; the whites will look lumpy, like cotton, and this texture will ruin your final product. You can overbeat whites with sugar added as well, but the dry peak stage comes up more slowly and it is easier to judge when the meringue is done.

To fold whipped egg whites or a meringue into a batter, proceed as follows: Scrape the egg whites onto the batter. Use a large balloon whisk to cut down into the batter and fold up over the top of the whites, continuing to do so until no streaks of whites remain. You may also lighten the batter initially by folding in about one quarter of the meringue mixture; then add the remaining whites. Follow the directions in specific recipes.

Many recipes in other cookbooks call for a large rubber spatula to be used when folding in egg whites. I usually start the folding process with a balloon whisk, which really preserves the volume, and finish off the folding with a large spatula. Try a combination of these techniques to see what works well for you.

Handling Chocolate

Chocolate is absolutely, without question, my very favorite food. If treated well, it will reward you fabulously. However, if not handled correctly, working with chocolate can be frustrating. Follow these tips and it will be smooth sailing.

Storing Chocolate: Chocolate should be stored at room temperature, well wrapped, in an airtight container. Dark chocolate will last at least 1 year. White and milk chocolates should be used within 6 months, due to their milk solids content. Keep all chocolates in an airtight container, free of moisture. Do not refrigerate or freeze.

Most chocolate is bought "in good temper," which means that the emulsion is stable and the chocolate looks shiny and proper. If it acquires grayish streaks during storage, it has developed "fat bloom," which simply means that the cocoa butter has become unstable and risen to the top. Don't worry; it looks unsightly, but the cocoa butter will mix back in upon melting. Do not, however, use this type of cosmetically impaired chocolate for creating decorative curls and the like.

Melting Chocolate: Chocolate can be melted successfully in a double boiler or in a microwave. Either way, it should first be chopped into small pieces. The best way to do that is with a chocolate chipper (see page 162). You can use a knife, but make sure it is a large heavy-duty chef's knife and never use the tip, which can break off.

To melt chocolate in a double boiler, fill the bottom of the double boiler with water so that it does not touch the bottom of the top pan. Place the chopped chocolate in the top pan and bring the water to a simmer, stirring the chocolate occasionally until almost completely melted. Turn the heat off and continue to stir. The residual heat will melt the remaining chocolate.

The two pitfalls with this technique are steam and overheating. Steam is created by the hot water in the bottom pot, and if water droplets get into the chocolate, it can seize. The chocolate will immediately clump up into a grainy mass and be unsalvageable at this point for most preparations. Prevention is the best medicine. Make sure that the top and bottom of your double boiler have a tight fit, which will lessen the chance of steam escaping.

Overheating will do one of two things. It may separate the fats (cocoa butter or oils) in the chocolate from the rest of its components, which will result in an oily mass, or it may burn the chocolate, which will make it grainy and lumpy. Bittersweet and semisweet chocolates should not be heated above 120°F; milk and white chocolates not above 110° to 115°F. Use a chocolate thermometer (see page 165).

To microwave chocolate, finely chop dark chocolate, place it in a Pyrex bowl, and set the microwave at about one third power (30%). For 1 pound of chocolate, heat the chocolate, uncovered, for 3 to 6 minutes, checking and stirring at each 2-minute interval until the bulk of the chocolate is melted. Then remove from the microwave and continue to stir (it may look as if a solid piece still remains), using the residual heat to complete the melting process.

I do not like to melt milk or white chocolate in the microwave because you do not have the same degree of control over the heat source as on top of the stove, and these chocolates are more temperamental. You also lose the ability to keep a constant eye on the melting procedure, which I find crucial with these trickier chocolates.

Whipping Cream

Always start with heavy cream (at least 36% fat), and chill the mixer bowl and the balloon whip attachment. Starting on medium speed, whip just until you can see marks left in the cream as the beaters are drawn across. Now you can proceed with the machine on low speed, or finish off by hand with a whisk. Beat only until soft peaks form. This keeps the texture silky, which is optimal whether you are using it to serve alongside a dessert or folding it into a mousse.

The cream found in most supermarkets is ultra-pasteurized. This means it has been exposed to a high heat, which kills off bacteria and therefore extends shelf life. It also has a slightly cooked flavor, and does not whip as easily as regularly pasteurized cream because a coagulating enzyme has been destroyed in the processing. See if you can find pasteurized cream.

Sometimes you may need your whipped cream to hold up for a prolonged period, or to hold up without refrigeration. To stabilize cream, dissolve a little bit of gelatin in water and fold it into the whipped cream. Use 1 teaspoon of gelatin to 1 cup unwhipped cream.

Sprinkle the 1 teaspoon gelatin over 1 tablespoon cold water and let it soften for 5 minutes. Then heat the gelatin mixture in a double boiler over hot water or in a microwave, and stir to dissolve. Cool to a barely warm temperature. Whip the cream until marks from the balloon whip attachment are just beginning to show. Fold the gelatin mixture into the lightly whipped cream, then continue whipping until the desired consistency is reached.

Shirley Corriher, a brilliant food scientist, mentions a great idea for stabilizing whipped cream in her book *Cookwise*. She advocates melting 1 large marshmallow and folding it into the whipped cream (cooling the melted marshmallow first) instead of using a gelatin/water mixture. Try 1 large marshmallow per 2 cups unwhipped cream; it works.

Rotating Pans During Baking

Most ovens have hot spots, that is, areas that are hotter and will cook baked goods faster than in other parts of the oven. To encourage even baking, many recipes suggest rotating pans from front to back, or even from upper rack to bottom rack while rotating. I suggest switching from front to back at least once during baking for most cookies, brownies and cakes. See the individual recipes for specific instructions.

Blind Baking Tarts with Foil and Weights

Some of the pie and tart recipes call for partially or completely baked shells. This is best accomplished if the chilled shell is lined with foil and filled with "pie weights," which can be purchased at cake-decorating stores. They come in ceramic and metal versions. I find that the metal ones conduct heat better. You can also use rice, dried beans or pennies if you don't have the weights. Basically, the tart or pie is baked with the foil and weights for a specified amount of time. The weight keeps the tart dough from puffing up. The term "blind baking" refers to the fact that the pie or tart is not yet filled. Follow the instructions in the individual recipes.

Common Pitfalls

The number one reason why recipes fail is that cooks do not read the whole recipe ahead of time and do not follow the directions. For instance, if the recipe calls for room-temperature buttermilk, make sure you don't use it straight out of the refrigerator, or the results will not be optimum.

Overwhipping cream: Many bakers unintentionally overwhip their cream. It will be unpleasantly buttery on the tongue if eaten as is, and if folded into other ingredients, it will yield a coarse texture. Stop beating before you think you are done. You may really be done, or you can gently finish whipping by hand. If you do end up with an overbeaten mess, don't give up yet. Gently stir in some liquid cream and you may be able to restore the texture.

Overwhipping egg whites: Egg whites, regardless of whether they are whipped to soft or stiff peaks, should never be dry. When dry, they will look lumpy, like cottage cheese. Stop whipping before you think you are done, and finish off by hand.

Overbaking: Bakers often leave their baked goods in the oven too long. With experience, you will learn how to count on residual heat to finish the cooking. The recipes here give time ranges and visual cues for doneness to help you avoid overbaking.

Burned baked goods: Many times, because of poor heat circulation or hot spots in one's oven, the bottoms of cookies and cakes will burn. Doubling up on pans will create an air pocket that will eliminate this problem, as will using high-quality heavy-duty pans. Before you go out and invest in new pans, try doubling your sheet pans or brownie pans (simply putting one on top of another) and see if that doesn't improve your results.

Storage: Some desserts should be refrigerated, some stored at room temperature. Sometimes an airtight container is best, at other times a loose wrapping is better. Follow the directions in individual recipes. Refrigerating desserts that should be stored at room temperature is particularly tricky because the baked item will dry out. Follow the directions.

Resources

Albert Uster
9211 Gaither Road
Gaithersburg, MD 20877
☎ (301) 258-7350
☎ (800) 231-8154
Fax (301) 948-2601

Large selection of equipment and ingredients, mostly imports. Great selection of candy-making equipment, spatulas and pans. Catalog available.

August Thomsen
36 Sea Cliff Avenue
Glen Cove, NY 11542
☎ (516) 676-7100

This is the wholesale distributor of Ateco products. They make wonderful tips, classic round cutters, icing spatulas and bench scrapers. Call for the retailer nearest you.

The Baker's Catalogue
King Arthur Flour
P.O. Box 876
Norwich, VT 05055
☎ (802) 649-3366
☎ (800) 827-6836
Fax (802) 649-5359
Website www.kingarthurflour.com

This constantly updated catalog has flours of all description, vanillas, Merckens chocolates, candied fruit rinds, scales, high-quality measuring cups, including ones in odd sizes, and more.

Beryl's Cake Decorating and Pastry Supplies
P.O. Box 1584
North Springfield, VA 22151
English and español
☎ (703) 256-6951
☎ (800) 488-2749
Fax (703) 750-3779
e-mail beryls@beryls.com
Website www.beryls.com

Beryl herself answers the phone and provides highly personal, professional and confidential customer service. She offers cutters of all sorts, colors, pastes and powders, cake pans, pastry tips, books, videos and more. Catalog available.

Bridge Kitchenware
214 East 52nd Street
New York, NY 10022
☎ (212) 688-4220
☎ (800) 274-3435
Fax (212) 758-4387

This New York institution has almost everything you need to outfit your kitchen: pans, tubes, decorating equipment, knives, spatulas, tart pans and more. Many French imports. Catalog available.

Broadway Panhandler
477 Broome Street
New York, NY 10013
☎ (212) 966-3434

This store has an entire section devoted to cake baking and decoration equipment—tips, pans, parchment, etc. No catalog.

Chandré
14 Catherine Street
Poughkeepsie, NY 12601
☎ (914) 473-8003
☎ (800) 3-CHOCLA
Fax (914) 473-8004
Website www.chandre.com

This mail-order company manufactures and sells the Sinsation, a small chocolate tempering machine that is perfect for home use. It is compact and hundreds of dollars less than any other on the market. It automatically tempers white, milk or dark chocolate perfectly every time. They even have a technical support line that is answered by knowledgeable staff. If you work with chocolate a lot, this is a must-have piece of equipment.

The Chefs Catalog
151 Skokie Boulevard
Northbrook, IL 60035
☎ (847) 831-1100
☎ (800) 338-3232
Website www.chefscatalog.com

Great mail-order catalog offering KitchenAid mixers, Cuisinart equipment, large professional-size rubber spatulas, bench scrapers, tart pans, extra-long hot mitts, parchment paper, and more. And all at very competitive prices.

Cooking by the Book
13 Worth Street
New York, NY 10013
☎ (212) 966-9799

This cooking school sells the Microplane, which is hands-down the best grater/zester on the market. They will mail-order.

A Cook's Wares
211 37th Street
Beaver Falls, PA 15010
☎ (724) 846-9490
☎ (800) 915-9788
Fax (800) 916-2886
Website www.cookswares.com

This mail-order company has a small catalog that packs a lot of ingredients and equipment into its pages. They offer scales, replacement parts for Cuisinart equipment, books and lots of baking pans.

Country Kitchen
3225 Wells Street
Fort Wayne, IN 46808
☎ (219) 482-4835
☎ (800) 497-3927
Fax (219) 483-4091

They offer pans, colors, cutters, tips, some ingredients, thermometers, squeeze bottles, etc. Catalog available.

Elegance Distributors
P.O. Box 275
Eaton Rapids, MI 48827-0275
☎ (517) 663-8152
☎ (800) 487-6157
Website www.elegancedistributors.com

This wholesaler specializes in edible flowers, such as pansies, and sells them in boxes of 50 for about $15. That may seem like a lot of flowers, but being able to sort through a box for color and size is important. And for around $15 delivered to your door, they're a bargain. Other edible flowers, such as sweetheart roses, rose petals, nasturtiums and fresh mint, are also available. They also sell dried cherries and cranberries.

J. B. Prince Co.
36 East 31st Street, 11th Floor
New York, NY 10016
☎ (212) 683-3553
☎ (800) 473-0577
Fax (212) 683-4488

Another New York supply house specializing in professional equipment. Great resource for pans, spatulas and racks. Catalog available.

Kitchen Arts & Letters Inc.
1435 Lexington Avenue (between 93rd & 94th
    Streets)
New York, NY 10128
☎ (212) 876-5550
Fax (212) 876-3584

This culinary bookstore will probably have any cooking-related book you want. If not, they will do a free search and find it for you. Whether you are looking for the newest bestseller, or for some obscure title, the friendly, helpful and knowledgeable staff is at your service. They ship anywhere.

La Cuisine
323 Cameron Street
Alexandria, VA 22314
☎ (703) 836-4435
☎ (800) 521-1176
Fax (703) 836-8925
Website www.lacuisineus.com

This very comprehensive supply house has excellent equipment, such as cake and tart pans, and high-quality ingredients, such as Valrhona chocolates and Tahitian vanilla beans. Catalog available.

Maison Glass, Inc.
725 Valley Brook Avenue
Lyndhurst, NJ 07071
☎ (201) 507-3557
☎ (800) 822-5564

This mail-order company offers specialty ingredients such as praline paste, chocolate-covered coffee beans and bulk chocolates. Catalog available.

Meadowsweets
Box 371
Middleburgh, NY 12122
☎ (518) 827-6477

This company makes the most exquisite crystallized flowers. If you do not want to make your own, this is the source to use. They are very well packaged in clear hard plastic boxes filled with shredded "grass" and come to you in perfect condition. Small catalog available.

Modern Chef
18 Wells Court
Bloomfield, NJ 07003
☎ (201) 338-0639
Fax (201) 338-0757

This company offers a small array of high-quality bakeware—what the pros use. You'll find rings, cake pans, loose-bottomed tart pans, rolling pins, pastry bags, dredgers, spatulas and cutters. Catalog available.

**N.Y. Cake and Baking Distributors/
The Chocolate Gallery**
56 West 22nd Street
New York, NY 10010
☎ (212) 675-CAKE
☎ (800) 94-CAKE-9
Fax (212) 675-7099

Here you'll find chocolates, including Valrhona, tips, molds, cutters, cardboard rounds, cake pans, Magi-Cake Strips, paste and powdered colors of all kinds, edible powdered gold and silver, professional baking sheets, books, magazines devoted to decorating, videos and more. This business also offers cake decorating classes through their School of Confectionary Arts. Visiting the store is a must when in Manhattan. Catalog available.

Parrish's Cake Decorating Supplies, Inc.
225 West 146th Street
Gardena, CA 90248
☎ (213) 324-2253
☎ (800) 736-8443
Fax (213) 324-8277

This company carries cake pans, decorating equipment, heavy-duty turntables, tips, etc. Catalog available.

Pearl Paint
308 Canal Street
New York, NY 10013
☎ (212) 431-7932
☎ (800) 221-6845
Website www.pearlpaint.com

This is a vast artist's supply house that also has a catalog. They carry gold and silver leaf, and plastic acetate sheets. They are the "world's largest discount art supplier."

Pfiel and Holing
58-15 Northern Boulevard
Woodside, NY 11377
☎ (718) 545-4600
☎ (800) 247-7955
Fax (718) 932-7513.
Website www.cakedeco.com

This company requires a minimum order (about $40), but they have loads of stuff: cake turntables, spatulas, thermometers, chocolate chippers, scales, rings, tart pans, ice cream scoops and heavy-duty hot-mitts. Catalog available.

Sur La Table
Pike Place Farmers Market
84 Pine Street
Seattle, WA 98101
☎ (206) 448-2244
☎ (800) 243-0852
Website www.surlatable.com

They have both a general catalog and a catalog devoted to baking. You will find pans, tips, rolling pins, half-sheet pans, spatulas and more. They also offer cooking classes at some of their retail stores throughout California and the Northwest.

Sweet Celebrations / Maid of Scandinavia
7009 Washington Avenue South
Edina, MN 55439
☎ (612) 943-1661
☎ (800) 328-6722
Website www.sweetc.com

This company used to be called Maid of Scandinavia; now it is called Sweet Celebrations. The catalog is much smaller now, but just ask for what you want. They have an extensive line of decorator equipment including tips, pans, Merckens chocolates and more. They carry coarse sugar, which they call crystal sugar.

Takashimaya
693 Fifth Avenue
New York, NY 10022
☎ (212) 350-0100
☎ (800) 753-2038
Fax (212) 350-0192

This great retail store will mail-order their products, including *matcha* tea and any of their specialty foods. Call for a catalog.

Williams-Sonoma
P.O. Box 7456
San Francisco, CA 94120
☎ (415) 421-4242
☎ (800) 541-2233
Fax (415) 421-5253
Website www.williams-sonoma.com

Famous for their mail-order catalog, they also have stores nationwide. You will find great measuring tools, a heavy-duty apple peeler, Boyajian oils, vanilla, some chocolate and cocoa, and other baking equipment.

Wilton Industries, Inc.
2240 West 75th Street
Woodbridge, IL 60517
☎ (708) 963-7100
☎ (800) 772-7111
Website www.wilton.com

Great catalog with heavy-duty cake pans, half-sheet pans, tips, colors, cardboard rounds and much more.

Bibliography

Inspiration can come from anywhere. Read constantly—cookbooks, food magazines, and food columns in newspapers. The ideas will flow.

Amendola, Joseph. *The Baker's Manual*. Rochelle Park, NJ: Hayden Book Company, 1972.

Amendola, Joseph, and Donald Lundberg. *Understanding Baking*. New York: Van Nostrand Reinhold, 1970.

Amernick, Ann. *Special Desserts*. New York: Clarkson Potter, 1992.

Beranbaum, Rose Levy. *The Cake Bible*. New York: William Morrow, 1988.

———. *A Passion for Chocolate*. New York: William Morrow, 1989.

———. *The Pie and Pastry Bible*. New York: Scribner, 1998.

Bloom, Carol. *All About Chocolate*. New York: Macmillan, 1998.

———. *The Candy Cookbook*. San Francisco: Chronicle Books, 1995.

———. *The International Dictionary of Desserts, Pastries, Confections*. New York: Hearst Books, 1995.

———. *Truffles, Candies and Confections*. Freedom, CA: Crossing Press, 1992.

Brachman, Wayne. *Cakes and Cowpokes*. New York: William Morrow, 1995.

Braker, Flo. *The Art of Perfect Baking*. New York: William Morrow, 1985.

Corriher, Shirley. *Cookwise*. New York: William Morrow, 1997.

Dannenberg, Linda. *Paris Boulangerie Pâtisserie*. New York: Clarkson Potter, 1994.

Desaulniers, Marcel. *Death by Chocolate*. New York: Rizzoli, 1992.

———. *Death by Chocolate Cookies*. New York: Simon and Schuster, 1997.

———. *Desserts to Die For*. New York: Simon and Schuster, 1995.

Gonzalez, Elaine. *Chocolate Artistry*. Chicago: Contemporary Books, 1983.

Goodbody, Mary, and Jane Stacey. *Pretty Cakes*. New York: Harper & Row, 1986.

Hannemann, L. J. *Pâtisserie, Professional Pastry and Dessert Preparation*. New York: Van Nostrand Reinhold, 1971.

Healy, Bruce, and Paul Bugat. *Mastering the Art of French Pastry*. New York: Barrons, 1984.

Heatter, Maida. *American Desserts*. New York: Alfred A. Knopf, 1985.

———. *Best Dessert Book Ever*. New York: Alfred A. Knopf, 1990.

———. *Book of Great Chocolate Desserts*. New York: Alfred A. Knopf, 1983.

———. *Brand-New Book of Great Cookies*. New York: Random House, 1995.

———. *New Book of Great Desserts*. New York: Alfred A. Knopf, 1982.

Hermé, Pierre, and Dorie Greenspan. *Desserts*. New York: Little, Brown, 1998.

Klivans, Elinor. *Bake and Freeze Desserts: 150 Do-Ahead Cakes, Pies, Cookies, Brownies, Bars, Ice Creams, Terrines, and Sorbets*. New York: William Morrow, 1994.

Lenôtre, Gaston. Faites Votre Pâtisserie comme Lenôtre. Paris: Flammarion, 1975.

Liddell, Caroline, and Robin Weir. *Frozen Desserts*. New York: St. Martin's Press, 1995.

Linx, Robert. *La Maison du Chocolat*. Paris: Robert Laffont, 1992.

Luchetti, Emily. *Four-Star Desserts*. New York: HarperCollins, 1996.

———. *Stars Desserts*. New York: HarperCollins, 1991.

Malgieri, Nick. *Chocolate: From Simple Cookies to Extravagant Showstoppers*. New York: HarperCollins, 1998.

———. *How to Bake*. New York: HarperCollins, 1995.

———. *Nick Malgieri's Perfect Pastry*. New York: Macmillan, 1989.

Medrich, Alice. *Chocolate and the Art of Low Fat Desserts*. New York: Warner Books, 1994.

———. *Cocolat*. New York: Warner Books, 1990.

Payard, François. *Simply Sensational Desserts*. New York: Broadway Books, 1999.

Purdy, Susan. *A Piece of Cake*. New York: Atheneum, 1989.

Rubin, Maury. *Book of Tarts*. New York: William Morrow, 1995.

Sax, Richard. *Classic Home Desserts*. *Shelburne*, VT: Chapters Publishing, 1993.

Silverton, Nancy. *Desserts*. New York: Harper & Row, 1985.

Stewart, Martha. *Martha Stewart's Pies and Tarts*. New York: Clarkson Potter, 1985.

Walter, Carole. *Great Cakes*. New York: Ballantine Books, 1991.

———. *Great Pies and Tarts*. New York: Clarkson Potter, 1998.

Welch, Adrienne. *Sweet Seduction.* New York: Harper & Row, 1984.

Index

cakes, decoration of:
    chocolate and marzipan roses and leaves, 116–117
    decorative piped borders in, 141
    equipment for, 126, 162–164
    finishing touches in, 126–128
Calmyrna figs, in raspberry fig rugelach filling, 33
Calvados applesauce date cake, 55–56
caramel:
    chocolate buttercream, 157
    devil's food cake, 125–130
caramel sauce, 146–147
    on gingerbread roll with sautéed apples, 142–144
cardamom rice pudding, 84–85
    topping of, 85
cardboard rounds, 126, 162
carrot honey maple muffins, 59–60
cheesecake, crème fraîche, in walnut crust, 119–122
cherries, dried:
    in cherry pecan rugelach filling, 33
    in florentines, 42
    in fruity paradise bars, 70–71
cherry(ies), sour:
    bars, 74–75
    canned vs. fresh frozen, 6
    chocolate *bûche de noël,* 122–124
    cranberry pie, 6–7
cherry pitters, 74
chocolate:
    banana pecan pie, 10
    bittersweet, 165
    bowls, toasted coconut ice cream in, 96–98
    buttercream, 157
    caramel buttercream, 157
    chipper, 162
    in coffee pecan oat shortbread, 51
    in cognac apricot rugelach, 33
    couverture, 82, 124–125, 134, 166
    in double-layer truffle brownies, 69–70
    dressing up plate with, 28, 29
    espresso cream puffs, 99–100

in espresso Kahlúa ice cream sandwiches dipped in bittersweet chocolate, 38
espresso shortbread, 40–42
espresso shortbread hearts with edible gold and silver, 40–42
in florentines, 42–43
in fudgy bittersweet brownies, 64
in gianduja truffle tart, 15–16
in hazelnut macaroons, 48
in hazelnut mocha crème brûlée, 90
and hazelnut tart crust, 15
in lemon espresso bars, 67
in marzipan apricot brownies, 64–66
marzipan pound cake with cognac apricots, 118–119
melting of, 170
in ménage à trois cookies, 45
milk, 165–166
in mocha almond dacquoise, 138–140
in mocha *coeur à la crème,* 82
mousse, B&B frozen, 87–88
peanut butter tart, 12–15
pie crust, 158–159
raspberry mousse cake, 130–133
sauce, bittersweet, 147–148
semisweet, 165
sorbet, bittersweet, two ways, 110–111
sour cherry *bûche de noël,* 122–125
storing of, 169–170
tart crust, 20
tempered, 124–125, 160
thermometer, 165
in toffee fudgies, 70
truffle raspberry tart, 20
truffles, 104
unsweetened, 165
in white chocolate espresso *pot de crème,* 78
chocolate, white, *see* white chocolate
chocolate almond biscotti, 49–50
    in espresso biscotti ganache ripple ice cream, 100

crumb coat, application of, 127

crust:

    walnut, crème fraîche cheesecake in, 119

    see also pie crusts; tart crusts

crystallized ginger:

    in chocolate chunk ginger bars, 66–67

    pear tart, 21–23

    in spiced peach crisp pie, 5–6

dacquoise, mocha almond, 138–140

date(s):

    blond, 71–72

    cake, Calvados applesauce, 55–56

    chopping of, 56

    dried, in fruity paradise bars, 70–71

decorating tips, 116–117, 126–128, 141, 162–164

decorating turntable, 126, 162

devil's food cake, caramel, 125–130

double-layer truffle brownies, 69–70

dredgers, 29, 162

dry ingredients:

    dressing up plate with, 29

    measuring of, 168

Earl Grey tea cream, 88–89

    Easter egg molding of, 89

eggs, separating of, 168–169

egg whites, whipping of, 168–169, 171

equipment, 126, 162–165

espresso:

    beans, chocolate-covered, 70

    biscotti ganache ripple ice cream, 100

    buttercream, 157

    chocolate cream puffs, 99–100

    chocolate shortbread, 40–42

    chocolate shortbread hearts with edible gold and silver, 40–42

    hazelnut crème brûlée, 89–90

    lemon bars, 67

    white chocolate chunk cookies, 37–38

    white chocolate *pot de crème*, 78

espresso Kahlúa ice cream, 99

    in ice cream sandwiches dipped in bittersweet chocolate, 38

fat and sugar, creaming of, 168

fig(s):

    raspberry filling for cognac apricot rugelach variation, 33

    tart, with lemon honey mascarpone, 17–19

Fiori di Sicilia, in shortbread Fiori di Sicilia, 34–35

florentines, 42–43

flours, 166

flowers, dried:

    crystallizing of, 108–109

    dressing up plate with, 29

    glazing of, 120–122

four-berry crisp, 24–25

    with crème fraîche sorbet, 25

frappe, skinny black and white, 110–111

frostings:

    honey vanilla cream cheese, 60

    white chocolate cream cheese, 120–122

frozen desserts, 93–113

    chilling and freezing of, 93

    storing and serving of, 94

    see also granitas; ice creams; sorbets

fruit oils, *see* lemon oil; lime oil; orange oil

fruity paradise bars, 70–71

fudgy bittersweet brownies, 64

ganache:

    bittersweet chocolate, 100, 122–125, 154

    ripple ice cream, espresso biscotti, 100

    whipped chocolate, 122–125, 154

gianduja:
    chocolate chunk cookies, Adrienne's, 35–36
    truffle tart, 15–16
ginger, crystallized, *see* crystallized ginger
gingerbread roll with sautéed apples, 142–144
ginger chocolate chunk bars, 66–67
ginger crackle cookies, 46
    pumpkin ice cream sandwiches with, 46–47
ginger ice cream, 100–101
    with roasted plum compote and sesame lace
        cookies, 101
gingersnap crust, pumpkin brûlée tart in,
        16–17
gold and silver powder, 167
    in chocolate espresso shortbread hearts with edible
        gold and silver, 40–42
    dressing up plate with, 29
gold leaf, 167
gold powder, in mocha *coeur à la crème*, 82
graham cracker crust, 9
Grand Marnier:
    in crème Anglaise, 146
    in marmalade butter, 59
granitas, 113
    merlot cinnamon, 113
    plum wine, 113
graters/zesters, 85, 162
gratin, three-berry mascarpone, 88
green tea:
    ice cream, 107–108
    jasmine sorbet coupe with crystallized flowers,
        108–109
grilled peach tart, 25–27

hazelnut(s):
    in Adrienne's gianduja chocolate chunk cookies,
        35–36
    and chocolate tart crust, 15
    espresso crème brûlée, 89–90
    in gianduja truffle tart, 15–16

macaroons, 47–48
    peeling and toasting of, 151–152
    in praline buttercream, 157
hazelnut liqueur:
    in crème Anglaise, 146
    in gianduja truffle tart, 16
    in praline chocolate cake with chocolate roses,
        128–130
honey:
    ice cream, 106–107
    lemon mascarpone, fig tart with, 17–19
    vanilla cream cheese frosting, 60
honeydew sorbet, minted, with lime, 112–113
honey maple carrot muffins, 59–60
    frosting for, 60

ice cream makers, 94
ice creams, 93–109
    banana, 106
    coconut, 96
    espresso Kahlúa, 38, 99
    ganache ripple, espresso biscotti, 100
    ginger, 100–101
    green tea, 107–109
    honey, 106–107
    lemon velvet, 103
    making of, 95
    pumpkin, 98
    toasted coconut, in chocolate bowls, 96–98
    vanilla, 94
    white chocolate mint, 104
ice cream sandwiches:
    espresso Kahlúa, dipped in bittersweet chocolate,
        38
    pumpkin, with ginger crackle cookies,
        46–47
ice milk, 109–110
    lemon, 110
    triple vanilla, 109
icing spatulas, 126, 163

ingredients, 165–167
    measuring of, 168
instant-read thermometers, 165
Italian meringue buttercream, 155–157
    in caramel devil's food cake, 125–130
    in mocha almond dacquoise, 138–140
    in praline chocolate cake with chocolate roses, 128–130
    in strawberry almond genoise, 135–138
    in strawberry marzipan dome, 137–138
    variations, 157

jasmine tea sorbet, 112
    in green tea jasmine sorbet coupe with crystallized flowers, 108–109

Kahlúa:
    in crème Anglaise, 146
    in espresso buttercream, 157
    espresso ice cream, 99
    in mocha almond dacquoise, 138–140
    in mocha *coeur à la crème*, 80–82
key lime pie à la Ravenna, 9–10
Kirschwasser, in chocolate sour cherry *bûche de noël*, 122–125
KitchenAid mixer, 162

lace cookies, sesame, 43, 101
leaveners, 167
lemon:
    espresso bars, 67
    ice milk, 110
    velvet ice cream, 103
lemon oil, 67, 166
leveling, of cake layers, 126
lighter bittersweet chocolate sorbet, 110
lime:
    curd, cocomac shortbread with, 72–74

key lime pie à la Ravenna, 9–10
    minted honeydew sorbet with, 112–113
lime oil, 166
liqueur-accented buttercream, 157
liqueur-flavored pastry cream, 151
liqueur-flavored sugar syrup, 151

macadamia(s):
    in cocomac shortbread with lime curd, 72–74
    shelling and toasting of, 152
macadamia oat crisps, 47
    with lemon velvet ice cream and raspberry coulis, 103
macaroons, hazelnut, 47–48
Magi-Cake Strips, 163
maple honey carrot muffins, 59–60
marmalade butter, as accompaniment to buttermilk poppy seed muffins, 59
Marsala, in Amaretto *zabaglione* with fresh apricots, 78–79
marzipan, 152–153
    apricot brownies, 64–66
    chocolate pound cake with cognac apricots, 118–119
    strawberry dome, 137–138
marzipan roses and leaves:
    making of, 116–117
    for marzipan chocolate pound cake with cognac apricots, 119
    for strawberry marzipan dome, 137–138
mascarpone, 167
    fig tart with lemon honey, 17–19
    gratin, three-berry, 88
    in grilled peach tart, 25–27
matcha (green tea powder), in green tea ice cream, 107–108
ménage à trois cookies, 45
meringue nests, with vanilla ice cream and roasted fruits, 94–95

Merlot:
    cinnamon granita, 113
    in meringue nests with vanilla ice cream and
        roasted fruits, 94–95
Microplane, 85, 162
microwave ovens, 163
milk chocolate, 165–166
mint, minted:
    crystallized, 113
    honeydew sorbet with lime, 112–113
    white chocolate ice cream, 104–106
mint sauce, 148
    on polka-dot truffle white chocolate mint ice
        cream, 104–106
mixers, heavy-duty vs. handheld, 162
mocha:
    almond dacquoise, 138–140
    coeur à la crème, 80–82
mousse, 77–90
    B&B frozen chocolate, 87
    cake, chocolate raspberry, 130–133
    white chocolate pear, 83–84
muffins:
    apricot vanilla bean, 60–61
    buttermilk poppy seed, 58–59
    honey maple carrot, 59–60

nonstick cooking spray, 2, 168
nuts:
    application of, to buttercream, 128
    peeling and toasting of, 151–152
    see also specific kinds of nuts

oat:
    coffee pecan shortbread, 50–51
    macadamia crisps, 47
    scones, 54
orange oil, 166
    in buttermilk poppy seed muffins, 58–59

orange peel, candied, in florentines, 42–43
ovens, 163
    hot spots in, 171–172
    microwave, 163
    thermometers, 163, 165

pans:
    pie, 2
    preparation of, 168
    rotating of, 171
    sheet, 2, 34, 164
    tart, 2, 164
pansies under glass, in crème fraîche cheesecake in
        walnut crust, 120–122
papaya, dried, in fruity paradise bars, 70–71
parchment cone, making of, 14
parchment paper, 2, 34, 163–164
pastry bags, 126, 164
    using of, 128
pastry cream, 150–151
    variations, 151
peach(es):
    crisp pie, spiced, 5–6
    in meringue nests, with vanilla ice cream and
        roasted fruits, 94–95
    tart, grilled, 25–27
peanut butter:
    chocolate chunk banana crunch cake, 56–58
    chocolate tart, 12–15
peanuts, in chunky raisin chip cookies, 36–37
pear(s):
    bread, 54–55
    crystallized ginger tart, 21–23
    mousse, white chocolate, 83–84
    and red wine sorbet, 111
pecan(s):
    cherry filling for cognac apricot rugelach variation,
        33
    coffee oat shortbread, 50–51
    in espresso white chocolate chunk cookies, 37–38

rum:
  in chocolate banana pecan pie, 10
  in chunky raisin chip cookies, 36–37
  in coconut ice cream, 96
  in crème Anglaise, 146
  in crystallized ginger pear tart, 21–23
  in grilled peach tart, 25–27

sauce(s), 145–148
  bittersweet chocolate, 99–100, 147–148
  blood orange, 107, 148
  bourbon, 80
  caramel, 142–144, 146–147
  dispensing of, 145, 164
  dressing up plate with, 28
  mint, 104–106, 148
  raspberry coulis, 103, 147
scales, 164
scones, oat, 54
semisweet chocolate, 165
sesame lace cookies, 43
  with ginger ice cream and roasted plum compote, 101
sheet pans, 2, 34, 164
shortbread:
  chocolate espresso, 40–42
  cocomac, with lime curd, 72–74
  coffee pecan oat, 50–51
  Fiori di Sicilia, 34–35
  hearts, chocolate espresso, with edible gold and silver, 40–42
skinny black and white frappe, 110–111
snack time treats, 53–61
sorbets, 108–109, 110–113
  bittersweet chocolate, two ways, 110
  crème fraîche, 111–112
  minted honeydew, with lime, 112–113
  pear and red wine, 111
sour cherries, see cherry(ies), sour
spatulas, icing, 126, 163

spiced peach crisp pie, 5–6
squeeze bottles, plastic, 145, 164
stencils, for tuiles, 51, 52
storage of desserts, 172
strainers, 164
strawberry(ies):
  almond genoise, 135–138
  marzipan dome, 137–138
  in meringue nests with vanilla ice cream and roasted fruits, 94–95
  tart, blackberry cream, 19
  in three-berry mascarpone gratin, 88
Sucanat:
  in fruity paradise bars, 70–71
  in oat scones, 54
sugar and fat, creaming of, 168
sugar crystals (coarse sugar), 61
sugar syrup, 151
  Amaretto-flavored, in strawberry almond genoise, 135–138
  Amaretto-flavored, in strawberry marzipan dome, 137–138
  hazelnut-flavored, in praline chocolate cake with chocolate roses, 128–130
  Kahlúa-flavored, in mocha almond dacquoise, 138–140
sweet tart dough, 159

tart(s), 11–27
  apricot almond, 23–24
  blackberry cream strawberry, 19
  chocolate peanut butter, 12–15
  chocolate truffle raspberry, 20
  cranberry sour cherry pie as, 7
  crystallized ginger pear, 21–23
  decoration of single-crust, 2
  fig, with lemon honey mascarpone, 17–19
  gianduja truffle, 15–16
  grilled peach, 25–27
  open-faced, 7